MW01292581

The 4th Fighter Wing in the Korean War

THE 4TH FIGHTER WING
in the Korean War

Larry Davis

Schiffer Military History
Atglen, PA

Dust jacket artwork by Steve Ferguson, Colorado Springs, CO.

THE CO's FIGHT AT FENCHENG
The cover depicts the 5 June, 1953, mission led by 335 FIS commander LtCol. Garrison to Fencheng, China, and their hair raising low-level sweep of the MiG base there. Garrison has just broken off from his gunnery pass on his second victim of the sortie as wingman Lt. Harry Jones in the background pulls into firing position on the next MiG.

Book design by Robert Biondi.

Library of Congress Catalog Number: 00-111511.

Printed in China.
ISBN: 0-7643-1315-0

Published by Schiffer Publishing Ltd.
4880 Lower Valley Road
Atglen, PA 19310
Phone: (610) 593-1777
FAX: (610) 593-2002
E-mail: Schifferbk@aol.com.
Visit our web site at: www.schifferbooks.com
Please write for a free catalog.
This book may be purchased from the publisher.
Please include $3.95 postage.
Try your bookstore first.

In Europe, Schiffer books are distributed by:
Bushwood Books
6 Marksbury Ave.
Kew Gardens
Surrey TW9 4JF
England
Phone: 44 (0)208 392-8585
FAX: 44 (0)208 392-9876
E-mail: Bushwd@aol.com.
Free postage in the UK. Europe: air mail at cost.
Try your bookstore first.

Contents

one

The World War II Years

The history of the 4th Fighter Interceptor Wing begins during the dark days of the Battle of Britain. Before America's entry into the war, Americans had already chosen sides. In early 1940, young American men were actively recruited for service in the British armed forces. Many young Americans crossed the border into Canada and joined the Royal Canadian Air Force. Names like Glover, Gentile, Garrison, and Blakeslee, all entered the war on the service rolls of the RCAF.

From the training bases in Canada, the fledgling American pilots went to England and the war. But instead of being posted to one of the RCAF squadrons, or being integrated into one of the Royal Air Force squadrons already involved in the war, the RAF formed them into not one but three all-American squadrons. They would forever be known as The Eagle Squadrons.

On 19 September 1940, Luke Allen, Bob Sweeny, Chesley Peterson and Gus Daymond, reported for duty in No.71 'Eagle' Squadron, based at Church Fenton Landing Field. Within four months, No.71 Squadron was completely manned with American 'volunteers'. Initially, they flew the Hawker Hurricane, but transitioned into Spitfires in August 1941. By then, there were so many American pilot trainees coming to England, that the RAF was forced to create two more 'Eagle' Squadrons.

On 14 May 1941, No.121 'Eagle' Squadron was formed at Kirton-in-Lindsay, followed on 1 August with the formation of No.133 'Eagle' Squadron at Coltishall. Flt/Lt. Donald Blakeslee was one of the first pilots to report to No.121 Squadron. The 'Eagle' Squadrons crowned their first 'ace' on 27 August 1941, when Pilot/Officer William Dunn shot down a pair of Fw 190s for his fifth and sixth victories of the war. Eagle Squadron pilots shot down a total of 73 1/2 Luftwaffe aircraft during the two years they were in existence. No.71 Squadron led with forty-one victories, followed by 121 Squadron with eighteen and 133 Squadron had 14 1/2.

On 12 September 1942, a brand new unit was activated at Bushey Hall, England. It was the U.S. Army Air Force 4th Fighter Group, which was one of the first units assigned to the brand new 8th Fighter Command. On 29 September, a ceremony took place at Debden involving the eighty-three pilots that had been assigned to the three Eagle Squadrons.

When the ceremonies ended, the Eagle Squadron pilots were now in the U.S. Army Air Force as part of the new 4th Fighter Group. No.71 'Eagle' Squadron became the 334th Fighter Squadron, No.121 Squadron became the 335th FS, and No.133 Squadron became the 336th FS. Home base for the new 4th FG was Debden Airdrome, an RAF field located about two miles from Saffron Walden, and forty-five miles north of London.

Debden was an established RAF base, complete with heated brick buildings, sports arenas for squash, billiards, tennis, and, of course, baseball. There were civilian orderlies, waitresses, flowers, and even its own chicken farm. The pilots even had RAF silverware to eat with. It was certainly a lot more plush than most of the fighter group stations in England. The first commander of the 4th was Colonel Edward Anderson.

The 'new' 4th FG retained their beloved Spitfires until 1 February 1943. On that day, the men returned from a mission to find these huge, pot-bellied aircraft sitting on the Debden tarmac. These were the first of the brand new Republic P-47 Thunderbolts. On 10 March, the Group flew its first mission in the Thunderbolt. One month later, all the Spitfires were gone.

No.71 Squadron pilot Joe Kelly on the wing of his Mk V Spitfire named "Little Joe", which also carries the Eagle Squadron badge on the nose. Debden, England 1942. No.71 Squadron was the first Eagle Squadron to be formed. (Jeff Ethell)

Left: No.121 'Eagle Squadron' pilot William J. Daley talks with his hands explaining to other 121 Squadron pilots how he scored his victory over a German Me 109 in 1941. He claimed eight victories. (Jeff Ethell) Right: Air Marshall Sholto Douglas, with 8th AF Commander Maj.Gen. Carl 'Tooey' Spaatz right behind, reviews the assembled Eagle Squadron crews at Debden on 29 September 1942, during the transfer ceremonies which took the Eagle Squadrons out of service with the RAF, and put them into U.S. Army Air Force service as the 4th Fighter Group. (Jeff Ethell)

The first victories for the group in the new uniform of the U.S. Army Air Force came on 2 October 1942, when Oscar Coen and Stan Anderson each got a kill. On 15 April 1943, Major Don Blakeslee shot down a German Fw 190 for the first 4th FG victory flying the new P-47 Thunderbolt. Five months later, on 8 October 1943, the new group crowned its first P-47 'ace' when 1/Lt. Duane Beeson shot down two German fighters to bring his total to six confirmed victories.

Colonel Chesley Peterson, one of the original Eagle Squadron pilots, took over command of the Group on 20 August 1943. His tenure was short-lived as Colonel Donald J.M. Blakeslee took over the Group on 1 January 1944. The era of the 'Blakesleewaffe' had begun.

In early December 1943, while the rest of the 4th Group was 'Ramrodding' (i.e. flying a fighter sweep mission) in P-47 Thunderbolts, Col. Blakeslee was leading the 354th FG on their first mission in the brand new North American P-51B Mustang. Col. Blakeslee had only fifteen minutes flying time in the Mustang at the time. When he landed he had shot down an Me 110 for his sixth victory of the war. It was love at first flight between the Mustang and Col. Blakeslee. So impressed was he with the P-51B that he went directly to 8th Fighter Com-

A pilot from No.121 'Eagle Squadron' prepares to climb aboard his Spitfire Mk V at Rochford in June 1942. No.121 Squadron was the second Eagle Squadron to be formed, being activated in May 1941. (Author)

A name forever on the lists of famous 4th Fighter Group pilots – Lt. Vermont Garrison, 336th Fighter Squadron. Garrison scored 7 1/3 victories with the 4th in World War II, and ten MiG-15s in Korea. (USAFM)

Right: Capt. John Godfrey leans on the wing of his 336th FS P-47D "Reggie's Reply", with his dog "Lucky." A painting of "Lucky' adorns the engine cowling on Godfrey's P-47. Debden, 1943. (James V. Crow)

mand Headquarters and asked that the 4th Group, his 4th Group, be converted to P-51s. If 8th FC concurred, Blakeslee guaranteed to have his pilots proficient in the P-51 within twenty-four hours!

On 27 February 1944, the first P-51Bs arrived at Debden. The Thunderbolt era had ended. 4th Fighter Group pilots scored 201 victories in Spitfires and P-47s before the transition into P-51s. Seven days after their arrival, Col. Blakeslee led the Mustang-equipped 4th FG on an escort mission to Big B – BERLIN! It was the first time that fighters had escorted the bombers to Big B. Hermann Göring is quoted as saying he "knew the war was lost when I saw those red-nosed Mustangs over Berlin." He was so right.

In March 1944, the 4th FG, flying a brand new aircraft, destroyed an amazing 156 German aircraft – the most by any unit in the 8th AF up to that time. Colonel Blakesleee told his pilots that he wanted to see 200 victories in April. 4th Fighter Group pilots responded with 215 victories. The group scored

Capt. Don Gentile flew Spitfire Mk V MD•T, when he transferred into the 336th Fighter Squadron at Debden in late 1942. The 4th FG flew the Spitfire until 1 February 1943, when the Republic P-47 arrived. (Author)

P-47Ds with the 336th FS prepare for the morning Ramrod (escort mission) into Germany during August 1943. The range of the P-47 was so short that one group would escort to the German border then go home, and a second group would meet the bombers on the way home. (Art Krieger)

Capt. Duane Beeson gives the thumbs up to his crew chief prior to another mission in "Boise Bee", the P-51B he flew when he was in the 334th FS. His scoreboard on the nose shows twenty victories, but his final total would be 24 1/3. (Dwayne Tabatt)

its 300th victory on 1 April, and the 400th just nine days later. The 215 victories in April brought the group total to 503 1/2.

By June 1944, the group had worked out most of the bugs in the still-new P-51 Mustangs. The new D models equipped with the bubble canopy had started arriving in late Spring. And it was a good thing too, as the group was heavily involved in supporting the invasion of Festung Europa on 6 June. The group put up three maximum efforts on that day. But since the Luftwaffe didn't make an appearance (Hitler was adamant that the Normandy Invasion was a diversion!), most of the missions were fighter bomber to keep German reinforcements from reaching the Second Front.

The fighter bomber missions continued into late June, usually two missions per day – one fighter bomber and one escort. The group had begun flying two separate groups, A and B Groups, to put a maximum number of airplanes into the air for any one mission. On 21 June, pilots of the 4th Group pioneered another new innovation in air tactics – the long range shuttle mission. Colonel Blakeslee led the group from Debden to Piryatin, Russia, escorting three groups of B-17 Flying Forts that had bombed targets at Ruhland in eastern Germany.

On 26 June, Colonel Blakeslee led the group on the second leg of the shuttle, landing at Lucera, Italy. They returned to Debden on 5 July. The entire mission had covered a total of over 6,000 miles, flying over ten countries, and the pilots were in the air for a total of 29 1/2 hours of combat flying. Although this was the first 'shuttle mission', 8th AF fighters and bombers, including the 4th FG, would fly many more such missions before the war ended in 1945.

Lt. Robert Wehrman flew "Lollapoluza", a P-47D with the 336th FS at Debden in the summer of 1943. Note the belly tank, commonly called a 'baby', which carries a very appropriate slogan. With the 'baby' under the fuselage, the P-47D was just able to penetrate the German border. (L. Krantz)

Lt. Joe Higgins flew "Meiner Kleiner", a 336th FS P-51B at Debden in the Fall of 1944. The first P-51Bs were delivered to Debden on 27 February 1944. (Art Krieger)

Operations continued throughout the remainder of 1944. On 17 September, the group took part in escorting the massive air drop of British and U.S. paratroopers involved in Operation MARKET GARDEN, the failed attempt to liberate most of Holland by airborne assault. On 21 September, 4th Group pilots shot down five German fighters to bring the group total to over 700 victories – the first group in any theater to score that many victories.

Throughout the rest of 1944 and the four full months of combat in 1945, the 4th Group continued to dominate the Luftwaffe. By now the Germans had unveiled the jet fighters in their arsenal. But it didn't matter. Top scoring pilots and leaders throughout 8th Fighter Command developed tactics to counter the tremendous speed advantage that the German jets had over the Allied fighter types – hit them on the ground!

On 16 April 1945, with the war rapidly winding down to a victory, the 4th Fighter Group was returning from a regular escort mission into Germany. The Luftwaffe made no appearance again as they had very little fuel to fly with. The group swept in low over Rosenheim-Gablingen Airdrome and found it filled with German aircraft of all types, just sitting on the ramps like so many ducks on a pond. When the 4th finally left,

Col. Donald J.M. Blakeslee and Maj. Claiborne Kinnard at Debden during the change of command ceremonies. Col. Blakeslee commanded the 4th FG from January 1944 until November 1944, when Col. Kinnard took command. (Author)

The 335th FS poses for a squadron photo on and around Maj. Pierce McKennon's P-51D, "Ridge Runner", on the Debden ramp in late 1944. The 335th FS finished the war with 262.50 victories. (Author)

Capt. Don Emerson escorts an 8th AF B-17 home to England in his P-51D "Donald Duck" during the late summer of 1944. Capt. Emerson finished the war with seven victories flying with the 336th FS. The 4th FG began receiving P-51Ds just prior to D-Day. (Author)

both airdromes were ablaze with the wreckage of 105 German aircraft.

On the following day, 17 April 1945, Major Fred Glover, and Lieutenants Wilmer Collins, William Meredith, and Douglas Groshong, each destroyed a German aircraft on the ground at Pilzen Airdrome. Although the war would last another three weeks, it would be the last victories that pilots from the 4th Fighter Group would score in World War II. On 25 April 1945, the group took part in a fighter sweep to the Linz-Prague-Dresden area. It was the final mission of the war for the 4th Fighter Group.

The 4th Fighter Group finished the war with a total of 1058 1/2 victories according to 8th Fighter Command statistics, to finish ahead of the 56th Fighter Group for top scoring honors of any unit in World War II. This was later downgraded to 1016. It was here that the motto for the 4th was borne – "Fourth But First." By the end of World War II, twenty-six 4th Fighter Group pilots were crowned 'ace', including thirteen 'double aces' (ten or more victories) and six with more than fifteen victories. This was only air-to-air victories. Ground victories would add another twelve aces to the total.

Capt. Carl Payne (left) and Capt. Thomas Bell wait on the Debden ramp for the call to action. The day was 24 March 1945, and Patton's troops had just crossed the Rhine River into Germany. Capts Payne and Bell both ended the war with 5.50 victories. (Art Krieger)

The 4th Fighter Group was led by Major John Godfrey with 30.60 victories, a fraction more than 1/Lt. Ralph Hofer and Major James Goodson. Major Don Gentile had the most air-to-air victories with 19.83. The 334th Squadron led the squadron totals with 395.42 victories, while the 335th had 262.50, and the 336th had 358.08. None of these totals includes victories with the Eagle Squadrons.

Throughout the Spring and Summer of 1945, the men of the Group celebrated their victory over Germany. Parades were held throughout England and France. And 4th pilots flew airborne salutes and took part in the massive Paris victory celebration. In late May, the group was notified they would be going to war again, against the Japanese in the Pacific.

But the atom bomb ended the Pacific campaign for the 4th Fighter Group before it even began. Aircraft and crews were rotated home or to other units in the summer of 1945. On 27 July, all remaining 4th Group personnel were transferred to Steeple Morden and their beloved Debden was returned to the RAF. On 4 November, the RMS Queen Mary departed England with all that remained of the 4th Fighter Group, docking in New York on the 10th of November, and the 4th Fighter Group was officially inactivated at Camp Kilmer, New Jersey. It wouldn't last long.

Opposite: "Mr. Inside" and "Mr. Outside" were Capts. John Godfrey (left) and Don Gentile. They're seen standing beside Gentile's P-51B "Shangri-La." The two 336th FS pilots accounted for 57 1/2 German victories in World War II. (USAF)

two

Entering the Jet Age

It had been less than a year since the group had been inactivated at Burtonwood. But events in the world were changing so rapidly that the 4th would again be needed. The Soviet Union was now recognized as the new bad guy in a world that was thought to be clear of bad guys after Hitler and Tojo were gone. But here was Joe Stalin, fresh and flushed with victory over the vaunted German Army, now flexing his muscles in Eastern Europe. He refused to give up the countries that his armies 'liberated' in the drive to Berlin. Poland, Czechoslovakia, Eastern Germany – all were now part of the Soviet Union. President Truman saw this and began a slow reorganization of the U.S. military, which had just been down-sized after the end of World War II.

One of the major things that President Truman and the War Department wanted to do, was create a 'new Air Force', a new JET Air Force. The Lockheed P-80 Shooting Star was well into production and the only jet fighter available in the US. The Army Air Force already had two P-80 groups, the 1st Fighter Group at March Field, California; and the recently activated 56th Fighter Group at Selfridge Field, Michigan. The third combat group would be a re-activated 4th Fighter Group.

On 9 September 1946, a small group of officers entered a low, long building at Selfridge Army Air Field. Under authority of General Order 57, Headquarters 15th Air Force, and General Order 21, Headquarters Selfridge Field, the 4th Fighter Group was re-activated. Commanded by Colonel Ernest Beverly, the entire 4th FG was comprised of seven officers, slightly over 100 enlisted men, and eleven tired ex-56th FG P-47N Thunderbolts.

But Selfridge was never intended to be the home of the 'new' 4th FG. As soon as the group had enough personnel to fly and maintain the P-47s properly, they would transfer to their permanent home at Andrews Field. That move came in the Spring of 1947. On 9 May 1947, the 4th officially opened Andrews Field. They were now re-designated a jet fighter unit as they had begun transition training into the P-80 Shooting Star. And the new 4th FG(Jet) was now assigned to Strategic Air Command. Which was very strange since the mission of the 4th was the air defense of the nation's capitol. And they had very few of the new P-80 jets.

While Andrews Field was an active base both during and after the war, no operational unit had been stationed there in quite some time. The few men assigned to the 4th had to rebuild all the living quarters, as well as the maintenance hangers and parking ramps. The same three squadrons would be assigned to the 4th as in World War II – the 334th, 335th, and 336th Fighter Squadrons.

The 334th FS(Jet) was the first squadron to begin operations. They were re-activated on 7 April 1947 with four officers and 42 enlisted men. Lt.Col. Jacob Dixon was the squadron commander. The other three officers were Lt.Col. Herschel Green – Deputy Commander, Maj. Howard 'Deacon' Hively – Asst. Group Operations Officer, and Maj. Ben Emmert was the Engineering Officer. The 334th would certainly not lack in combat experience as these four officers had some forty victories between them.

On 21 April 1947, several pilots were sent to March Field, California, home of the 1st FG(Jet), to receive on-the-job training in flying and maintaining the Lockheed jet. The first of the new P-80 jets started arriving at Andrews in late April, and the training began in earnest. Pilots began checking out in the P-80 in early May. But not at Andrews. Because the Andrews

The 4th Fighter Group was re-activated on 9 September 1946 at Selfridge Field, with seven officers, 100 enlisted personnel, and eleven ex-56th FG P-47N Thunderbolts. When the 4th moved to Andrews Field in May 1947, they took the war-weary Thunderbolts with them. (Warren Bodie)

Field runway was only 5400 feet long, all initial check flights were done using the Langley Field runway, which was 8000 feet long. This offered the pilots many chances at correcting a potentially deadly mistake. Flying the new jets was unlike flying anything else most of these pilots had ever done. The jets were very unforgiving, especially these early models. But once they got the hang of it, most of the pilots said that flying a jet fighter was easier in every way than flying a propeller-driven bird.

On 9 May 1947, Captain Vermont Garrison, an ace with the Eagle Squadron and the original 4th FG, and Captain Staranick, were sent to Williams Field for a sixty day course on the maintenance, performance, and flight capabilities of the P-80A. But many of the pilots were becoming proficient in flying the P-80s enough to began demonstration flights to show the public what the new jets could do. On 31 May 1947, members of the 4th FG(Jet) put on their first air demonstration at Georgetown Airport, Delaware.

June was a very hectic month for the members of the 4th. Captain's Garrison and Staranick returned from Williams and began setting up regulation schools for jet mechanics, armament specialists, and other ground duties on the P-80s. The P-

A 334th FS(Jet) P-80A on the Andrews Field ramp in August 1947. In the Spring of 1947, the 4th FG received their first Lockheed P-80A Shooting Stars, and the unit was redesignated 4th FG(Jet). The 334th FS(Jet) was the first squadron operational in the P-80A. (Dave Lucabaugh)

47Ns were phased out of service by the end of June. Lt.Col. Ben Preston was named CO of the 336th FS. And the 4th performed their first air show at Andrews on 4 June.

July started with a bang, or rather a crash. On the 4th of July, Lt. Webster was forced to bail out of an out-of-control P-80, which crashed near Glen Burnie, Maryland. Lt. Webster was unhurt, and although the airplane was totally destroyed, no one on the ground was hurt either. That same day Captain Alex Melancon (336th FS) set an unofficial speed mark when he flew from Mitchel Field, Long Island, to Andrews Field in twenty-four minutes fifteen seconds, an average speed of 562 mph.

In August, a pilot would be assigned to the 4th FG(Jet) who would forever be remembered in the annals of Korean War history. Major Bruce Hinton, was re-assigned from Panama, to the 335th FS. Maj. Hinton recalls those early days; "I went to the 4th in August of 1947. There was considerable combat experience in the 4th at that time, no doubt due to the energetic effort of Col. Beverly and his close contacts in the Pentagon."

"Checking out in the P-80 in those days was an interesting program. The runways at Andrews were not considered long enough for a summer checkout program. So the checkout program was done at Langley Field, which was much longer. After studying the TO (tech order) on Pilot Operating Procedures,

A 335th FS(Jet) P-80A is towed from the hanger at Andrews in the Summer of 1947. The first P-80s were delivered in an overall gloss gray paint to increase top speed. However, it peeled badly at transonic speeds and actually cost maximum speed. (Author)

A 335th FS(Jet) P-80A at the National Air Race held at Cleveland Municipal Airport on 30 August 1947. Major Clayton Albright flew this 335th P-80A in the Jet Division of the Bendix Trophy race. The aircraft were completely stripped of the gloss gray paint, polished with steel wool pads, and then waxed. And after all that work was accomplished, the race was canceled because of bad weather. (Dave Lucabaugh)

The 4th FG(Jet) had a few P-51Ds in the inventory, which were used as target towing 'tugs' when the Group practiced air to air gunnery over the Atlantic Ranges. Note the tow target (commonly known as 'the rag') attachment under the rear fuselage. (Dave McLaren)

P-80As from the 334th FS(Jet) start engines on the ramp at the Miami Airport in January 1948. The 4th FG(Jet) was invited to take part in the All-American Air Maneuvers and flew many aerobatic shows during the three day event. (Bruce Hinton)

15 May 1948, Capt. Vermont Garrison flew a bag of Special Air Mail letters from Andrews Field to LaGuardia Airport in New York City to celebrate the 30th Anniversary of the introduction of Air Mail to the U.S. Postal Service. (Ron Picciani)

my checkout was a discussion of the peculiarities of flying the P-80, followed by assistance in starting the engine!"

"The Air Force hadn't yet developed a hard helmet for use by jet jockeys. So I had to resort to wearing a football-type helmet borrowed from the tank corps. It had ear flaps that contained the radio receiving headset. Once in the air, I found that the helmet was so loose on my head that when I turned to either side, looking for landmarks or at equipment in the cockpit, I found myself looking right into the ear flaps!"

In the late summer of 1947, a major air show was held at the Cleveland Airport. It was the National Air Races, and featured the best in both military and civilian aircraft and pilots. The 1947 Cleveland race had all three major aviation trophies on the line, the Bendix Trophy, the Thompson Trophy, and the Allison Inter-City Race. The 4th FG(Jet) entered all three races. Contestants included Maj. Clay Albright (335th FS) in the Jet Division of the Bendix race. Lt.Col. Ben Preston (336th FS) and Lt. Joe Howard (335th FS) entered the Thompson Trophy run; and Capt. William Whisner (335th FS) and Lt. La Rose (334th FS) competed in the Allison race.

The Bendix Race was a flight from California to Cleveland. All the aircraft were 'slicked down' prior to the race, i.e. the P-80s were scrubbed down, then polished with Brillo pads before being waxed. This brought the "metal skin" to a high degree of shine with a minimum of drag. But alas, after all that work, the Bendix race was called off due to weather in the Cleveland area. Lt. Howard placed second in the Thompson Trophy Race, and Captain Whisner was fourth in the Allison race.

Squadron insignias were rendered and approved in the late summer of 1947. The 334th FS(Jet) would use the old fighting Eagle insignia from World War 2 days. However, they were always known as the 'Pissed-Off Pigeons'. The squadron color would be yellow. The 335th adopted the indian head as the squadron emblem, called themselves the Chiefs, and had the color red. The 336th designed a totally new emblem showing a jet fighter cockpit attached to a skyrocket. They were known as the Rocketeers, and their color was blue. The aircraft had the nose painted in the squadron color, with the squadron insignia applied in the curve of the color scallop.

In November, the first of many modifications to the P-80 were begun. The aircraft were flown to Lockheed where water injection was installed on the J33, new heating and air conditioning equipment was installed to alleviate pilot discomfort, Jet Assisted Take-Off (JATO) brackets were installed, the pitot head was re-located from the fin tip to under the nose, the gun firing mechanisms were adjusted so that all the guns could be fired at any speed, and the wingtips were beefed up to handle larger drop tanks or bombs. And the gloss gray paint was stripped from all aircraft.

Bruce Hinton; "In November, the P-80As were returned to Lockheed for modifications. We flew the birds into Van Nuys in small groups, then flew them back once Lockheed finished the modifications. The most important of these was installation of a larger hydraulic system accumulator. In those days, we still used the fighter 'pitch-up' for landing. And we found that the hydraulic system, which ran both the landing gear retraction as well as the aileron boost, had insufficient power to handle both. With the airplane at idle during pitch-up, the ailerons lost all boost until the landing gear cycled to full down. The mods corrected that."

The modified airplanes were re-designated P-80A-10. With the removal of the glossy grey paint, Col. Beverly approved a new marking and the nose was painted black, again having the squadron emblem inside the curved part of the nose scallop. Squadron colors were applied to the tip tanks, which had the forward portion painted black, with the squadron color on the aft portion, divided by a thin white line.

The first U.S. Air Force jet aerobatic team was a team of pilots in the 4th FG(Jet). They flew their initial air show at Georgetown Airport, DE, on 31 May 1947, some seven months before the Air Force formed the Acrojets team at Williams Field. (Left to right) Lt. Sandy Hesse (R Wing), Capt. Vermont Garrison (Lead), Lt. Larry 'Mac' McCarthy (Slot), and Lt. Beriger Anderson (L Wing). (Tom Ivie)

In January 1948, the Group was invited to take part in the All-American Air Maneuvers at Miami Airport, one of the premier air shows in the U.S. at the time. Col. Beverly took forty-eight P-80As to the event. The Group left Andrews on 7 January, flying non-stop to Miami. At the show, the Group flew multiple air show schedules, with several different 'teams' performing for the crowds. The remainder of January, February, and March saw the rest of the Group's P-80s brought to A-10 standard.

In April, the three squadrons were all TDY, but to three different events. The 334th left on 5 April for a very long range mission to Spokane AFB, Washington and back to Andrews with a single refueling on each leg. It proved the range of the P-80 could be extended to well over 1000 miles when flown at

A 336th Squadron P-80A starts the engine on the snowy ramp at Ladd Field in November 1948. Col. Ben Preston took sixteen P-80As from the 336th Squadron, deploying to Ladd Field, Alaska on 6 October 1948. The 336th FS(Jet) was in place at Ladd on 10 October 1948, following a 2000 mile flight and seven refueling stops. (Bruce Hinton)

maximum efficiency. The entire flight was performed at 40,000' or better.

On the morning of 7 April, the 336th Squadron went back to Florida. This time the destination was MacDill AFB, and the squadron was not going for a good time on the air show circuit as the purpose was gunnery training. Dive bombing was also improved as the squadron used the Avon Park Bombing Range. Air-to-air targets were towed by the group's lone Douglas A-26 Invader.

The 335th went to Davis-Monthan AFB for joint fighter and bomber missions with B-29s from the 43rd BG(VLR). The 335th P-80s would be the 'aggressor' aircraft, 'attacking' the B-29s in simulated combat. It was something the B-29 crews would experience again about two years in the future, i.e. being attacked by enemy jet fighters. But by a much more formidable foe.

In June, the P-80s once again returned to Lockheed for modifications – winterization for very cold weather operations. The major modifications included; 1.) The left leading edge fuel tank was modified to use 100 octane aviation gasoline in place of the normal JP-1 jet fuel. This alleviated cold weather starting problems as the Avgas had a much lower ignition temperature. 2.) All hose connections were replaced with rubber, which wouldn't crack during extreme cold weather operations. 3.) All aircraft slated for operations over snow-covered regions, had their outer wings and aft fuselage painted bright Insignia Red for visibility in case the airplane went down in the snow.

But the Arctic operations weren't slated until the Fall of 1948. And the men of the 4th didn't have winter on their minds yet. Lt.Col. Preston took four 336th P-80s to Kindley AFB in Bermuda on 29 June. It was a demonstration to the world, and the Soviets in particular, that SAC fighters could perform the long range escort mission anywhere in the world, including vast distances over water. Col. Preston's P-80s made the 720 mile trip in slightly less than two hours, averaging 446 mph. They returned to Andrews on 3 July.

On 10 July, the advance party for the coming winter operations took the group C-47 to Ladd AFB, Alaska. Since the first contingent was slated to be from the 336th Squadron, Headquarters sent Lt.Col. Ben Preston, Maj. Ben Emmert – Group Operations Officer, and Major Bruce Hinton to check out Ladd for any possible problems. While they were gone, Tony Levier brought the first of the new TF-80C two-seat jet trainers to Andrews, taking pilots and ground crew personnel for rides.

The 336th Squadron P-80As remained at Ladd for the entire five months of the Alaskan Maneuvers. Squadron personnel from the other two squadrons were rotated through Ladd every six weeks or so, using the Group C-47 for movement. In April 1949, pilots from the 334th Squadron ferried the Shooting Stars back to Andrews. (Bruce Hinton)

On 31 July, the Group was invited to the opening of Idlewild Airport. It would be a big air show tied in with the airport grand opening. The 4th FG pilots were invited to put on a flying demonstration for the thousands of civilians in attendance. Lt.Col. Ben Preston and Maj. Bruce Hinton, both returned from Ladd, performed a two-ship daily aerobatic show. It was the forerunner of the formation of the first U.S. Air Force jet aerobatic team in history.

With all the air shows that were scheduled, Headquarters decided to form an 'official' team. At first, only two-ship demonstrations were performed with Capt. 'Mack' Lane and Lt. 'Mac' McCarthy. These short demonstrations began on 13 July, continuing into early August. On 10 August, the word came down for the team to begin four-ship flights and get ready to do a show at the Cleveland National Air Races in September.

The team was made up of four pilots from the 334th Squadron. Lead was Capt. Vermont Garrison, Lt. Erwin 'Sandy' Hesse flew Right Wing, Lt. Beriger Anderson was on the Left Wing, and 'Mac' McCarthy flew both the Slot position and was the Solo pilot. This team performed almost seven months prior to the formation of the Acrojets team, which is generally accepted as the first jet team in the Air Force. The 4th FG team had no name, it was simply the 4th FG team.

The first show was performed on 4 September. 'Mac' McCarthy: – "We were allotted 5 minutes for the demonstration. We would start with a loop. At the bottom of the loop I would break out of formation and go into another direction. The remaining 3 ship 'V' would start to get into position for the next maneuver as I rolled upside down and cruised past the reviewing stands at an altitude of 50-100 feet."

"The 'V' would then do a trail roll, after which I did a four point roll before rejoining the other ships for a four ship roll in a tight diamond formation. We then went into an inverted Cuban Eight, ending with another four ship loop. At the bottom of the loop, I'd throttle back to clear Lead's tail, then I'd 'square turn' into a tight climbing roll, continuing as high as I could go. By that time, the rest of the team had performed a 'V' formation landing, after which I'd land and join the others."

"My 'square turns' eventually got me into hot water with Col. Preston, when he found out I was pulling so many 'Gs' on the breakaway that the G-meter was bending on the peg! And I was pulling some of the fillets on the bottom of the airplane right through the rivet heads!"

The Alaskan Maneuvers began on 6 October. Col. Preston took sixteen 336th Squadron P-80s and both Headquarters C-47s, to Ladd AFB. The flight was long and arduous, and made in multiple legs. The first leg was Andrews to Chanute, where the crews stayed overnight. The morning of the 7th, the Squadron went first to Smoky Hill AFB, Kansas, then to Weaver AFB, South Dakota, and finally stopped at Great Falls AFB, Montana. On the 9th, the Squadron went to Edmonton, Alberta, on to Fort Nelson in British Columbia, up to Whitehorse in the Yukon Territory, and finally arrived at Ladd.

The first eight aircraft arrived at Ladd at 1600 hours, flying the 2000 miles from Great Falls to Ladd in a single day. The Squadron was in place by the end of the 10th. Lt.Col. Ben Emmert had gone ahead with 175 ground personnel that were waiting to service the airplanes and get them ready for the training, which started the next morning. This cold weather training didn't end until March 1949.

The cold weather training involved at least one squadron every month, between October 1948 and April 1949. This duty was even more hazardous than normal, and the Group suffered five accidents during the period. Sadly, Lt. Meinzen flew into the ground with P-80A #44-85250A after declaring an unknown emergency. He was killed in the crash.

The 4th FG(Jet) Headquarters building at Langley AFB in 1949. The 4th moved to Langley on 25 April 1949. (R.F. Raasch)

Bruce Hinton: "We, the 335th FS, went back to Ladd in December for another TDY. Ben Preston and I took two additional F-80s up the Alcan Trail to replace a couple of airplanes that had been destroyed in accidents. The winterized F-80s had a separate fuel tank in the wing leading edge, containing 100 octane Avgas, which was then switched over to normal JP-1 jet fuel after we got the engine started."

"We decided early on, to leave the original batch of airplanes from the 336th at Ladd, then simply change the pilot rotation. Pilots were ferried in and out on C-47s, which were flying a non-stop shuttle between Andrews and Ladd, bringing

A 336th Squadron P-80A on the Andrews ramp in the Fall of 1948. The Shooting Star has red wingtips and tail which were applied for operations in Alaska, with black 4th FG nose scallop and tip tanks. The blue tank and fin tip are 336th squadron colors. (via Ken Buchanan)

Capt. Vermont Garrison flew this 334th Squadron P-80A during the UHF tests in early 1949. By this date, the red Arctic markings had been repainted in black. Note that the buzz number has been changed from 'P' for Pursuit, to 'F' for Fighter, which was done after Congress created the new U.S. Air Force in October 1947. (USAF)

in personnel and supplies. Of course, all the F-80s modified for the cold weather tests, had red aft sections and wingtips. This was for high visibility in case they were forced down in the snow." That same month, December 1948, the 4th FG was transferred from SAC to Continental Air Command in the 14th AF, and given an air defense mission.

In February 1949, the Alaskan Maneuver ended, with most of the personnel coming home by 12 March. The pilots from the 334th went to Ladd in March and April, to ferry the remaining sixteen 336th FS Shooting Stars back to Andrews. The last airplane returned on 16 April.

A big air show was flown on 15 February – the Air Force Air Demonstration Show. The purpose was to show off the 'new' Air Force, its progress, and the new aircraft within the Air Force. It wasn't open to the public, and the invited guests included only President Truman, senators and congressmen, and a few high ranking officers from around the world. The F-80s of the 4th FG were the focal point of the demonstration, although several of the brand new North American F-86A Sabres came in from the 1st FG in California, easily putting the F-80s in their place. It was the first time the men of the 4th got a good look at the airplane that would figure very prominently in their future.

April saw the Air Force move the entire group from Andrews to Langley AFB, Virginia. The move was supposed to take place by 25 April. But the squadrons weren't in place until May, with Headquarters and the 335th FS(JET) ready on 1 May, the 336th on 15 May, and the 334th ready for operations on 25 May.

While the move from Andrews to Langley was taking place, the group was notified of two impending events: 1.) They would participate in Operation BLACKJACK, a program to train the crews for the air defense mission. 2.) The 4th FG(J) would be the next unit to transition into the new F-86A Sabre.

BLACKJACK revealed that ground controllers had effective radar control of the group's F-80s at 40,000 feet, to a distance up to 200 miles. This was something else that would come in handy when the 4th moved to the Far East. The 334th and 335th flew the BLACKJACK mission until the middle of the month, at which time it was handed over to the 336th.

On 13 May, the 4th FG(J) gunnery team returned from Las Vegas AFB and the Air Force 1949 gunnery competition. Captain Vermont Garrison's team of Captains Cal Ellis and J.O. Roberts brought home the First Place trophy, with Garrison himself, placing second in individual scoring.

The Sabre Arrives

In late May, several pilots went to March AFB, California, to be checked out in the F-86A Sabre. The Sabre was head and shoulders above everything else in the Air Force. But it could be a handful with an inexperienced pilot. The Sabre flew right on the edge of the Mach, even in level flight. But the controls were still basically those of previous types, i.e. mechanically actuated with a hydraulic boost. And they were simply not able to handle the higher performance of the Sabre. Plus the swept wing made it a very hot landing airplane. The slightest miscalculation by a pilot, could result in immediate disaster.

The first F-86A, #48-200, was delivered to Langley on 6 June 1949 and was flown in by Capt. Dick Creighton, who would become the fourth ace in Korea. By the end of August 1949, the 4th Wing had sixty-seven F-86As in the inventory. (via David Menard)

On 6 June 1949, Captains Dick Creighton, 'Mac' McCarthy, and Bill Mathews ferried in the first F-86As. The first aircraft to land at Langley was F-86A #48-200. But even though the group was rapidly transitioning into the Sabre, all new pilots continued to train in the remaining F-80As. The F-80As would eventually be transferred to the 81st FG(J) at Kirtland AFB, NM. By the end of July, the aircraft status of the 4th stood at forty F-80As, forty-seven F-86As, six F-51D target tugs, three T-6F Texan trainers, and a pair of C-47s. By the end of August, only nineteen F-80s remained in the 4th inventory, with F-86As numbering sixty-seven.

Col. Al Evans, who took over as group commander just as the Sabre was arriving, emphasized the importance of the group becoming combat ready at the earliest possible date. The Soviets had exploded an atomic bomb, and they had the airplane to deliver them to the continental United States – the Tu-4, a copy of the B-29 Superfortress.

As with all new aircraft and systems, problems with the Sabre surfaced almost immediately. Actually, most of the problems were with the J47 engine, not the actual airplane. Turbine wheels started to fail, resulting in several engine fires and explosions. General Electric supplied new turbine wheels, which seemed to alleviate the problem. The leading edge slat was a constant problem, not the least of which was the 'slat lock', a mechanical device that held the slat closed after takeoff.

Bruce Hinton: "I checked out in one of the very early F-86A-1s in June. It had the loose slats which had to be locked in place after takeoff. If you failed to have enough speed to get the slats fully retracted, the lock might not engage. This created some very interesting conditions. One slat could come out on you during high G maneuvers, resulting in some very unequal, and unexpected, roll conditions. The airplane would often snap-roll without any warning at all. Thank God, this was soon eliminated!"

By the end of August, the 4th FG(J) was ready to demonstrate how good both they and the Sabre were. Col. Evans got permission from Air Force to enter a team in the Thompson Trophy Race, held at Cleveland during the National Air Show. Captains Bruce Cunningham (334th) and Martin Johansen (335th) entered the Thompson, while Capt. 'Mac' McCarthy

A trio of 334th FIS F-86As on alert at the Laurenberg-Maxton AB during Exercise SWARMER in April 1950. SWARMER was a 'war game' held in April 1950 for all branches of the U.S. armed forces. Personnel lived in tents during the exercise, a portent of things to come only six months and 9,000 miles later. (USAF)

and Lt. J.O. Roberts went to Cleveland to lead an aerobatic team.

Capt. Cunningham won the Thompson at a record speed of 586.1 mph, which was over sixty mph faster than the 1948 record. Capt. Johansen finished Second. The race could have been even more exciting as Cunningham felt a 'jolt' during lap fifteen in the tail. When he landed, a shiver went down his spine when he noticed that over 2.3 feet of his elevator had been torn off.

North American and Air Force were ecstatic that a.) the Sabre had won the race. and b.) that the damage incurred showed the Sabre to be structurally sound enough to survive the high G loads encountered in combat maneuvers at near Mach One speeds. However, Group Operations restricted flight speed to less than 500 knots below 10,000' until the elevator problem was checked out.

By the end of the month of September, the group had eighty-one F-86As in service, plus nineteen F-80s. But only three of the Sabres were in commission! Recurring problems with the J47, plus a new problem with fuel cell deterioration, caused Air Material Command to ground all the F-86s until the problems were corrected. Ruptured emergency fuel regulator diaphragms allowed the RPMs to exceed limits, causing the turbine to fail. Replacing the fuel cells and regulators cured that problem.

In October, just as the previous problems were being ironed out, the Sabres were again grounded. In all, nine TWXs from AMC were received, each one grounding the F-86s, not just in the 4th but throughout Air Force. Oxygen systems, elevator replacement (a result of the Cunningham incident), more faulty fuel regulators, and other TCTO orders all had to be taken care of.

In November, the group adopted new unit markings. The rudders were painted the squadron color, along with two 4" stripes on the elevators, and two 6" stripes on the wingtips – red for the 334th Squadron, yellow for the 335th, and blue for the 336th. In addition, a 24" squadron insignia was painted on the fuselage, with the 4th FG flaming arrow running through each unit insignia.

By the end of November, the group had eighty-one Sabres on inventory, but were averaging only nine per day in commission. A new problem arose with failure of the nose gear actuating cylinder. Bob Hunter, the North American Tech Rep assigned to the 4th since June, was transferred to the 33rd FG(J) at Otis AFB, the latest unit to transition into the Sabre. Einar 'Chris' Christopherson took Bob Hunter's place in mid-December, inheriting all the latest problems.

Lt.Col. John Carey briefs pilots from the 334th Squadron on Exercise Swarmer held at Laurenberg-Maxton AB, NC. (Left to right) 1Lt. Bertram Anderson, 1Lt. Dick Becker, and 2Lt. T.C. Smith. Lt. Anderson would be killed in action in September 1950, flying F-51D Mustangs in Korea. (Dick Becker)

Armed Forces Day was 20 May 1950, and the personnel of the 4th held an Open House at Langley AFB. The local citizenry lined up for their first close look at the new F-86A Sabre jet. The sign on the nose explains it all – "This Is A F-86 Saber." (Al Evans)

In the Summer of 1950, a famous pilot was given his checkout in the F-86A Sabre by a pilot that would become the first 'jet ace' in history within 10 months. On the left is Col. Hubert 'Hub' Zemke, leader of the famous 56th FG "Wolfpack" in World War II; on the right is Capt. James Jabara, who would shoot down fifteen MiGs in Korea. (Al Evans)

(Left to right) John Henderson – North American Tech Rep, Col. Al Evans, a 4th FG crew chief, and Capt. Harry Casselman on the ramp at Langley AFB in early 1950. Col. Evans was 4th Group Commander in June 1949, and Wing Commander in August 1949. (Al Evans)

The 4th FG(Jet) aerobatic team that performed during the gunnery competition held at Las Vegas AFB in August 1949. (Left to right) The Silver Sabres team – 1Lt. J.O. Roberts, 1Lt. Don Stuck, Capt. Vermont Garrison, and Col. Al Evans Jr. (Al Evans)

On 13 December, Air Force began holding practice alerts with the 335th Squadron, to see how much time it would take the squadron to re-arm and refuel following a mission. It was another piece of the training schedule that would be necessary a year later. The group had ground strafing practice at Bloodsworth Island. And the 336th sent fourteen pilots by C-47 to tour the North American plant. With most of the Sabres grounded, the pilots used the C-47 to perform necessary flying time requirements. But by the end of the year, sixty-eight of the eighty-one F-86s were back in commission.

On 20 January 1950, the 4th FG(JET) was re-designated the 4th Fighter Interceptor Group (FIG), and assigned to Air Defense Command. All the squadrons were also re-designated as fighter interceptor squadrons (FIS).

In March, the group was alerted to participate in a 'war game'. This was Exercise SWARMER, a three week maneuver held jointly with the Army. The 4th moved their Sabres to Laurinburg-Maxton AB on 10 April. It was a bare-base facility, and not a whole lot better than the Korean bases they would occupy in seven months – just a lot warmer. The 4th was to provide top cover for elements of the 314th Troop Carrier Group.

The 4th returned to Langley on 6 May, just in time to receive several of the new '49 model F-86A-5s. The '49 model Sabres had fully automatic leading edge slats, which retracted into the wing leading edge as the aircraft speed increased. No more troublesome slat locks! The new Sabre also had the improved J47-GE-13 engine, which offered greater thrust, and was much more reliable than the -7 engine.

By June 1950, the group had already flown its allotted flying time for Fiscal Year 1949. They were ordered to 'Stand Down!' on the 24th and await the beginning of the next Fiscal Year on 1 July. Bruce Hinton, CO of the 336th Squadron, recalls what happened next: "We were supposed to have a whole week off before resuming operations in July. However, at midnight of the 24th, we received orders to get the entire group together for a briefing."

"After shaking out the bars, homes and whatever, my squadron assembled in the Operations Room. I was handed orders to take my squadron to Andrews, and go on immediate alert. Two Sabres would be on five minute alert to guard the nations capitol against any airborne threat. AIRBORNE THREAT! What was going on? We found out later that the Communists had invaded some country called South Korea."

"Well, after flying up to Andrews, we set up our alert operation using the Andrews Base Ops building. I had a long distance telephone line to the GCI radar site serving as our controller. We held that line open for over forty-eight hours as our 'scramble line', until a secure, direct line was installed. Initially, the alert aircraft was a pair of F-86s stationed at the taxiway entrance to the main runway. We had to leave the engines running since we didn't have any starter carts yet. The airplanes were refueled as needed – with the engines still running!"

"When a "Scramble!" came in over the phone, a standby pilot would race out the door, jump in a jeep, and tear off down the taxiway, yelling and waving at the alert pilots to scramble the airplanes. Of course, all the scrambles were in vain, being off-course airlines, flocks of birds, or some kind of weather anomaly."

"That lasted about two weeks before we were ordered back to Langley. The Korean situation looked like a local deal, and

334th FS(Jet) crew chiefs on the ramp at Las Vegas AFB in August 1949. (Al Evans)

In September 1949, the 4th FG(Jet) entered the Thompson Trophy race Jet Division held at the Cleveland National Air Race. This is Captain Martin Johansen's 334th Squadron F-86A on the ramp at Cleveland Municipal Airport. Johansen finished second behind 4th FG team mate Capt. Bruce Cunningham. (William J Balogh, Sr)

the Russians weren't going to launch an all-out attack against the US. Back at Langley, I received orders to prepare for a Permanent Change of Station (PCS) to Dover AFB, Delaware. DOD was preparing for an attack from any direction. We went to Dover, the 334th and Wing headquarters went to Newcastle County Airport, and the 335th went to Andrews. The date was 13 August."

"There were terrible problems at Dover when we arrived. The base was completely run down, and we had to make it livable again literally overnight. As I put the first bunch of F-86s onto the Dover runway, I noticed the place was overrun with Air Guard P-47s on summer maneuvers. Since it was a short TDY for the Guard guys, they'd been living in tents and other broken down buildings. Most of the base hadn't been inhabited since the end of the war."

"I landed and went directly to their Headquarters. There was a major general sitting at the desk. I rendered him a right smart salute, and calmly stated "Sir, I'm taking command of this base!" I'll never forget the surprised and humorous look on his face as he replied to me, a lowly major, "Yes sir!""

The situation in Korea became very bad during the late summer of 1950. The UN forces attempting to repel the North Korean invasion, had been driven into a small pocket in southeastern Korea, around the town of Pusan. The F-80s, F-51Ds, and F-82s of the 5th Air Force, the Far East Air Force (FEAF) B-29s, and Navy and Marine carrier air forces, had driven the North Korean Air Force (NKAF) from the skies over the entire Korean peninsula. But the ground war was still very much in doubt.

1Lt. Phil Janney was a pilot in the 335th FS(Jet) in 1950, and went with the Group when they deployed to Korea in November. (Phil Janney)

But the Pusan Pocket held long enough for General Douglas MacArthur to come up with a strategic surprise for the Reds. On 15 September, MacArthur's troops surprised the hell out of the Reds by making a sea-borne invasion at Inchon, just west of the South Korean capitol of Seoul. Within a couple of weeks, the communists were in full retreat. UN troops drove them back across the 38th Parallel.

But MacArthur didn't stop there. The UN ground forces, supported by elements of FEAF and 5th AF, chased the fleeing Reds back towards the Yalu. MacArthur was going to re-unite Korea under the UN flag. He was so confident of success, that he told the press that his troops would probably be home by Christmas. However, Joe Stalin and his gang had other ideas.

However, the men with the 4th Wing had problems of their own. On 18 October 1950, three F-86s were lost, and two pi-

Capt. Bruce Cunningham flew this 335th Squadron F-86A, #48-254, to first place in the Thompson Trophy race at Cleveland Municipal Airport, averaging 586.1 mph, some sixty mph faster than the record set at the 1948 Thompson Trophy race by a Lockheed F-80. (Warren Bodie)

lots were killed in a bizarre accident near Washington, D.C. 1Lt. Joseph Russell, with 2nd Lts. Luther C. Barcus and Carnelius P. Mills on his wing, left Andrews AFB on a routine training flight. After an eighty minute flight during which the three pilots practiced formation flying and engaged in some good-natured camera gunnery on each other, the flight began their return to Andrews.

Letting down over the Potomac River on final back to Andrews, the flight ran into a haze layer at about 1000 feet. But they continued their letdown through the fog, hoping to break out just over the end of the runway. Lt. Barcus was concentrating on keeping a tight formation when suddenly the other two Sabres disappeared in two violent explosions. Barcus himself, thought he had just flown into a brick wall. Regaining his senses and control of the damaged Sabre, Barcus radioed Andrews Control that the other two Sabres had crashed.

Barcus continued flying until he ran out of fuel near Aden, Virginia, about thirty miles southwest of Andrews. He picked out a large farmers field and made a wheels-up landing, destroying the Sabre. Two farmers found Barcus wandering around in the field, with a broken leg and multiple cuts and bruises.

The three Sabres had let down through the haze in a tight 'V' formation, with the wingmen concentrating on the leader. As Lt. Russell searched through the haze for the ground, he made a slight bank. The three Sabres were so low that both Russell and Mills' aircraft struck the Potomac River with their wingtips. Lt. Barcus had slightly more altitude and ricocheted off the water like a flat stone. Both Russell and Mills were killed in the crash. Lt. Barcus survived but never flew with the 4th again.

In early October the Chinese Reds began moving large numbers of troops into North Korea, both in front of and behind the UN forces that were steadily moving toward the Yalu River border with Manchuria. At the same time, Stalin committed units of the Soviet Air Force to the conflict. These units were equipped with the Mikoyan-Gurevich type 15 jet fighter – the MiG-15.

1Lt. Dick Merian lost hydraulic power in his 336th Squadron F-86A, resulting in the nose gear not extending. He crashed just off the runway at Andrews in October 1950. The Sabre, #48-227, could not be repaired in time to make the STRAWBOSS deployment to Korea and was replaced with an aircraft from the 33rd FIG. (Dick Merian)

At 1345 hours, a flight of four 5th AF F-51Ds escorting an RAF Mosquito photo reconnaissance aircraft, were jumped by two swept wing jet fighters with red star markings. Although the Mustangs and Mosquito easily maneuvered away from the Red jets, the arrival of the MiGs changed the air war dramatically. Literally overnight, the MiG had obsoleted everything 5th AF and the Navy had in the theater. The MiGs did something that hadn't occurred since 1942 – wrested air superiority away from a U.S. force.

The 5th AF F-80 pilots, flying an inferior airplane, put up a good fight against the much faster MiG. Indeed, they shot down a couple of the speedy Red jets using greater pilot skills. But FEAF knew the F-80s were out-classed. And the Reds could do whatever they wanted, when they wanted. It's a good thing the Reds didn't realize it. FEAF needed something to counter the MiG threat – and they needed it yesterday! That something was the F-86 Sabre. Air Force Headquarters concurred. On 9 November 1950, a TWX went out from the Pentagon to Headquarters, 4th Fighter Interceptor Wing at Newcastle. The 4th was going to Korea – The Land Of The Morning Calm.

three

"A Short TDY": Operation Strawboss

RESTRICTED
HEADQUARTERS
4TH FIGHTER-INTERCEPTOR WING
New Castle County Airport
Wilmington, Delaware

CT 370 11 November 1950

SUBJECT: Movement Order

TO: See Distribution

1. In accordance with provisions of Warning Order, Headquarters Eastern Air Defense Force, dated 9 November 1950, and Operations Order Serial Number 28-50, Headquarters Continental Air Command, dated 10 November 1950, the following named units at the approximate personnel strength indicated will proceed from stations indicated to a theater of operations in a temperate climate for an indefinite period of TDY. Provisions of AFR 75-37 "Preparation for Overseas Movement POM", are waived except for immunization as outlined in paragraph 4a, below.

Unit	Shipment No	Approx Str Off	Approx Str Amn	T/O&E
Hq & Hq Sq, 4th Ftr-Intcp Wg	5259A	30	64	1-1011, 24 Mar 48, 1 x colm 5, 1-00P1c, 1 Jul 49
Hq 4th Ftr-Intcp Gp	5259B	11	25	1-1212, 24 Mar 48, 1 x colm 5
334th Ftr-Intcp Sq	5259C	30	108*	1-1233, 24 Mar 48, 1 x colm 5, 1-0001D, 1 May 49
335th Ftr-Intcp Sq	5259D	30	108*	1-1233, 24 Mar 48, 1 x colm 5, 1-0001D, 1 May 49
336th Ftr-Intcp Sq	5259E	30	108*	1-1233, 24 Mar 48, 1 x colm 5, 1-0001D, 1 May 49
Hq 4th Maint & Supply Group	5259F	4	10	1-7012, 24 Mar 48, 1 x colm 5, 1-0001D, 1 May 49
4th Maint Sq	5259G	9	126*	1-7213, 24 Mar 48, 1 x colm 5 as modified by P&E1L 1-7213 & 1-0001C

Copies of the movement orders that sent the 4th Fighter Wing to Korea in November 1950.

With those simple words the men, aircraft and equipment of the 4th FIG went to Korea, The Land Of The Morning Calm. But it was certainly not calm almost any morning anywhere in Korea, what with the scream of bullets, bomb explosions, and the whine of jet engines. And it was definitely not a "temperate climate." When the Sabres touched down at K-14, the temperature was sub-zero, snow would blanket the area almost every morning. and temperatures on the flightline would often touch -40° in the early morning hours.

Operation STRAWBOSS was put into effect on 10 November, and the pilots began ferrying the aircraft west to the points of embarkation on the 11th. The 334th and 335th Squadrons took forty-nine Sabres to San Diego Naval Air Station, where they were loaded aboard the Navy escort carrier USS Cape Esperance. The 336th Squadron ferried seventeen F-86As to McClellan AFB, then to the naval air station at Oakland, where they were loaded onto at least four commercial tankers.

Both before and during the flights to the embarkation points, STRAWBOSS orders called for all the other F-86 groups to give up their newest F-86A-5s to the 4th FIG. The 4th, being the second unit to convert to F-86As, had very few of the new '49 FY Sabres. The 1st FIG gave up eight new Sabres, the 33rd traded twenty-one to the 4th, Col. 'Gabby' Gabreski's 56th Group turned over eighteen Sabres, the 81st FIG gave the 4th five F-86As, and The Fighter School at Nellis traded eight Sabres to the 4th.

Their wasn't time for proper maintenance prior to shipment to the Far East. The newer aircraft that had been transferred from other units, weren't even inspected. Nor was there time for proper preparation of the aircraft for the coming two

10 November 1950 – personnel of the 4th FIG load equipment and supplies aboard a C-46 at New Castle County Airport, for the 'short TDY' to a 'theater of operations in a temperate climate'. What a crock! -40° is not temperate! Neither is a seven year deployment!(Troy White)

week ocean voyage. Paper and masking tape was used to cover openings and control surfaces that might be damaged by salt spray. But these quickly tore off during the voyage. And many of the birds aboard the aircraft carrier had wings or tail surfaces that extended beyond the edge of the deck, making resealing virtually impossible. On top of that, Navy personnel damaged quite a few aircraft during loading and unloading, including one aircraft that was dropped.

Bruce Hinton: "On the 9th of November, we received orders to prepare to move to Japan. We had to be out of Dover by 1100 hours on the 11th. The 334th and 335th would go to San Diego to be loaded onto a Navy aircraft carrier. My squadron, the 336th, was to fly to McClellan AFB near Sacramento, to be loaded onto a tanker. We had to be at our destinations within forty-eight hours – or else!"

"I left Dover with the last four F-86s at about 1030 hours on the 11th, a Saturday. By eight that evening (2200 hours), I landed at Amarillo, Texas, which was an Air Material Command base. One of my pilots was down there with a sick bird. His '86 needed an engine change. An engine change on a Saturday night at an AMC base! The base commander calmly and firmly told me 'No Way!'"

"I followed our priority letter and asked to use the phone. I called Headquarters Air Force at the Pentagon. The priority letter said quite simply to use the word STRAWBOSS to whomever answered. Hearing who I was and the word 'STRAWBOSS', the general on the other end said 'Where are you?' And then asked to speak to the AMC base commander. In slightly over an hour, a civilian crew from General Electric was on base – with a brand new J47."

"I ordered the rest of the flight to go on to Sacramento as the new engine was being installed. At 0400, the F-86 was ready for a test hop. The GE rep told the pilot to 'Circle the field for an hour, land, and we'll re-check everything.' Since we only had eight more hours to get to McClellan, I told the pilot to tell the GE guys 'OK'. We both took off at 0430. Once airborne, I asked him if it looked OK. He said yes as we circled the field

The 334th and 335th Squadrons flew their Sabres to North Island NAS in San Diego, where the aircraft were loaded onto the flight deck of the USS Cape Esperance. Prior to embarkation for the Far East, the 4th traded several of their older, high-time Sabres for newer aircraft taken from the inventories of the 1st, 33rd, and 56th Groups. (John Henderson)

one time. We straightened out and started west – with the GE guys screaming at us over the radio."

"We caught the rest of my gang at Nellis, refueled and departed for Sacremento. I led the squadron on the final leg. We went due west into California, then turned north. Since we didn't know what the results would be from our upcoming new adventure, I did something I'd never done before or since. I buzzed my home town of Stockton, California. Twenty-five F-86s in combat spread! It probably would have gotten me grounded except that our next stop was a little outside the normal official circles."

The tankers departed San Francisco the week of 15 November. The Sabres were lashed to the top deck and covered with a light film of oil. The USS Cape Esperance, with forty-nine Sabres and several F-84Es tied down to the flight deck, left San Diego almost two full weeks after the tankers carrying the 336th Squadron. The ground crews and tech reps went with the airplanes. But the pilots went to Travis AFB, and were flown to Japan aboard Air Force C-54s.

The Cape Esperance arrived at Yokosuka on 10 December, about two weeks after the tankers carrying the 336th Squadron Sabres. North American Tech Rep John Henderson recalls the condition of the airplanes:

"We dropped anchor in Tokyo Bay across from Kisarazu AB. The carrier could not pull into the docks because of her deep draft. So we had to double handle the airplanes, first off-loading them onto barges for the trip to the dock, then off-load them again from the barge onto the dock. Handling aircraft with a sling and hoist is a worrisome thing. But in this case there wasn't any other way."

"As soon as the airplanes were on dry land, they were taken to the wash rack for de-greasing and cleaning. We were met by a large contingent of 4th FIG maintenance and supply troops, along with men from the 6408th Maintenance Squadron from Kisa. The 6408th guys supervised the large compliment of Japanese movers and cleaners that worked at Kisa."

"All the Sabres suffered, to some degree, a galvanic corrosive action caused by salt water action between magnesium and aluminum metals that were in direct contact. It was mainly trailing edges of the wings and tail. When the first 'clean' Sabres got to the hangers, the Air Force inspectors began listing all the 'squawks' that had to be corrected before the aircraft could go to the flightline for pre-flighting."

"My chief concern was the condition of the aircraft extremities. Dents in the wing tips and trailing edges, abrasions on the canopy glass caused by the slings – everything that had to do with hoisting and swinging the airplanes from one level to another. We really lucked out on the handling problems, as we had none of great consequence."

"Chris (North American Tech Rep 'Chris' Christopherson) and I had been warned by the 6408th guys to look for places of corrosion. Oddly enough, we'd noticed an F-84 with a flat tire that was still tied down to the deck. Closer inspection revealed

4th FIG Sabres on the deck of the USS Cape Esperance are covered with a thin layer of cosmoline to retard the corrosive effects of salt spray during the Pacific crossing. The aircraft with the three tail stripes are from the 33rd FIG, while the tri-color tail came from the 56th FIG. The cosmoline wasn't near enough as corrosion was extensive on all the flying surfaces when the Sabres arrived in Japan. (John Henderson)

Lt.Col. John Meyer, Commander of the 4th FIG, is greeted by Capt. Maitland, the CO of the 6408th Maintenance Squadron at Kisarazu AB, Japan on 10 December 1950. In the background are some of the Sabres assigned to the 4th, including an ex-1st FIG Sabre. (Bruce Hinton)

that the steel axle had went through the magnesium wheel, the result of extreme corrosion, and the axle was resting on the top of the flat tire! Electrolytic action had caused this failure in only thirteen days at sea!"

"The airplanes all had much the same degree of corrosion damage. Some of the trailing edges were cleaned and provided with a protective coating. They could be flown until the next regular inspection. Others had to have the corrosion reworked by chemical treatment. Still others had much worse problems and were down until the corroded part was removed from the airplane, and either repaired by cutting out the damage, or replaced."

The 336th airplanes, although suffering from similar damage, were rushed through the cleaning process and pre-flighted. Since the airplanes were in a variety of markings from the previous units they had served with, all markings were removed. The airplanes then had new 4th FEAF approved combat mark-

When Detachment A movëd into Kimpo AB on 13 December 1950, the base was a mess, having been fought over twice already. There were eight to ten Class 26 (scrap) F-80C air frames on the base, which were cannibalized for parts. John Henderson 'borrowed' some aluminum tubing and armor plate for use on the Det A Sabres. (John Henderson)

Below: With similar silhouettes in the air, the F-86 and the MiG could be mistaken for one another during the heat of battle. Far East Air Force ordered all the F-86s to have 6" black and white stripes painted around the fuselage and wings to make identification in the air easier. (Bruce Hinton)

ings applied. Since the airplanes bore a striking resemblance to the MiGs, it was decided to apply some quick ID stripes such as those applied to Allied aircraft prior to the D-Day landings in World War II. They even chose the same colors. All the 4th FIG Sabres had three white and two black bands painted around the wingtips and the fuselage behind the canopy. In addition, a black stripe was painted on the rudder. Squadrons would be identified by a single color band just behind the nose intake – red for the 334th FIS, yellow for the 335th, and blue for the 336th.

As soon as the airplanes were painted, Lt.Col. Bruce Hinton led them directly to Korea. Staging through Taegu for the last leg of the flight, the first seven F-86As arrived at Kimpo AB (K-14) on 13 December 1950. What they found wasn't exactly conducive to high performance jet aircraft operations.

It was, in fact, the roughest conditions many of them had ever seen. And more than one had been in some of the rough North African and Pacific bases during the last war. Opposing armies had fought through Kimpo at least twice in the past six months. Permanent buildings and hangers, those that still stood, were gutted and windowless. They might be usable as a windbreak from the terrible frigid winds blowing in from the north.

John Henderson recalls: "The blowing dust of summer was now frozen mud from the bitter cold that blew out of Manchuria. The temperature was sub-zero the entire length of the peninsula. The base was crowded, had very little hard stand area for parking, and a single 5,000 foot runway with no overrun. The changes between stateside duty and Korea took a lot of getting used to, not just the austere working conditions, but the change in working demands from peacetime to war conditions taxed all the personnel."

Army road graders were pressed into service to plow the runways at Kimpo on the afternoon of 16 December. (Irv Clark)

"The Sabres were maintained on the open ramps. There were no hangers, not even revetments to break the wind. We had a specific area in which to park and maintain the airplanes. We had enough intake and exhaust plugs to keep foreign objects out of the intakes while parked. But foreign object damage (FOD) was a constant threat as the Sabres taxiied for takeoff. The best the crews could do was to 'police up' their own

Snow covers the Kimpo runway and the aircraft of Det A on 16 December 1950. Lt.Col. Bruce Hinton took seven Sabres of Det A into Kimpo on 13 December, flying an orientation flight on the 15th. The first mission to MiG Alley was scheduled for the 16th but was canceled because of the weather. (Bruce Hinton)

The runways are plowed and the sun came out on 17 December. Col. John Meyer led the morning mission to Kanggye, escorting a force of B-29 Superfortresses. No MiGs were sighted on the morning mission. (Bruce Hinton)

Lt.Col. Bruce Hinton led a flight of four F-86As on the afternoon mission, with Capts. 'Mo' Pitts, Ray Janaczek, and 1Lt. Paul Bryce in his flight. Flying to the Yalu River, the Det A Sabre pilots used F-80 radio call signs and cruising speeds, in an attempt to trick the MiGs into thinking they were Shooting Stars. The ruse worked and Bruce Hinton shot down one of the intercepting MiG fighters. (Bruce Hinton)

areas all the time. We also had a walking party police the taxiways prior to takeoff or landing."

In spite of the horrible conditions at K-14, Detachment A of the 4th FIG was in place the night of 13 December 1950. The next mooring, the aircraft were completely checked over and made combat ready. The first mission was slated for the following morning, 15 December. That first mission turned out to be an orientation flight of the area, and the route to and from MiG Alley in northwest Korea. MiG Alley was the term the pilots used for an area south of the Yalu River, down to about the Chong Chon River, and east to the Suiho Dam area. This was based on known information about the range of the MiG. The Yalu River was approximately 230 miles from K-14.

The first combat mission to MiG Alley was scheduled for 16 December. But a snow storm completely blanketed Kimpo, shutting down all operations until the Army could get the runways plowed. And by the time the Army plows were in place and had the runways open, the day was over. The first mission would have to wait until the following morning.

The First MiG Kill

The morning mission was led by Col. John C. Meyer, Group Commander of the 4th. The mission took off at about 0900 and proceeded north, where they rendezvoused with a flight of B-29s. The B-29 target was Kanggye, North Korea. All went well, the B-29s hit the target, and no MiGs were sighted. The Sabres returned to Kimpo more than a little upset at the lack of action.

The afternoon mission was a different story. At 1405K (local time), Creature Baker Flight lifted off the runway at Kimpo. The four F-86s were flown by Lt.Col. Bruce Hinton, Capt. 'Mo' Pitts, Capt. Ray Janaczek, and Lt. Paul Bryce.

Bruce Hinton: "Our F-86s blasted a cloud of snow as they powered away from the parking ramp at K-14. With two 120 gallon tanks hung under the wings and 1800 rounds of .50 caliber ammunition, each Sabre had its full combat load. Our mission was CAP 04 Baker, the second combat air patrol (CAP) flown that day."

"At 1405K, Baker 1 and 2 splashed down the Kimpo runway, followed six seconds later by 3 and 4. Join-up was delayed by a landing gear that failed to retract on my aircraft – probably due to water splashing up onto the gear door lock and freezing during takeoff. I operated the gear retraction system several times and finally broke it loose. We were on our way, and we were motivated. We joined up, switched to combat channel, checked in, and I slid the rudder pedals causing my bird to fishtail, the signal for combat spread formation."

The weather at Kimpo was lousy, even when it was at its best, with temperatures reaching -40° on the ramp. A snow storm blew in during the morning of 18 December, blanketing all the aircraft with snow. But the ground crews cleaned the aircraft off, and the Army plowed the runway again, and Col. Meyer took the Sabres up to the Yalu against the MiGs on the 20th. (John Henderson)

"Climbing out to 25,000 feet, we took a heading directly for Sinuiju, about 200 miles away on the Yalu. Somewhat symbolically, we tested our guns as we crossed over the North Korean capitol of Pyongyang. We had clear skies, and visibility all the way to Moscow. Below us was the rugged Korean landscape of ragged mountain ridges and peaks, all covered with fresh snow."

"As we approached Sinuiju, I motioned for the rest of the flight to drop the speed down to about .65 Mach, approximating that of a flight of F-80s. We knew they had radar at Antung, and possibly a GCI (intercept) controller that would call the MiGs down to engage the "F-80s" that were intruding into their air space. We wondered if they knew that we were even in the theater, and how much they knew about our airplanes as opposed to the F-80s."

"About five miles south of Sinuiju, we turned right in combat spread, and began a patrol parallel with the Yalu River, the well advertised border between the MiG sanctuaries and the combat of MiG Alley. They could attack us from their side of the Yalu, but we weren't permitted to cross the Yalu under any circumstances for fear of spreading the war. Although we suspected the MiGs were being flown by Russian pilots, we had no proof."

Kimpo, 22 December 1950. Snow still covers the ramp from the storm on the 16th, but all aircraft are in the air for the morning mission. The 'Witches Tit' or 'Mt. Useless' is in the background, a welcome sight to pilots returning from the Yalu. "If you can see Mt. Useless in the morning, you were flying!" (John Henderson)

Hot start! During the extremely cold weather at Kimpo, it was not unusual to have a false start, resulting in fuel pooling in the tailpipe. John Henderson often physically pulled the airplane down by the tail, so that the fuel would drain out. (John Henderson)

"With the sun high behind us, someone broke radio silence – "Baker Lead, I have bogies at nine o'clock low and crossing." Slightly below us at about 20,000 feet and climbing, I saw a flight of four swept wing fighters moving very fast, crossing our path about a mile ahead. It was a completely startling sight. They were in loose fingertip formation. Their speed was astonishing. I punched the mike button – "Baker, drop tanks now!" But the rest of the flight didn't react. My transmitter was dead!"

"The MiGs went across to our right side and started a climbing turn back into us. No time to lose, I thought, and I punched off my drop tanks, and firewalled the throttle. Upon seeing my tanks come off, the rest of the flight did likewise. A hard pull into their turn brought me in at five o'clock to them and closing."

"The MiGs, looking more white than silver against the snow, were climbing to meet us, at the same time that we were diving slightly on them. I picked out the lead element to attack. Baker 3 and 4 were headed for the other MiG element. As I closed to within about 4,000 feet, the MiG drop tanks came off."

"I checked my air speed as I moved into the six o'clock position on the MiG element I had staked out. Our Sabres were red-lined at .95 Mach, and my mach meter indicated a pretty good gap over the red line as I started to close. It was the highest speed I'd ever flown a Sabre at."

"At this point the MiG flight began to spread. MiGs 3 and 4 seemed to be breaking off under the lead element. MiG Lead and 2 slowly rolled from a right climbing turn, into a level left bank, with Lead going slightly high. That settled it. I picked up the closest MiG, No.2, put my pipper on his left fuselage about where I thought the fuel tank should be, and closed. I was using stadiametric ranging on the gun sight, with a 30' span on the setting."

The maintenance crews at Kimpo in December 1950 worked under some of the worst conditions ever encountered by any Air Force crews. Here are two mechanics pulling the aft section from an F-86A at Kimpo even as the snow flies. The rear fuselage section was held to the forward fuselage with four hardened bolts and was reasonably easy to remove. But not in the snow and below 0 temperatures. (John Henderson)

"All this time I could hear the rest of my flight on the radio. They were trying to call me keeping me advised of my position, the rest of the MiGs positions, and their moves to counter any threat against me. But of course I couldn't answer them. But about now I was almost within good gun range and I stopped hearing them at all."

"At about 1500 feet I let go with a short burst, and saw strikes against the middle left fuselage, and from the right wing where my bullet pattern had sprayed across the MiG. The holes caused some kind of leak, possibly from the MiG fuel tank. I waited for a few seconds and watched."

"The MiG leader had drifted higher, sitting at about two o'clock and 200 feet higher than his No.2 and myself. Could he get into position to hit me? Where was he going? Was he going to work a defensive split (US pilots would), which would draw me off. Or was he trying to pull a high attack on my wingman and me?"

A Det A F-86A on the Kimpo ramp in late December 1950. By the 20th, Det A had grown to almost a full squadron and could put up several flights of four for each mission. The 4th suffered its first loss on 22 December when the MiGs came up in strength and shot down 1Lt. Larry Bach, a 336th Squadron pilot. (Bruce Hinton)

Navy Lt.Cmdr. Paul Pugh was 'on loan' to the 4th FIG when the unit deployed to Korea, remaining with the unit until mid-1951. Cmdr. Pugh would score his only victory of the war on the same day the Group lost Lt. Bach. (Author)

Det A crew chief Sgt Henry Price points to the small red victory star painted on Col. John Meyer's F-86A, #49-1210. Following the loss of Lt. Bach on the morning mission of 22 December, Det A pilots shot down six MiGs on the afternoon mission. (Henry Price)

"Wingman? Where was Baker 2? He wasn't with me. Then I knew. We'd initiated a break into the MiGs just as my transmitter quit. And I had momentarily straightened out as I tried to get the radio to work. Baker 2, 3, and 4 had continued the hard break into the MiGs. My pause had caused a separation between them and myself. I was alone!"

"I decided to watch MiG Lead, but continue to work on MiG 2, who suddenly popped his speed brakes, then retracting them immediately. That momentary lapse in flight discipline on the part of MiG 2 allowed my closure rate to increase dramatically. I put the pipper right on his tailpipe, hoping to get at his engine."

"I started bouncing and twisting violently in his jet wash. So I slid slightly inside and out of his turbulence. At about 800 feet, I pressed the trigger and put a good long burst into his engine. Pieces flew off the MiG and smoke filled his tailpipe. Then a long flame started coming out of the opening. His air speed dropped abruptly and I put out my speed brakes and throttled back to idle – but I was still closing. We just hung there in the sky, turning left, with my airplane tight against the underside of the MiG in a show formation."

"We were about five feet apart and I got a good close look at the MiG. It was a beautiful, sports car of an airplane. The silver aluminum was clean and gleaming. No dirt on the underside anywhere. The rivets and structure looked first class. After hanging close together for a seemingly long time (actually only seconds), I moved out and over him looking for the other MiGs. No one in sight – we were all alone. The MiG was losing altitude rapidly in a 45° left bank, and slowing."

"Moving further to his inside, now about 2,000 feet above me, I thought, 'Why doesn't he blow?' The MiG was smoking from several places and fire was still coming out the tailpipe. 'OK', I thought, 'I'll finish him off.' In a diving left turn, I put the pipper on the forward fuselage and fired a long, long burst. The API flashed and twinkled on the left and right wing roots and cockpit area. The MiG rolled on his back and went into a dive, trailing smoke and flames toward the snow-covered ground below."

"It was then that I started hearing the radio again. Baker 3 and 4 had just broken off their chase of the other MiG element. To our surprise, the MiGs had simply outrun the Sabres back across the Yalu and sanctuary. Baker 2, my wingman, had joined up with 3 and 4, asking them if they had seen me. No one had. They had seen an airplane go down, but didn't know who or what it was. And I couldn't tell them."

"I finally caught up to them during the flight back to Kimpo. It was a long flight home, especially long since I couldn't tell anyone about the outcome of my MiG fight. But I let the troops on the ground know as soon as we entered the traffic pattern at Kimpo. I rolled my Sabre up and over, putting the Sabre into a long fast dive over the active runway. I leveled off at about 150 feet and well over 500 knots, and performed the customary victory roll over the field."

Lt.Col. Bruce Hinton had scored the first MiG victory by an F-86 pilot. It wouldn't be the last. 5th Air Force pilots would shoot down well over 800 MiG-15s during the war. Pilots from the 4th FIG would account for over 500 of those victories. But Lt.Col. Hinton's was the first.

Interestingly, Capt. 'Mo' Pitts, who had been the Officer In Charge of the advance party into Kimpo, also had a problem which should have prevented his takeoff on the mission. In his haste to get ready for the flight, Mo had jumped into his flight suit, grabbed his helmet and parachute, and went to his airplane. He was in the airplane, hooking up his equipment, when he realized that he didn't have a mike hookup for his radio. They were already starting engines for the mission.

The flight was already starting to taxi out. Rather than delay the takeoff, or even abort his element because of defective equipment, Mo Pitts started to taxi. With radio silence all the way to the Yalu, Mo's silence wasn't noticed by Hinton or anyone else. Upon landing, Mo could be heard saying "There was no way I was going to miss going on that flight!"

The die had been cast. The 4th FIG Sabres had regained control of the air in Korea. And the weather started to cooperate. Missions were flown, usually two a day, from that day forward. Of course, the MiGs didn't always come up. And many times when they did, they simply 'hid' on their perch, high above where the F-86A could go.

On 18 Dec, the morning mission went to MiG Alley, only to find the MiGs didn't want to come out and play. Weather canceled the afternoon flight. On the 19th, the MiGs came up against Lt.Col. Hinton, Lt. Rudy Holley, Lt.Col. Glenn Eagleston and Lt. Al Upchurch. Hinton got in some hits but the MiG didn't go down. On the afternoon of the 19th, the MiGs again came up, but only Col. Eagleston was able to draw within range. He claimed one Damaged.

The weather was lousy on the 20th, although Capt. Howard Lane did take eight Sabres through the clouds to MiG Alley, only to find the MiG fields were also socked in. Two missions were flown on the 21st, with Col. Eagleston getting another Damaged on the mooring mission. Col. Meyer led the afternoon mission, but the MiGs ran away and hid.

The fuel 'dump' at Kimpo during the first few weeks of the conflict before fuel trucks were flown in. Fuel was delivered to Det A in fifty-five gallon drums, which had to be hand-pumped into the airplanes. Each Sabre had a capacity of 675 gallons with empty drop tanks, requiring at least twelve drums of fuel per mission. (John Henderson)

Drop tanks were delivered in wooden crates, then stacked alongside the runway for the next mission. Being out in the open in the elements, the tank release mechanisms suffered from problems with wiring and water, which often caused the tanks not to drop in a combat situation. (John Henderson)

"Burr Head" a 334th Squadron Sabre in the snow at Kimpo in December 1950. Det A was made up of any aircraft that were flyable after the corrosion damage caused by the Pacific trip. It would be Spring 1951 before all the aircraft were declared back in commission. (Henry Price)

The First Loss

By the 22nd, Det 'A' had grown to almost squadron strength. Flights to the combat arena were now flown by up to eight aircraft. On the morning of 22 December, Lt.Col. Nance led Red Flight with Captains Ed Farrell, Joe Brooks, and Capt. Larry Bach; while Capt. Ray Janeczek led White Flight, with Lt. Hubert Shackelford, Lt. Simpson Evans, and Lt. Arthur O'Conner. After patrolling the Yalu in the Sinuiju area for a few minutes, Nance's flight was jumped by eight MiGs at about 35,000 feet. The MiGs were already in position at six o'clock high when Col. Nance called, "Red Flight, break right and drop tanks now!"

The MiGs were at about 1000 yards range and closing rapidly. The MiGs opened fire on Col. Nance's element and hit Capt. Bach's Sabre several times with heavy cannon fire near the wingroot. Bach's Sabre immediately began a series of violent snap rolls, while heading toward the ground. The MiGs continued to press the attack against Col. Nance, but Captains Farrell and Brooks, took up a covering position on Nance and started calling the breaks.

These MiGs were not like the previous ones encountered since Hinton's victory. They were extremely aggressive, and knew what their airplane could and couldn't do. With Farrell and Brooks calling the breaks and trying to get into position on the MiGs firing on Nance, another flight of MiGs started in for a head-on pass against the remainder of Red Flight. But they missed and Red Flight, now at 'Bingo' fuel, started to exit the area.

Janeczek's White Flight was just pulling into the area as Red was exiting. The MiGs were back on their perch, high above the inbound Sabres, and flying a lazy circle as if taunting the Sabres. Janeczek's flight started to close on the high-flying MiGs, when they suddenly broke into them and attacked. Janeczek's flight did get off several rounds, but the MiGs had built up too much speed and flew straight threw White Flight, headed toward the deck and crossed the river. White Flight was now also at 'Bingo' and headed for home.

The CO of the 336th FIS, and the first Sabre pilot to shoot down a MiG, was Lt.Col. Bruce Hinton. Hinton would end the war with two confirmed victories and many 'probables'. (Bruce Hinton)

Because of the aggressive nature of the MiG attacks, and the fact that Red 3 and 4 were busy trying to cover Red Leader, no one was able to see whether or not Captain Bach got out of his airplane. Capt. Bach's Sabre, #49-1176, was last seen spinning to the left at about 35,000 feet, with flames coming from the aft fuselage section, about 25 miles northwest of Sanchon. Captain Bach was officially listed as missing in action. Capt. Laurence Bach was actually a POW with the Chinese Reds, and was returned under Operation BIG SWITCH, the repatriation of U.S. prisoners at the end of the war.

The loss stunned the men of the 4th. They knew it could happen, but they had been untouchable until now. It also made them mad. And the afternoon mission would make the MiGs pay. Lt.Col. Eagleston would lead Red Flight, with Lt. John Odiorne, Lt.Cmdr. Paul Pugh, and Lt. W. Yancey as Red 2, 3 and 4. Lt.Col. John Meyer was White Lead, with Lt. Ward Hitt, Capt. J.O. Roberts and Lt. Arthur O'Conner as White 2, 3 and 4. The results were not the same as the morning flight.

Right: Even though Lt.Col. Hinton was CO of the 336th Squadron, M/Sgt Raymond Sherry was the real 'boss' – the First Sergeant. (Bruce Hinton)

Red Flight encountered five MiGs at five o'clock low, about ten miles SE of Sinuiju. Now it was the Sabres that had the altitude advantage. Col. Eagleston, (Eagle), ordered red Flight to drop tanks, and broke right and down onto the MiG formation. Eagle pulled in behind one of the MiGs and gave him a short spray, scoring quite a few hits on the fuselage, and the MiG went into a sudden dive with pieces coming off the airplane.

But Eagle and Odiorne couldn't follow him as they were busy with another MiG that had tacked onto 'Eagle's' tail. The MiG had broken down in between Eagle and Odiorne and was quickly getting into a firing position. O'Diorne was screaming for Eagle to "Break now!", as the MiG was almost within range. Eagle broke into the MiG and got off a quick 90° deflection shot. The sudden movement by the American, and hits on his airplane, caused the MiG driver to give second thoughts to continuing the fight. The MiG immediately shot up into the sun and was gone.

Odiorne called Eagle and told him he was at 'Bingo' fuel, and Red Flight started for home. But before they got out of the area, they spotted another pair of MiGs below them at about 10,000 feet. The Sabres broke into a left dive, and pulled in behind the MiG element. Once again, the Sabres had the element of height and speed advantage. The MiGs saw them just as Eagle and O'Diorne were pulling into position, and immediately broke in opposite directions.

The MiG leader broke right with Col. Eagleston in hot pursuit. The wingman broke left and O'Diorne followed him. Eagle fired a good long burst that caught the MiG in the fuselage and wing. The MiG went into a sudden, lazy and out of control spin, with smoke and pieces streaming from the airplane. Eagle followed him down to 3,000 feet before breaking off. O'Diorne was in good position on the #2 MiG and began firing. He too saw strikes on the fuselage and pieces started to come off the MiG, which went into a 90° dive at less than 1000 feet altitude.

By now, both Eagle and O'Diorne were well below 'Bingo' and started for home. Cmdr. Pugh and Capt. Yancey also had their hands full after the initial encounter. A MiG had staked out Pugh and was just beginning to pull in range when Eagle warned him of the MiG at his six. Pugh broke right and saw the MiG behind him. But instead of holding his position, the MiG suddenly broke away and started into a dive, Pugh and Yancey in hot pursuit.

Pugh closed the range and got off a good burst, which struck the MiG between the cockpit and the wing. Pugh and Yancey watched as the MiG went into a slight dive, dropping below the cloud deck at about 2,000 feet. When the MiG leveled off at 500 feet, Pugh again pulled in behind him and gave him another squirt. The MiG immediately went into a hard vertical dive from which their was no recovery.

The ground crews built 'fire pits' to stay a little warm on the flightline at Kimpo in late December 1950, using drop tank crates as a wall, and jet fuel in the stove. The C-119 in the background has just delivered the first two fuel trucks to Kimpo. (John Henderson)

Col. Meyer's White Flight was just entering the area as Red Flight was leaving. O'Conner called out "Two Bogies at five o'clock!", at the same time that J.O. Roberts saw another pair of MiGs at twelve o'clock low. They were about 3000 feet below White Flight and climbing. Meyer started into a slight dive and the MiGs and Sabres passed each other about 1000 feet apart. Meyer and Hitt pulled up into the sun and reversed course, pulling in behind the MiGs.

M/Sgt Jack White on the snow covered Kimpo ramp in late December. As the Red Chinese advanced, the 4th FIG was ordered to evacuate Kimpo. As the afternoon mission returned from MiG Alley on 2 January, they refueled with the sound of Chinese artillery in their ears, then took off and flew to Johnson AB, Japan. (Jack White)

Left: On the morning of 1 January 1951, as the Group rushed to evacuate Kimpo, Sergeant Witherspoon was checking drop tank feed pressure, ducked under the nose and came up in front of the intake. The engine sucked him into the intake, killing him instantly. John Henderson and several crew chiefs worked through the night to have the Sabre flyable for the evacuation. (John Henderson) Right: Detachment A pilots at Kimpo just before the 'bug out' in January 1950 (Left to right) John Ironmonger, Mac Lane, Dick Ransbottom, 'Mo' Pitts, 'Black Jack' Wingo, and Max Weill. (Bruce Hinton)

Just as the MiGs split, Hitt called for his leader to "Break left!" as there were two more MiGs on their tail. Meyer and Hitt went left and back up into the sun, then reversed and came down right behind the MiGs that been on their tails only moments before. Meyer pulled the trigger and watched as his .50 caliber bullets caught the MiG near the engine. The MiG rolled over onto his back and suddenly exploded.

But Meyer couldn't enjoy the moment of victory just yet as Hitt was again screaming for him to "Break now!." There were two more MiGs at their seven o'clock and moving into position. Meyer and Hitt again broke left and went up into the sun, reversing to the right on the way. The MiGs did not follow.

J.O. Roberts and O'Conner, White 3 and 4, were busy with a pair of MiGs that attacked them from head-on. The closure rate was much too fast for either side to get off any shots, and the MiGs turned left after flying past J.O. and O'Conner. J.O. and O'Conner broke left too, and started pulling in behind the MiGs, with all four airplanes scissoring back and forth trying to gain some type of advantage.

Suddenly the MiGs split. J.O. took the one that broke left, O'Conner the one that went right. J.O.'s MiG started into a dive and J.O. followed, unable to close the range. The MiG pilot was frantically trying to shake J.O. off his tail. The MiG dove, leveling off at 20,000 feet, then dove again. The speeds were in excess of .95 Mach as the MiG started turning and rolling. The MiG driver then made a fatal mistake.

The MiG went into a left chandelle and J.O. was able to pull within range, frame the MiG in the gun sight reticle, and pull the trigger. J.O.'s fire struck the MiG all over the forward fuselage and cockpit, and the MiG snap-rolled to the left, rolled over to the right and went straight into the mountains below. As J.O. pulled back up to altitude, he suddenly noticed small balls of white smoke passing over his right wingtip.

He was under attack! The other MiG had followed J.O. down as his leader was crashing into the mountains. When J.O. pulled back up, the MiG pulled in behind him and started firing. J.O. started screaming for O'Conner. Calmly, O'Conner called his leader and told him that he was in position on the MiG and firing. O'Conner's fire struck the MiG and it immediately snap-rolled, and went into the mountains inverted. J.O. sighed with relief when he looked over his shoulder and saw the MiG spinning out of control.

The loss of Captain Bach that morning had caused the MiGs to come up with a new confidence. It also made the pilots on the afternoon mission more aware of what the MiGs could do when flown properly. With good flight integrity and aggressive flying on the part of the 4th pilots, the results were stunning. Of ten MiGs sighted that afternoon, six had been shot down and two more damaged. It would be a long time before the MiGs were again that aggressive.

The rest of the month the MiGs and the weather combined for little action. Although the MiGs made appearances through the remaining days of December 1950, no claims for Destroyed were filed. Each time the Sabres got into position, or started making hits on the little Red fighters, the MiGs would suddenly turn and run back across the river. The year ended with the 4th having flown 236 sorties to MiG Alley, shooting down eight MiGs, damaging at least a dozen more, for the loss of a single 4th Group pilot. And this was just the beginning.

four

Crowning the First Ace

The new year of 1951 didn't start out well for the 4th FIG. It started with a bang all right, but the bang was provided by the Red Chinese Armies. The UN forces had been retreating back down the Korean Peninsula since the Chinese attacked in full force in late November. Now they were about to break across the Han River and overrun Seoul again – and Kimpo.

Bug-Out From Kimpo

The last two days of the existence of Detachment 'A', 4th FIG were much the same as the previous nineteen days. Leave Kimpo in the morning or afternoon, fly 230 miles to the Yalu, patrol up and down looking for MiGs for about 20 minutes, then fly home again. The end of Detachment 'A' came on 2 January 1951 when Kimpo AB was evacuated in front of the Chinese advance. The last mission was a sixteen aircraft sweep of the Yalu River. But no MiGs came up. The official notes in the 4th FIG History read as follows about the lack of MiG activity; "Who could blame them for not coming up. They always emerged from the dogfights defeated, having been out-maneuvered, out-thought and out-fought."

In the eighteen days that Detachment 'A' had been in existence, 4th FIG pilots had scored eight victories – one each by Lt.Col. Bruce Hinton, Lt.Col. Glen Eagleston, Col. John Meyer, Lt. Arthur O'Conner, Capt. John Odiorne, Capt. J.O. Roberts, and two confirmed victories for Lt.Cmdr. Paul Pugh, the Navy exchange pilot. They also had two probables and three damaged.

John Henderson recalls: "The order to 'pack up and bug out' was probably ordered on the 30th or 31st of December. The Red Chinese were advancing down the Korean Peninsula and Kimpo was right in their path. I don't recall how I got the word, maybe it was one of the pilots I bunked with. But we flew on both days, finally standing down on New Years Day."

"Detachment 'A' flew their last sortie on the 31st, and sent the first aircraft back to Johnson the same day. I don't recall how many went initially, but I do remember that it was a much shorter distance, walking from airplane to airplane, checking its status. We probably sent eight aircraft back as soon as the word came down for the bug out."

"We had one sick bird on the line. There had been a fatal accident on the evening of the 1st. One of the 334th crew chiefs had been sucked into the intake of a Sabre. We were checking the fuel transfer from the drop tanks to the main tank on each airplane. The engine was run up to 70% to pressurize the tanks and make them feed. Usually, there were two members of the ground crew to check, one on each drop tank. This precluded having to go from one tank to the other during tests. But in this case, we were short of personnel, and their was only one airman, Sgt. Witherspoon, making the check on this Sabre."

"As we started the feed check, we had five or six engines running at the same time. I walked down the line, well in front of the Sabres. About fifty feet past the second Sabre, I heard the sound of one of the engines change from a high pitched whine to a deadened, muffled roar. It got my immediate attention and as I turned around, I had a fleeting glimpse of someone's legs disappearing into the intake."

"Sgt. Witherspoon had checked the tank on one side, then ducked under the nose in front of the landing gear to check the other side. How or why he did it, I'll never know. He'd probably done it a many times. But this time, he made a mistake.

Maybe his parka affected his ability to bend over and scoot under the nose, and he went a little farther out in front."

"Sgt. Witherspoon was dead before the violent vortex slammed him into the engine accessories cover. His body tore off the pitot tube that was in the air intake. And the pitot tube assembly went through the compressor, destroying the engine. We removed Sgt. Witherspoon's body from the intake and sent for Graves Registration."

"The airplane was a mess and needed a new engine. We had a spare engine ready for installation. But it was going to be a tough job in the dead of night, on that cold, windy tarmac. We couldn't use the 'cherry picker' to lift the engine, so we had to roll the airplane onto the engine. It was a very risky operation. We may have to destroy the airplane before leaving Kimpo."

"But the decision was made for us. We would replace that engine in the dark and cold. We pulled the damaged engine out and set it on some sand bags, then uncrated our spare. The sheet metal guys worked on a 'scab patch' in the intake where the pitot head had been. We had to wash out the entire intake and forward fuselage as it was filled with blood. By dawn, the new engine was installed, checked out, and made ready for a test hop."

"Capt. 'Mac' Lane from the 336th Squadron, climbed in and taxiied out for the test. We knew if everything went right, he would simply fly on to Johnson. Capt. Lane took off with Max Weill on his wing. We saw them later at Johnson. LtCols Zack Taylor and Bruce Hinton, Capt. Quay, the armament officer, one crew chief and myself, were left behind to tidy up the odds and ends before we abandoned the base. Everything was finished by early afternoon, but no one came to get us, or rather ME! About supper, Hinton, his jeep, Taylor, and the others, were loaded onto a C-119 and flew out of Kimpo. It got kinda scary as the night wore on and we were still at Kimpo. We could actually hear shooting in the distance. But about midnight, a C-54 air-evac bird arrived and my name was on the manifest." Detachment A was finished!

On 2 January 1951, Det A aircraft and personnel 'bugged out' from Kimpo with the sound of Chinese guns coming through the air. (Left to right) Lt.Col. Bruce Hinton, Lt.Col. Zack Taylor, and Capt. Deck drink a toast to leaving Kimpo (and to coming back!) as Hinton's jeep is loaded aboard the last C-119 out of Kimpo. (Bruce Hinton)

Following the bug-out from Kimpo, their wasn't a lot of combat activity for the crews since Johnson AB was much too far from Korea to conduct operations where the guys could get at the MiGs. The range of the F-86A was only about 500 miles, and MiG Alley was close to 800 miles from Johnson. The first few weeks of January 1951 were spent bringing the aircraft and records up to date. All necessary maintenance was done,

F-86As from all three squadrons line the ramp at Johnson AB in early 1951. Lt. Scotty Hanford (336) flew "Billie", Capt. Lee Fisher flew the 334th Sabre with the winged star. The red nose is not paint but the natural color of the fibreglass nose on the F-86A. (Lon Walter)

as well as repairing both combat damage and shipping damage that hadn't already been performed.

Thoughts of returning to Korea began in the middle of the month as the Chinese advance slowed. But not before they had overrun both Kimpo and Suwon. Major Billy Hovde, Captain J.L. Brooks, Captain J.O. Roberts, and Lieutenant Ralph 'Hoot' Gibson, took four 335th Sabres into Taegu (K-2) on the 14th, becoming Detachment 'B'.

Taegu was a horrible place to operate Sabres from. It was very rough, the roughest many of the World War II vets had ever seen. It made Kimpo at its worst, look like a resort. Both the runway and all the taxiways were pierce steel plank (PSP). Parking areas were simply frozen mud.

One of the major problems at K-2 was the PSP runway, which actually 'rolled up' when the airplanes were taking off or landing. And as the runway rolled up, it exposed the very sharp edges of the PSP, which ate tires up constantly. And the high pressure tires the F-86 used, weren't exactly easy to come by in Korea.

Detachment B began operations from K-2 with between four and eight aircraft. They still couldn't reach MiG Alley, so the pilots began flying armed reconnaissance missions with 5" HVAR rockets and bombs. Det B flew two missions a day, all under the control of the T-6 Mosquito Squadron that was flying forward air control over the front lines.

Lt. Lon Walter recalls: "I counted myself one lucky 'second balloon', when I found myself at Taegu in the quarters we shared with pilots from the 49th FBG. We were at Taegu to both practice air to ground rocket and bombing, and to build up flying time. At Johnson, there was literally nowhere to practice either air to air or air to ground."

"So when the group sent a small detachment back to Taegu, all of us youngsters wanted a piece of the action – experience or not. It was a bitter cold January day (No Korean January could ever remotely be considered warm!), and the pot bellied stove was working overtime to keep our hut livable."

"This would be my first ever combat mission. I drew a flight led by Capt. Martin 'Joe' Johansen. I was typical of the new pilots in the 4th – ninety-five hours in the F-86, and had never fired a gun or rocket from any type of airplane. Let alone the F-86. But 'Joe' briefed us on all the switches and tactics to be used."

The maintenance facilities at Johnson were superb compared with what the Group had left at Kimpo. Johnson had hangers to work on the airplanes. This F-86A is undergoing a complete engine change in early 1951. (via David Menard)

From the look on the pilots face to the right, this Sabre must have been the one he was supposed to fly. If the nose gear locks were not installed exactly right, it was possible for the gear to fold up after hydraulic pressure bled off. However, little damage was done and the Sabre was simply jacked up and the nose gear lowered into place – and locked. (Author)

Right: Det A Personnel at Johnson felt as if they were at a hotel compared with Kimpo. Johnson had Quonset huts for all the personnel, and even concrete buildings for the headquarters. (Jack White)

"We were to take off from K-2, proceed to the Suwon area, and contact a T-6 Mosquito controller. Our Sabres were armed with 1200 rounds of .50 caliber and two 5" HVAR rockets, plus the usual 120 gallon drop tanks. During the briefing we were told to expect anything when firing the 5" HVARs, as they were very unpredictable."

"Taking off from K-2 was a story in itself. So were landings and taxiing. The entire base was PSP. That's Pierced Steel Plank. The PSP would ripple and roll up under the weight of an airplane, sometimes coming apart and destroying the tires. But it was wide enough for four ship takeoffs, which were accomplished but not often."

"We climbed out from K-2 to about 20,000 and Joe contacted the Mosquito, who told us about a large group of Chinese troops dug in on the hillsides overlooking K-13 (Suwon). The Mosquito marked the target with Willie Pete (white phosphorous), then cleared us in on our firing passes."

"We all saw the Willie Pete smoke, and set up our switches for a gun attack. We would use the guns until the ammo got low, then fire the rockets. We got into a trail formation, and set up a gunnery pattern. But I'll tell you this – I didn't see anything! No foxholes, no troops, no sign of life anywhere on that hill."

"Capt. Joe rolled in, followed by Jack Bryant, 'Flash' Gordon and myself. I watched as Capt. Joe's tracers cut a path on the hillside. But I still didn't see anything! We all made three gunnery passes each, then Capt. Joe called for us to change the switches for a rocket attack. Joe went into a slight dive, and fired his rockets, followed by the rest of us. All I could say was that we hit the hill! Suddenly Jack Bryant called out – "Look at that! They're coming out of their holes and running up the hill!""

"Capt. Joe acknowledged that he saw them and started in on his second run. Me? I still couldn't see anything! But I lined up again on where everyone else was firing, and let go with my last rocket. Bryant yelled "Good shot Lon! You hit right in the middle of them!" Yeh, right."

"About that time, everyone was out of ammo and rockets. The Mosquito pilot thanked us for doing a good job, and cleared us back to Taegu. As we debriefed the mission, an intelligence guy came into the room waving a piece of paper and yelling at us. "You guys must have really done the job! The Mosquito called back and estimated 200+ enemy troops KBA (killed by air)." I was astounded but gratified that we had actually done some good. Two weeks later, we were again flying out of Suwon with a counter-air mission. Flying over the area we had attacked, I kept looking for any signs of our rocket mission but never saw anything."

(Left to right) Lieutenants Denny Dennison, Jack Kemp, and Gene Holley at Johnson in March 1951. Kemp would fly Capt. Jim Jabara's wing on 20 May, while Holley would chase a MiG off Jabara's tail that same day. Jabara shot down two MiGs to make 'ace' on 20 May. (Lon Walter)

A detachment of eight Sabres from the 336th FIS went to Chitose in February 1951, to guard against any MiGs coming across the straits into Northern Hokkaido. (Left to right) 1Lt. 'Shack' Shackelford, 1Lt. Al Reeser, 1Lt. Don Torres, 1Lt. Ward 'Turkey' Hitt, Lt.Col. Hinton (sitting), Navy Lt. Simpson 'Swabby' Evans, Capt. Max Weill, Capt. Don Stuck, and Capt. Dale Hudson. (Bruce Hinton)

Back at Johnson, 5th Air Force ordered the 4th to reopen Niigata AB on 16 January. Communist air threats were very real with the possibility of Tu-4s, the Russian copy of the B-29, being based at Vladivostok, which was well within range of anywhere in Japan. Men of the 334th FIS became Detachment E when they re-opened Niigata for air defense duties. Again, it was a very rough field. Niigata had no hangers at all, and didn't even have a control tower.

Duty at Johnson was quite boring for most of the crews. Even flying the ground attack missions out of Taegu was better than sitting around Johnson. The entire group was on alert all the time, with two Sabres on five minute alert, two on fifteen minute alert, and the rest standing ready for thirty minute alert.

A pair of 335th FIS F-86As take off from Taegu (K-2) in February 1951. The 335th FIS deployed to K-2 in mid-January after UN ground troops had stopped the Chinese advance just beyond Suwon. The first four Sabres were in place at Taegu on 14 January, and were designated Detachment B. (Paul Vercammen)

But most of the day was taken up with combat training. Tactics, combat formations, combat responsibilities of the wingman, GCI controlled intercepts, cross-country navigation, and of course aerial gunnery were constantly being improved. The ground troops in Korea were slowly pushing the Chinese back, and it wouldn't be long before Suwon would again be in UN hands – and ready for operations into MiG Alley.

By the end of the first month of operations from K-2, Det B had flown 158 sorties – 101 with HVARs in the armed recce mission under Mosquito Control. The rest were top cover over the F-80 and F-51 fighter bombers. Det B pilots fired 115,380 rounds of .50 cal ammunition in that first month – none of that at enemy aircraft. And the runway at K-2 destroyed nineteen tires!

On 22 February the 334th squadron relieved the 335th at K-2, which promptly became Detachment C at Niigata. Suwon (K-13) was again in UN hands and Colonel Meyer sent a re-arming and refueling crew to the base. The 334th pilots would stage through Suwon to begin immediate operations in north-west Korea. But not quite into MiG Alley. Missions staged through K-13 could only penetrate as far as Pyongyang.

By 10 March, Suwon was ready for full operations by the 334th Sabres, and the squadron moved into place. At the same time, the 336th FIS moved into Taegu and began flying mis-

"Minimum Effort", a 336th FIS F-86A on the taxiway at K-2 in March 1951. Both the taxiways and the runway were pierce steel plank or PSP, which would roll up under the weight of an airplane, and tear open the tires. By the end of operations at Taegu, the PSP runway had destroyed 19 tires. (Troy White)

sions staging through K-13. But Suwon was far from combat ready when the 334th began operations.

The runway was only 5200' long, but at least it was cement. Of course, the B-29s and fighter-bombers had cratered it quite a few times, which made for some interesting landings at first. The big problem initially was a total lack of paved taxiways. They weren't even PSP. That meant the F-86s returning from MiG Alley had to land in trail, touching down at 180 mph as other F-86s were using the side of the same runway to taxi back to a parking spot. Less than ten feet separated a landing Sabre from those taxiing! And the 86s that were landing also had to battle the jet wash of the preceding aircraft. It made the day interesting to say the least.

March 1951 claims were scarce as only a single MiG was destroyed. And that happened on the last day of the month when F/Lt. Omar Levesque, an exchange pilot from the Royal Canadian Air Force, shot down a MiG near Sinuiju. It was the ninth MiG shot down by 4th FIG pilots, but the first since the 30th of December. They also scored one probable (Lt. Dick Becker), and ten damaged including the second for Capt. Jim Jabara.

In April the war in MiG Alley started to heat up again. The 334th flew a total of 1,073 sorties that month, scoring sixteen victories, one probable, and twenty-one damaged. Captain Jim Jabara got four confirmed victories in the big fights of 3 April, 10 April, 12 April, and 22 April. Unknown to the pilots of the 4th, a new Russian air division had moved into Antung. They were led by Ivan Kozedub, the Russian World War II ace.

These new MiGs were from one of the elite Moscow Defense Sector units, and had some very colorful markings. Several of the MiGs had colored noses. This caused problems with combat identification between the F-86s of the 4th and the MiGs with colored noses. The F-86s flying from K-13 were a mixed bag of aircraft from all three squadrons. Thus some had yellow noses (334th), some red (335th), and some blue (336th). With the arrival of the new MiG units, 4th Headquarters ordered that all unit color stripes be removed.

The First Ace Is Crowned

In May, Lt.Col. Glenn Eagleston took over command of the Group from Col. John Meyer. On the 1st of May, the 335th relieved the 334th at K-13. The 334th pilots were sent back to Johnson AB for a well deserved rest. All except one – Captain James J. Jabara. Jim's score stood at four MiGs Destroyed and he was granted a extension to try to become the first 'ace' in the Korean War.

Four of the first pilots to return to Korea included (Left to right) Major Billy Hovde, Capt. Martin Johansen, Capt. Bruce Cunningham, and Capt. Nick Farrell, trying to warm his ears as the temperature was -10°. The conditions at Taegu made even Kimpo look good. And they had to share the base with F-80 and F-51 units. (Lon Walter)

It was Sunday, 20 May 1951, and history was about to be made. Back home the folks were watching Eddie Lopat win his seventh game in a row for the Yankees, who were leading the American League as usual. The National League was led by Brooklyn's Dodgers. People were watching Van Johnson in the theaters, as he led the Japanese-American 442nd RCT in the movie "Go For Broke", while Robert Mitchum was chasing Ava Gardner in the film "My Forbidden Past."

But at Suwon AB, the men of the 4th FIG were about to take off into history. Lt.Col. Bruce Hinton led PINTAIL ABLE flight with Col. Herman Schmid, Capt. Sam Pasecreta, Lt. Paul Bryce, Capt. 'Mo' Pitts, and LT Rudy Holley. PINTAIL BAKER was led by Capt. Max Weill, with Lt. John Ironmonger, Capt. Ray Janeczek, Lt. Howard Miller, Lt. Ward Hitt, and Capt. Dale Hudson.

A 4th FIG armorer attaches the safety wire to the nose of a 5" HVAR rocket at K-2. While the 336th was at Taegu, they flew a number of ground support missions against Chinese troop concentrations, despite the fact that the F-86A could carry only one HVAR under each wing when drop tanks were carried. (Lon Walter)

AWNING ABLE flight was made up of Lt.Col. Ben Emmert, Lt. Bill Ihrig, Lt. Milton Nelson, Lt. James Dennison, Lt. 'Hoot' Gibson, and Lt. Lon Walter. AWNING BAKER was led by Capt. J.O. Roberts, with Lt. John Hungerford on his wing; Capt. Jim Jabara led the second element, with Lt. Sam Kemp as his wingman; Capt. 'Sandy' Hesse and Lt. Stan Ahrends made up the third element. Lts. Hubert Shackleford, Dick Panter, Bobbie Lee Smith, and Phil Janney flew 'spare'.

It was the afternoon mission, a MiG sweep over Sinuiju, four flights of six with four 'spares'. Bruce Hinton and PINTAIL ABLE flight left Suwon at 1630 hours local time. Bruce Hinton: "We arrived over Sinuiju about 1700K (local Korean time), at about 36,000 feet. As soon as we arrived, the MiG sightings started to come in. I immediately gave the order to "Drop Tanks." Pasecreta and Bryce had tanks that wouldn't drop. Standing orders were that any Sabre with 'hung tanks' was to abort the mission and return to base, so I ordered them to return to Suwon."

"Mo Pitts and Rudy Holley tried to climb up to the MiGs, which were entering the area at about 40,000'. However, the MiGs kept out of range and they had to break off. But there were plenty of MiGs everywhere that day. As Mo broke off his attack on the high MiGs, he looked down to see several at about 17,000', flying a constant scissors formation. Evidently they were trying to find us."

"Pitts broke down onto the MiGs, pulled within range of the trailing MiG wingman and pulled the trigger. Mo's .50 calibres made some good hits on the MiG, which went into an immediate, violent dive. Holley squeezed off a few shots but saw no strikes on the fleeing MiG. As Mo was getting ready for another crack at the MiG, his A1CM gunsight went out and he had to break off the attack."

1Lt. Dick Merian strains a bit as he holds one of the 5" HVAR rockets at K-2 in February 1951. Each of the rockets weighed 140 lbs. (Dick Merian)

"Max Weill's flight entered the area at the same time that we did, but at 25,000' As soon as he heard we were sighting MiGs above him, he ordered his flight to drop their tanks. Again, two members of the flight couldn't drop their tanks. Ward Hitt and Dale Hudson had to break off and head back to K-13."

"Max and the remainder of Baker Flight began to close on the MiGs. Max Weill got within shooting range and fired a quick burst. Nothing! But it did wake up the MiG pilot, and he broke left, right, then went into a dive trying to get away from the closing Sabres. But Max had the advantage of height and speed and closed on the MiG."

"As he got within range, Max fired two long bursts, hitting the MiG in the fuselage near the engine area. The MiG

Five 334th Sabres on the concrete part of Suwon in March 1951. The 334th FIS moved into Suwon AB on 10 March 1951, when the runway also had to serve as taxiway as everything else was either mud or bomb craters. "Nosey Rosie" is Capt. J.L. Brooks' Sabre. Brooks was the first pilot to chase a MiG across the Yalu into Manchuria. (Australian War Memorial)

Col. Glenn Eagleston straps himself into his F-86A for a rocket-firing mission at K-2 in February 1951. The 5" HVAR can be seen inboard of the drop tank. The yellow nose band is a 334th FIS marking. Col. Eagleston shot down two MiGs in Korea, to go with the 18 1/2 German victories in World War II. (Wm. J. O'Donnell)

immediately began trailing thick, heavy black smoke. Max was still closing on the obviously wounded MiG. But when he fired again, one of his guns exploded (We were using experimental explosive .50 caliber ammo), and he had to break off the attack as the explosion in the gun bay blew off his radar access door. The MiG was last seen at about 8,000' and heading straight for Antung."

"Max and Ironmonger immediately started for Suwon. But about forty miles SE of Sinuiju, they were jumped by a pair of MiGs. Max turned sharply into the MiG, and the MiGs immediately broke off their attack and ran for the River. Janeczek and Miller, Baker 3 and 4, were busy about thirty miles E of Sinuiju. They sighted a lone MiG and closed to about 1200 feet. Janeczek got off a quick burst – nothing. He closed to 1000 feet and fired again. This time he hit the MiG right behind the wingroot and all over the wing. Fuel started streaming from the MiG's wing, and it flipped over onto its back and started into a steep dive."

"As Janeczek was watching the MiG start down, Miller suddenly called "Break!" A pair of MiGs had gotten in behind them and were in pretty good firing position already. For the next eight minutes, Janeczek and Miller were completely defensive, trying to shake this pair of MiGs off. Finally, another pair of Sabres came to their rescue and the MiGs broke away. Janeczek and Miller were both below 'Bingo' fuel, and started for Suwon."

The Awning Flights, led by Lt.Col. Ben Emmert, left Suwon about fifteen minutes after Pintail. They arrived over Sinuiju at 1720K, entering the area at 26,000'. Emmert had been monitoring the radio talk from Pintail, and the excited voices during the fight. He immediately ordered the flights to "Drop tanks." Several members of Awning Flight had problems with their tanks, including Emmert. He and Bill Ihrig had to start for home just as the fight was getting heated up.

The remainder of Able Flight found the MiGs. Nelson, Dennison and 'Hoot' Gibson spotted a pair of MiGs about thirty miles east of Sinuiju, and started to close. Gibson, against 4th Group SOP, was flying a solo as his wingman, Lt. Lon Walter, had mechanical problems and had to turn back to K-13. Nelson pulled within range and fired a short burst. Missed! But the MiG was now alerted and went into a dive to get away. Nelson, not being in position to follow the lead MiG, started to close on his wingman.

But 'Hoot' was in position to follow the MiG leader. He had anticipated the MiG diving away, and had started into a dive himself. He closed rapidly on the MiG, firing two long bursts which struck the MiG on the wings and all over the aft fuselage. The MiG snap-rolled and started a long glide toward the Yalu, with pieces coming off the wings and tail, then suddenly slowed down, probably a flameout, and Gibson overshot the Red jet. Hoot was starting to get into position to finish him off when another pair of MiGs interrupted him and he had to break off his pursuit. The MiG Hoot had staked out, continued toward the Yalu streaming heavy black smoke.

Meanwhile, Lt. Nelson had pulled in behind the second MiG. When his leader went into the sudden dive, with Gibson right behind him, Nelson's MiG also broke down and away. But Nelson was able to follow. He closed to within 1,000' and opened fire. The range gate continued to close and Nelson continued to fire. In fact, Nelson didn't stop firing until he had used up all his ammunition, 1500+ rounds. The MiG suddenly snapped into a violent dive, spiraling down to 5,000', with flames streaming from the fuselage.

Awning Baker flight was in position over Sinuiju at 1715K, flying at 30,000'. The air was full of the talk of the earlier fights, and the ongoing battles of Nelson and Gibson. J.O. Roberts called for the flight to "Drop tanks", and immediately called out "Bandits!" The MiGs, about twenty of them, were just starting across the Yalu at about 35,000'. J.O. and his wingman, John Hungerford, turned left into a flight of four MiGs, which went into a Lufberry defensive circle.

Two of the MiGs broke away from the circle suddenly, zooming up into the sun and literally 'sat on their perch' watching the rest of the fight develop. J.O. and Hungerford began a game of 'who can get into a firing position first' with the MiGs. J.O. couldn't get into position on any of the MiGs, but one of

As soon as the 334th moved into Suwon, a 'tent city' sprung up for all the personnel. Again, initially, the squadrons shared the base with the 51st FIG and their F-80s. (Dick Merian)

1Lt. Bernard Moore leans on the wingtip of his heavily damaged F-86A at Suwon in Spring 1951. The MiG-15 had two 23mm and one 37mm cannons, which could heavily damage a Sabre with a single round. But Lt. Moore brought the damaged Sabre back to K-13 using his ailerons to turn the airplane since his rudder was completely shot away. (Col. Bernard Moore)

The pilot of "Minimum Effort' taxies past a 315th AD C-54D ambulance aircraft at K-2 in March 1951. The 336th Squadron Sabres remained at Taegu, but staged through Suwon, stopping just long enough to top off the tanks before heading for northwest Korea and 'MiG Alley'. (USAF)

the MiGs did get off a few rounds toward Hungerford. Finally, after several 360s with the MiGs, the MiG leader got tired of the game and the MiGs started climbing into the sun.

As the MiGs started to climb, they split, one left and the other right. J.O. and Hungerford tacked onto the MiG that split left. The MiG went into another Lufberry, but J.O. was ready this time, and in a much better position. J.O. caught the MiG with several short bursts into the tail and tailpipe. The MiG went into a tight spin and headed down, suddenly pulling out of the spin at about 8,000', and headed straight back towards Antung.

As J.O. and Hungerford started back for altitude, they found another pair of MiGs at 20,000' about eighteen miles ESE of Sinuiju. Again, the MiGs went into a Lufberry to stay out of J.O.s fire. As soon as J.O. got into position, the MiGs broke out of the Lufberry and ran for the River. J.O. and Hungerford gave it up and turned south. But the MiGs crossed the Yalu, turned and started to get into position on J.O.

J.O. went into the defensive circle this time, and he had enough speed to begin closing on the MiGs that started out behind them, but were now in front of them. That's one of the things about a Lufberry circle. You can be defensive one minute and offensive the next. Pulling the stick tighter and tighter, J.O.s element closed within range, when suddenly the MiGs realized they were now the pursued, and broke out of the circle, diving back across the Yalu. J.O. and Hungerford were now at 'Bingo' fuel and started south.

About fifteen miles SE of Sinuiju, another fight was starting to take shape. Baker 3 and 4, Jabara and Jack Kemp, had just dropped their tanks when two things occurred. First, Jim's right wing tank did not drop. And second, they sighted a large gaggle of MiGs in their area. Orders were that any airplane with tanks that wouldn't drop, especially one with only one tank that didn't drop, that element was to immediately depart the area and head for home. But this might be Jim Jabara's last mission, and he wasn't going to let one hung tank interfere with his possibly making ace.

Jim Jabara: "We heard Col. Hinton call out "many bandits crossing the river." We were still approaching the area, coming up the west coast to the mouth of the river. Col. Emmert ordered us to "Drop tanks!" just as we made landfall. As we approached Sinuiju, I saw about twelve MiGs, which turned and started toward us. It was then that I noticed that my right tank hadn't dropped."

"They were maybe 3000' above us. We were at about 27,000'. The MiGs continued closing as we turned into them. Two of the MiGs fired on us as we closed in a head-on pass. I fired and missed as we passed each other. They missed and overshot badly. I tried to turn and get on their tail. But with that right tank still 'hung', I couldn't get into any kind of position. That tank really screwed me on that pass."

In the late Spring of 1951, FEAF authorized testing of explosive .50 caliber ammunition in the Sabres. The problem was that the explosive .50 ammo, often blew up in the gun breech, which also took out the main hydraulic system, including the brakes. Capt. 'Mo' Pitts' Sabre "Punkin-Head" slid off the runway at K-13 following a gun breech explosion in April 1951. (Phil Janney)

Sgt Jesse Hendley, armorer on Lt. Phil Janney's Sabre "Vida Mia", cleaning the barrels of one of the six .50 caliber machine guns. One of the first things that the armorers did, was to permanently fix the automatic gun doors in the open position, or remove them entirely. The doors were very prone to freezing closed in the extreme cold of Korea. (USAF)

1Lt. Jim Leatherbee (FU-217) and Capt. Jim Jabara (FU-259) over the rugged, snow-covered North Korean mountains in April 1951. Capt. Jabara, a 334th FIS pilot, shot down his first MiG on 3 April 1951. 'Jabby' would have four by the end of the month – and 100 missions, which should have sent him home. (USAF)

"Kemp called to tell me about three more at our five o'clock, getting into position. That made twelve of them to the two of us. As these three MiGs overshot, Kemp and I cranked her around and broke into them. I picked out the No.3 MiG, which seemed to be slightly behind the other two. The MiG went into a constant left turn, and we went round and round for awhile."

"At about 25,000' I started to pull within range, fired once, then again. The second burst caught the MiG right below the cockpit, through the wing root, and across the left wing. It suddenly burst into flames, did a couple of snap rolls, and went into a spin. I could see him the whole time because he was trailing heavy black smoke."

"I kept watching it and thought it was going to go straight in. But at about 10,000', the MiG leveled out just for a minute, and I saw the pilot bail out. The MiG then just exploded. I don't think there was a big piece of it left at all. I made a pass at the pilot with my camera rolling. I almost hit him when I bent down to turn on the camera, and had to pull up to avoid him. He was twirling in the 'chute, and all dressed in black."

"We were down to about 7,000' when the MiG exploded. Jack and I started to climb back to altitude. About 20,000' I spotted 6 more MiGs, four in a fingertip formation, and two more trailing. Somewhere in the climb Kemp and I had separated. I don't know where he was. They were in a left turn and evidently didn't see me at all. I pulled in behind the No.6 MiG and fired."

"The first four MiGs dove down and away. The guy I had staked out just kept climbing straight ahead. His leader was also nowhere to be seen, and I figured he would be coming back at me. I had to keep one eye out for him, and the other on the MiG ahead of me."

Jim Jabara explains to (Left to right) 2Lt. Hamp Miller and 1Lt. Bill Yancey, how he maneuvered into position for a shot on a MiG in March 1951. This day resulted in a damaged credit for Jabara. Jabara always had a cigar in his hand when he wasn't flying, thus earning him the nickname "Ceegar Kid" in World War II. (USAF)

"My MiG was still climbing and probably would have gotten away if he'd continued. But he suddenly dove down to the left. I had no trouble catching up with him. I started shooting as soon as I got within range. I got several good strikes. I don't know whether he was on fire or if he flamed out. But he was pouring white smoke out of his tailpipe."

"I overshot him right away, and he started a turn, well sort of a spiral – half spin, half spiral to the left. I looked around to see if anybody was on my tail, and put on my speed brakes. I knew he was in trouble, and I wanted to see if he was going to hit. I followed him down to 6500'. I think he was on fire, but I'm not sure because he was smoking like mad. He had definitely flamed out, going very slow, maybe 170 knots."

"All of a sudden, there was popping all around me. There were MiGs back there, and they were shooting at me! I broke real hard to the left, as hard as I could, pulled in the brakes and put on full power. I couldn't do much more than 500 knots because the airplane was very hard to control. I had to use both hands on the stick. It kept wanting to dip down to the left, probably because of the hung right tank. Every time I would straighten out, the MiGs would shoot at me. Those reddish pink tracers were coming awfully close."

"Above me, a pair of F-86s were heading for home. It was 'Mo' Pitts and Rudy Holley. Pitts called Holley on the radio and said, "There's an F-86 down there getting bounced by two MiGs." I said, "I know it too damned well!", and Pitts called me and asked who the pilot was. I must have been in a 10-G turn when I hollered into the radio, "Jaaabbbaaarrraa!" Mo then said, "Call us if you need help." And I calmly replied that I could sure use some now!"

"I kept breaking, then building up my air speed and breaking again. Mo and Holley came down and Holley started firing on the MiGs. One of the MiGs broke for the river. But the other was intent on getting me. He nearly had me now, and was closing the gap the whole time. Holley and Pitts pulled in behind the MiG that was behind me."

"Holley got off a couple of good bursts, hitting the MiG in the fuselage. The MiG started to smoke and dove away from us, heading straight for the Yalu. None of us could chase him down, even though he was crippled, as we were all way below 'Bingo'. We joined up and headed back to Suwon, landing on fumes."

Three of the F-86As had been testing a new M23 high explosive .50 caliber round, including the aircraft of Mo Pitts. The tests were inconclusive as far as the destructive power was concerned against the MiG. But all three aircraft suffered damage when the M23 rounds exploded in the breech, which sev-

9 April 1951, Capt. Max Weill congratulates 1Lt. Arthur O'Conner on his 2nd MiG kill of the war. Lt. O'Conner also shot down a MiG on 22 December 1950, the day the pilots of Det A shot down six MiGs in retaliation for the loss of Lt. Bach. (USAF)

On 20 May 1951, Capt. James Jabara shot down two MiG-15s becoming the worlds first jet vs. jet 'ace' with six victories. Capt. Jabara holds 'hands free' as the crew chief puts the safeties into the ejection seat on his Sabre, #49-1319. Note the gun smoke residue on the armored blast panel. (Irv Clark)

Opposite:
Top: 4th Group pilots talk about Jabara's achievement as the ground crew begins working on 'Jabby's' Sabre. The right wing tank is still attached. Existing orders were to head for home if your tanks didn't drop, but Jim wanted that fifth MiG to become an ace, and wasn't about to let a drop tank or orders keep him from it. (Irv Clark)

Bottom: General Electric Radar Tech Rep Leo Fournier beams with pride as he stands next to Jabara's 'ace Sabre' on the Suwon ramp in late May 1951. Jabara would later reveal that this day was one of the few on which he left the type A1CM gun sight turned on, and it worked like a charm. (Leo Fournier)

U.S. AIR FORCE
91319

U.S. AIR FORCE
91319
FU-319

ered the parking brake lines, taking out most of the hydraulics. All three aircraft made it back to Suwon however.

The score for the day was five damaged – Pitts, Holley, Weill, Janeczek, and J.O. Roberts; one probable by 'Hoot' Gibson, and three victories – Lt. Milton Nelson and two by Captain James J. Jabara. The two by Jabara were his 5th and 6th, making him the first ace in the Korean War, and the first jet vs. jet ace in history. Jabara's total was six victories, one probable, and four damaged. When Jabara landed at K-13, there was a crowd waiting for him, mostly his fellow pilots and ground crew. Almost as soon as Jim climbed out of the cockpit, Col. John Meyer, 4th Group Commander awarded him the Distinguished Flying Cross. Later, in his private office, he chewed Jabara's butt for violating orders with regards to having a 'hung' tank.

By order of 5th Air Force, Jabara was sent home on the 22nd. He flew first to Johnson AB, Japan. Or rather he was flown to Johnson by C-54. Air Force had their first ace and they weren't taking any chances. Air Force wanted him to be an instructor and show the other pilots bound for Korea, how it was done. But Jabara would return in 1953, much to the dismay of the MiG pilots. They'd already had enough of Captain James J. Jabara.

June was a very interesting month for the Group. The weather started to close down flying activities over both the north and south. The sorties for the month were down to 1250. An indication of the variety of missions that the Group was flying are the statistics for the first half of June. By 15 June, the Group had flown 645 sorties – 427 MiG Sweeps, 149 escort mission for the Superforts and fighter bombers, eight armed reconnaissance mission, thirty-seven weather reconnaissance missions (Operation STOVEPIPE), and twenty-four 'scrambles' against MiGs picked up by radar. Monthly totals included nine MiGs destroyed and twenty-five damaged.

On the 17th of June, the Group almost lost Col. Eagleston, when he tangled with a very good MiG pilot – the legendary "Casey Jones." And later that same night, "Bedcheck Charlie hit the base with a vengeance, destroying one Sabre, damaging eight others, and wounding a pilot and a tech rep from GE.

Opposite: 2Lt. Gene Holley and Maj. Ed Fletcher carry Capt. Jim Jabara away from his airplane following the twin MiG kills of 20 May 1951, which made Jabara the first ace in the Korean War. 5th Air Force immediately grounded Jabara and ordered him home. His final score was six destroyed, one probable, and four damaged. He would return in 1953 and score another nine victories. (USAF)

1Lt. W.D. 'Willie Dog' Taylor talks with his hands to explain his fight with the elusive MiG on 6 April 1951. Listening intently are (Left to right) Lt.Col. Eagleston, Capt. Martin Johansen, 2Lt. Roy McLain, and 1Lt. John Odiorne. All five pilots would score in the ensuing months. And Eagleston and Johansen would encounter the heralded MiG pilot known as 'Casey Jones'. (USAF)

"Casey Jones"

Lt.Col. Bruce Hinton recalls the day: "Ol' Casey, also known as "Honcho" or "The Professor", was an exceptional pilot, and definitely not an oriental. His normal procedure was to sit up high all by himself, then dive down at a very high rate, and attack any F-86 that seemed isolated and alone. It was quite similar to a tactic used by von Richthofen in World War I."

"Because of his tactics and flying, plus some close brushes with other 4th pilots, close enough for a visual ID showing the guys western features, we thought he might be an ex-Luftwaffe pilot flying for the Reds. The name "Casey Jones" came from the fact that he usually led the MiG flights, called 'Bandit Trains' by the radar site at Chodo. He was easily spotted in the air since his MiG had a significant paint job with a red nose and fuselage stripes."

"June 17th was a bright, clear, sunny day. We had a pretty heavy commitment for the day, with both squadrons involved. Lt.Col. Glenn Eagleston was leading the 334th Squadron. I had the 336th. The mission was nothing special, a MiG Sweep on the Yalu. But today, the MiGs were definitely ready to fight. About two minutes into the patrol, the MiGs came across the River. We quickly broke down into two-ship elements to take on the MiGs."

"My element was flying at about 25,000 feet over the eastern end of MiG Alley. There were lots of MiGs everywhere, and I soon spotted a 'loner' maneuvering with the swirl of the fight. Suddenly, the MiG turned away from the battle and

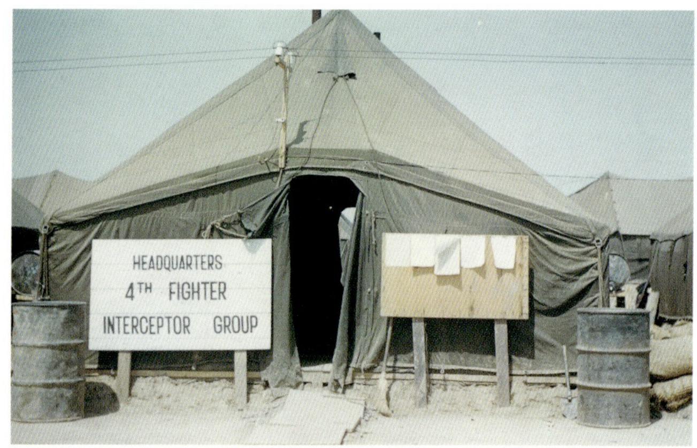

Left: As with almost everything else at K-13, the crash crew and trucks had nothing over them but camouflage netting. Of note are the fuel drum 'walls' to the crash station. (Leo Fournier) Right: The 'plush' Headquarters for the 4th FIG at Suwon in Spring 1951. (Leo Fournier)

headed north. I began to close the range, getting it down to a little less than 1500 feet. With the pipper on his tail, I was ready to hammer him. He was all mine!"

"Just as I started to pull the trigger, a Sabre appeared between me and the MiG I was about to clobber. He was flying 90° to my direction of flight, and he wasn't alone! About 500 feet behind him was a MiG, with a red nose and stripes on the fuselage. Casey Jones! And he was pounding the Sabre with cannon fire. As both airplanes flew directly between 'my MiG' and myself, I wondered how we had missed a mid-air collision."

"As the two aircraft passed in front of me, I could see the MiG fire, and see his shells hitting the Sabre, with flame and sparks marking the strikes on the fuselage. Pieces of the F-86 were flying through the air, some very large pieces. One unassailable rule that we had – no MiG was worth losing an F-86 pilot over. The Sabre was on fire, and I broke off a certain kill to try and take that MiG off the Sabre. I had no idea who was flying the Sabre, but I knew he was in deep kimchi."

"I pulled the nose around as hard as I could toward the Sabre and MiG. When I completed the turn, they were both about 1000 feet below. The MiG had overshot the Sabre, made a quick climbing reversal, and was now coming back to finish him off. The Sabre had lost most of his airspeed, and appeared to be just hanging there, waiting for the inevitable. Suddenly, the MiG started to pull up. He'd seen me coming and was now starting a head-on pass against me!. We passed head-on, about fifty feet apart."

"At that point we both tried to use all we had left to gain some kind of advantage over the other. We went into a Lufberry circle, in which I had a slight advantage, but not enough to get into a good firing position. I started a vertical yo-yo, with a slight reduction in speed to increase my turning rate. It began to work, and I started to close. The maneuvering Gs were extreme, so much so that my wingman left part way through, later telling me he'd become air sick."

"At this point I decided to try a high angle-off burst of fire. I had a little inside advantage by now, with Ol' Casey passing in front of me at about 60-70° angle off. As we approached the tight end of the circle, I watched over the leading edge of my wing for him to appear. When he did, I hauled back tight on the stick to bring my nose to bear on him. As he passed in front of me, I held the trigger down and gave him a good burst."

"On the next orbit, I did the same thing. This time Ol' Casey had to fly directly through the spray from my six .50s. That second burst got his attention real quick, and he suddenly broke away and dove toward the Yalu, easily pulling away from me. I broke off and started to look for the stricken F-86. I found him sort-of floating at about 20,000 feet. The fires had gone

The control tower at Suwon. (Troy White)

out, but he had some big holes in the fuselage. The aft section was holed, and his left gun bay door and all three .50s were gone."

"The guns had absorbed most of the cannon shell impact, saving the pilots life. I tried talking to him, but his radio had been hit by another cannon shell. We were flying at about .7 Mach, and he was steadily losing altitude. Pulling up next to him, I finally got his attention and signaled for him to head toward the Yellow Sea and get ready for a bailout. I'll never forget the pilot in that cockpit violently shaking his head "No!" I was sure he had to be one of the new lieutenants, but couldn't figure out his disregard of a possible life-saving instruction."

"We continued south, avoiding the flak traps, and trying to measure the angle of our flight path to see if we could make it back to Suwon before we ran out of altitude. It took forever, but we finally made it to friendly territory. I called K-13 tower, informing them that I was bringing in a cripple, and to clear the runway, and alert the meat wagon and fire trucks. He was going to have to make a wheels-up landing as the MiG had shot out all the controls."

"Flying a tight formation with the wounded F-86, I came down the final right beside him. The Sabre slowly settled onto the runway, finally touching down with a jolt. I watched the pilots head banging back and forth in the cockpit as he rode that airplane down the runway like a bucking bronco. The Sabre slid to a stop off the end of the runway in a big cloud of dust."

"I poured on the coal, went around, landed and rolled to a stop by the busted F-86. The airplane was a wreck. Not only was the engine hit, but the throttle controls were smashed by cannon fire. The left fuselage was a sieve, with some very large holes around the cockpit. It was then that I learned that the pilot was my very close friend, Glenn Eagleston." The Sabre was scrapped and towed to the far end of the runway, where it was placed on some drums with other 'Class 26d' F-86s. Here they sat, as decoys for the night raiders that had started to bomb Suwon lately.

Lt.Col. Eagleston is greeted by Brig.Gen. Edward Timberlake following an encounter with the MiGs in March 1951 when he scored a 'damaged' to go with his two victories and one probable. (USAF)

Following the article written about Jim Jabara in which Life Magazine made some rather derogatory remarks about the food at Suwon, this sign appeared at Mess Hall #1. (Leo Fournier)

Bedcheck Charlie Hits Suwon

Bedcheck Charlie had been a threat since World War II. The Japanese had used them against our troops throughout the Pacific campaign. They were usually a small light plane, with very loud exhaust. The Japanese used to make it even louder by deliberately putting the engine timing out of sync, causing the airplane to backfire constantly. The troops in the Pacific called them "Washing Machine Charlies'.

The antiaircraft positions at K-13 were M16 halftracks with four .50 caliber machine guns, in a fuel drum revetment. But the night of 17 June 1951, the gun commander left word not to fire unless he gave the order. 'Bedcheck Charlie' visited Suwon that night and didn't wait for the gun commander. (Leo Fournier)

In Korea, they were known as "Bedcheck Charlie." The aircraft was a North Korean Air Force Polikarpov Po-2 biplane trainer, developed by the Soviets during World War II. Charlie would usually enter South Korea at an altitude of between 50-100 feet, well below radar, and at speeds of less than 100 mph. The Po-2 usually had a crew of two, with the rear pilot having a box full of grenades or small bombs, which he dropped over the side as they passed over the bases. Sometimes they would drop leaflets telling our guys what bad people we were. Charlie had already made one big strike when he hit the fuel dump at Inchon Harbor, which burned for a couple days. You could see the smoke pillar as far away as Suwon and Seoul.

"De Ramblin Rebel" sits forlornly on old fuel drums awaiting its fate at K-13 in June 1951. Sabres that were so badly damaged that they would never fly again were 'Class 26d' and stripped of all usable parts, then towed to the end of the main runway to act as decoys in the hopes that 'Bedcheck Charlie' would bomb useless airplanes. (Dick Becker)

Mr. Leo Fournier was the General Electric Gunsight Tech Rep to the 4th FIG. Leo Fournier: "The night of 16 June 1951 is one I'll never forget. I was in a ten-man tent at K-13 that sat right next to the runway. Which meant the parked Sabre Jets were very close to our tent as Suwon didn't have parking ramps or taxiways at this time. We'd just left the new movie 'theater' (a screen erected in the open air), and were walking back to our tent."

"We stopped in another tent where the guys were listening to Radio Peking. The announcer was talking about how they'd bombed Suwon a few nights prior, and that they'd be back! Everyone laughed and we walked back to our tent. About 0200 in the morning of 17 June, which incidentally was Fathers Day, I was awakened by a very loud noise. An explosion!"

"Bedcheck Charlie had come calling again, just like the Chinese announcer had bragged he would. There'd been no air raid alert this night, because the power had been turned off to the siren! And the 40mm anti-aircraft guns hadn't fired because the gun crews had been given strict orders not to fire until the CO told them to! And of course, their CO was nowhere to be found when Charlie made his strike."

"The first bombs exploded near the end of the runway where we had several scrapped Sabres sitting on oil drums as decoys. (This was where Eagleston's F-86 had been taken) The decoys worked initially, but Ol' Charlie kept flying straight down the flightline towards us. The third bomb landed just outside my tent, so close that Capt. Paul Kominsky had the legs of his cot shot right out from under him."

"With the first explosions, we all grabbed our gear and headed for the nearest foxholes. Irv Clark, the GE engine rep, told me later that he 'knew' I was OK, because he could hear me cussing in the night. I was dressed only in my shorts, but I

Lt.Col. Glenn Eagleston's F-86A before his meeting with the legendary 'Casey Jones' over the Yalu on 25 June 1951. 'Eagle' had 18 1/2 victories in World War Two but met his match on this day. Col. Eagleston was 4th Group Commander. (Australian War Memorial)

grabbed my helmet, ran out of the tent and jumped into the nearest hole. There were already two or three other guys in it, including one guy that said "I'm hit! I'm dying!""

"It was about this time that I thought I'd better check myself out. I felt OK, but ... As I looked down at my stomach, I was startled to see a small hole in my abdomen with blood spurting out. John Henderson, the North American Tech Rep, ran out and yelled for the medics."

"In the meantime, there were lots of fireworks going on all over the base. The anti-aircraft guns had finally opened up (evidently someone had found the CO), and the night sky was full of tracers. Some of our F-86s had been hit and were on fire, with a lot of the rounds in their guns cooking off and sending still more tracers into the night. And these were all at head level!"

"In a few minutes the medics were in our trench checking on both myself and the other guy that'd been hit. They put a quick dressing on my wound, and carted me off to sick bay. The doctor on duty, a big guy smoking an even bigger stogie, and who hadn't shaved for quite a few days (he looked like Hawkeye Pierce from the MASH show!), took one look at me and said – "We can't do anything for this guy!""

"I looked at him and yelled "What the hell do you mean, you can't do anything for me?" He then told me that since I had an internal injury (aren't they all?), I'd have to go to the emergency hospital at Yong Dong Po, where they had the right equipment to fix me up. They transported me to the MASH unit by ambulance, and within a few minutes after my arrival, they had several IV bottles hooked up to me, and had wheeled me into the x-ray room to shoot pictures of my leak."

"After about ten minutes or so of doctors talking and looking at the pictures, they gave something called sodium pentathol, and told me start counting. I got to almost five and was out. The next morning, or maybe it was twenty-four hours later, I awoke. There was a big bandage on my stomach and I didn't feel the greatest. The doctor stopped by my bed and I asked him straight out if I was going to make it. He said sure, that I was the luckiest guy around. The shrapnel from Ol' Charlie's bomb had gone almost completely through me, with only my liver getting in the way."

"But my liver injury was a bad one. The doc calmly told me that 'with an injury like you have, you either live or die in the first twenty-four hours!' Oh great! But then he told me that I'd already slept the entire first twenty-four hours. I learned later that the other wounded guy was Capt. 'Jig Easy' Smith, and that he had also survived. The flightline was a mess however with one airplane destroyed, F-86A #49-1334; and eight other Sabres damaged."

Lt.Col. Eagleston checks over what's left of his Sabre following the encounter with 'Casey Jones'. 'Casey Jones" first rounds hit the left gun bay, blowing the guns out of the airplane and damaging Eagleston's throttle. There were also big cannon holes in the aft fuselage, wing, and engine. Eagleston had to belly the airplane in at K-13 following the fight. (Bruce Hinton)

"About a year later, I was completely recovered and back working for GE. One morning I was told to report to the base commander at Hancock Field near Syracuse. Much to my amazement, the general pinned the Purple Heart on me in front of the TV and press people. I didn't know that a civilian could get the Purple Heart! But there it was – "By direction of the President, under the provisions of AFR 30-14, and Section VII, General Order 63, etc., etc., the Purple Heart is awarded to Mr. Leo Edmund Fournier, Civilian Technical Representative, for wounds received in action against an armed enemy on 17 June 1951." I understand that Capt. Sandy Hesse was the guy that put me in for the decoration."

"Some time after the award ceremony, someone told me that a month or so after I was hit, a Marine night fighter had shot down one of the Bedcheck Charlie raiders. The pilot had a diary on him that confirmed that he was the guy that had bombed K-13 that night. He'd written in his diary that he'd damaged three airplanes. Funny he didn't even mention me. But I'll never forget him!"

"Clobber College"

In June 1951, with the influx of new experienced and brand new pilots straight out of The Fighter School at Nellis, the 4th set up a quick program to indoctrinate all the new pilots as to what to expect in the aerial combat over northwest Korea. Officially, it was known as the Combat Orientation Detachment. But it was known as the "Clobber College." Col. Bruce Hinton and 1 LT. Lon Walter tell what "Clobber College" was all about. Bruce Hinton: "Sometime in the late spring or early summer of 1951, a plan was set into motion to begin rotating combat pilots out of Korea, and bring replacements in. It was an attempt on our part to try and keep the combat experience level strong at all times, while gradually replacing all the veteran pilots."

Hinton: "Of course, some pilots chose to stay. But overall this rotation plan began to introduce a steady stream of incoming pilots – most of which were fresh from 'USA-shima'. What

When 'Bedcheck Charlie' visited Suwon the night of 17 June, he dropped three bombs. The first bomb hit the 'Class 26' Sabres at the end of the runway, the second hit the tent line and wounded Capt. J.E. 'Jig Easy' Smith and Mr. Leo Fournier, GE Radar Tech Rep. The third bomb hit the left wing of Lt. Phil Janney's F-86A, setting it on fire and completely destroying the airplane. (Leo Fournier)

Visitors at Taegu. A Royal Australian Navy Sea Fury from one of the Australian aircraft carriers operating in the Yellow Sea, visits Taegu in the early Summer of 1951. (Dick Merian)

rapidly became apparent was the lack of intimate knowledge on our part, the 4th Group, regarding the level of competence and relative tenacity of these replacements. Also, there was a real need to provide them with some 'feel' for the severe maneuvering conditions that our previous combat experience had found in the arena on the Yalu."

"Most of these conditions took all of us far beyond the kind of training that stateside schools provided. Out of this came a need to provide orientation briefings with some combat film, and combat experience lectures. After the lectures and briefings, there would be at least one local flight with a combat flight leader or higher experienced pilot."

5th AF tried everything to bring down Bedcheck Charlie until the end of the war – armed AT-6s, F-82Gs, F-94Bs, and even a B-26B light attack bomber. Nothing worked until the Navy and Marines brought in F4U-5N Corsair night fighters. "Yokosuka Annie" was one of the airplanes flown by Navy Lt. Guy Bordelon, the only non-Sabre ace in the Korean War. (via Jim Sullivan)

"Normally, the flight would include a local area mission, during which the leader would put the new pilot through extensive hard maneuvering – with the new pilot in the combat wing position – simulating the violent and unpredictable forces in changing attitude, direction, and airspeed which would be expected during contact with the wily MiG. If the flight was considered satisfactory, the new pilot would then fly his next flight as a wing man with a selected leader. Thereafter, the new pilot would fly three or four more flights, being carefully watched the entire time, before attention was relaxed on the individual new pilot."

"The procedure was followed for <u>all</u> pilots coming into the 4th Group. In fact, then Col. Frances Gabreski, the World War II ace with over thirty victories, came to the 4th following J.C. Meyer's departure, I put him through the 'college', and included flying him as my #3 man on a couple of missions!"

1Lt. Lon Walter was one of the instructors at "Clobber College." Lon Walter: "The "Clobber College" consisted of a couple of weeks flying at Johnson AB, Japan. All the new arrivals went through it. Some, but not all, of the newly arriving 'old heads' with lots of jet time and combat experience (read that: captains and up), simply bypassed the 'course' and went right to Korea."

"Commander Paul Pugh, a U.S. Navy exchange pilot with the 4th, was put in charge of the initial 'course'. Paul was an immensely popular and talented pilot, who might easily have become the first jet ace. The 'instructors' were drawn from all three squadrons within the 4th, and were generally first lieutenants. There probably were never more than five or six instructors at any given time while I was there. I was picked from the 335th Squadron by Captain Nick Farrell, our ops Officer, because I had more missions than the other lieutenants. He felt it was the only 'fair' thing to do. I bitched, begged, and pleaded, but to no avail. I never caught up with the other guys who passed me during the two or three weeks that I was 'instructing' at Johnson."

"The 'course' consisted basically of making sure the new guys could fly the kind of combat formations we were using up on the Yalu. And that their radio discipline was up to snuff. There was a lot of simulated combat, where the emphasis was on wingmen staying with their leaders, checking their six o'clock position, and making the proper radio calls. There was no actual gunnery training, not even 'camera combat'. Our gun cameras were so unreliable that we didn't even attempt to use them in the program."

"The first 'class' of fifty-eight new pilots, was held in June 1951, which included thirteen that had never even flown an F-86 before! Most of the new guys flew between ten and twenty hours, about an hour and twenty minutes per mission. Some flew more, some less. There was very little classroom work – possibly an intel briefing on what the MiG looked like, what it could do, MiG tactics, etc. And of course, what to expect if you were shot down over enemy territory."

"It was all pretty informal compared to what happens in today's Air Force. As the individuals demonstrated their readiness to the satisfaction of the 'staff', they would be sent to the combat squadrons in Korea. Often these 'new guys' would get to ferry an F-86 back to Korea. It was a pretty successful little program, since the new arrivals usually got only one 'local area' check-out flight in Korea, and then they were flying combat."

five

Maintenance during the War

John Henderson

John Henderson was a North American Aviation Technical Representative, Tech Rep for short. His job was to be a liaison between the factory and the operational units flying the F-86. But it was more than just that, especially in Korea. He had to come up with answers to questions that had never been addressed by the engineers or anyone else at the factory. They build airplanes to fly and do a specific job. But in combat, the pilots ask the airplanes to do things they were not intended or designed to do. And many times the crew chiefs had to fix things that just weren't supposed to be broken in the manner that they were. John Henderson, North American Tech Rep to the 4th FIW, not only came up with the answers, he also worked with the crew chiefs to make things work. In short he was an engineer/mechanic/secretary/politician/wizard.

John Henderson: I was assigned to the 4th FIW for thirty months, from July 1949 through December 1951. Eighteen months after arriving at Langley AFB, Virginia, I was in Korea. Korea was the purest environment for tech rep support by a contractor's representative. Everything was furnished by the government, including transportation, housing (nice, clean, warm tents) and sustenance by the finest cooks in the Air Force. But in spite of these extravagances, things were very basic. After my thirteen month foreign assignment was finished, I left the 4th FIW with a feeling of gratitude for the opportunity to work with the finest airmen and pilots the U.S. Air Force ever enlisted.

Korea for me started with the STRAWBOSS deployment in November 1950. I was alerted at the same time as the rest of the men in the 4th, for a "short TDY to a country of temperate climate"! Boy what a crock! For three days (including the day we were alerted) after we were alerted for the deployment, I helped the mechanics prepare the F-86As for the cross-country flight to North Island Naval Air Station in San Diego. Some of our birds were replaced by newer aircraft from other units, because they were out of commission for parts (AOCP) or had 'high time airframes', considered to have too many flying hours for combat. All these airplanes were left behind, repaired, and sent to the units that 'loaned' the 4th some of their newest and best airplanes. Those unit commanders weren't any too happy about that.

As soon as the birds were ready to fly, and no later than 1100 hours on 11 November, they departed for the West Coast. I traveled in the Headquarters Flight C-47, along with loads of equipment and other personnel. We followed the route of the Sabre's, making any stops to help with maintenance of any lagging aircraft, of which there were none, if you don't count Lt. Larry Latham's Sabre, which was at Williams AFB with the nose gear stuck in the well. That bird was also left behind and replaced with one from the 1st Fighter Wing at March AFB.

When we got to California, I went up to the factory and reported to my boss, John Casey, who informed me that I would have a teammate in Korea, my old partner Einar 'Chris' Christopherson. Chris and I scrambled to prepare all the paperwork so we could get back to North Island and help load the airplanes. North American sent a crew of technicians to assist us in preparing and loading the airplanes for the ocean trip to the Far East. One of the things we did was to work off all the time compliance tech orders (TCTOs) that were still open in the logs. This brought most of the airplanes up to the latest specs and peaked the electrical/electronic systems on each airplane. We were really glad that North American had sent the extra people then.

When the USS Cape Esperance, the Navy 'jeep carrier' which would transport the 334th and 335th squadrons Sabres to Japan, broke a propeller shaft, our end of the operation was set back three days. This allowed the 336th Squadron to leave ahead of us, as they were loaded aboard freighters out of San Francisco. It also allowed Chris and I to hit the March AFB PX to purchase needed military attire – dress uniforms and fatigues, with non-combatant shoulder patches and officers collar insignia and caps.

When we got back to North Island, the Navy was ready to load the Sabres (and a few F-84 Thunderjets) onto the carrier. Again, it was a scramble. All forty-nine F-86As (and the F-84s) were loaded onto the open flight deck. Crated, boxed, and containerized cargo and heavy equipment, all eighty-five tons of it, went into the hangar deck and the ship's hold. On 28 November 1950, we departed NAS North Island on a thirteen day voyage to Japan.

The voyage itself, was relatively calm. We were allowed topside several times to check the aircraft mooring lines and skin preservation. We'd applied a liberal coat of cosmoline to the entire airplane, but obviously not liberal enough. The salt spray coming over the bow even in calm weather, was enough to corrode many of the portions of the skin, especially the flight controls and any area where dissimilar metals were in contact with each other.

We arrived in Tokyo Bay on 10 December, anchoring across the bay, and immediately began off-loading the aircraft. The carrier had too deep a draft to pull up to the Kisarazu dock so we had to first off-load the birds onto barges, which took them across the bay to the docks at Kisarazu AB, where they were hoisted off and taken to the cleanup areas of Kisarazu. It was a very busy period for Chris and I. So much so that I left the Cape Esperance without having my passport stamped recording my entry into Japan. This wasn't a big problem while I was in uniform and had my military ID. But thirteen months later I wanted to go home and now there was a problem. I had no proof of entry into Japan. But thanks to an understanding MP captain, who diplomatically intervened on my behalf, I made my flight.

But that was later. Chris and I boarded a bus for the trip to Johnson AB, Japan, which would be 'home plate' for the Wing during the ensuing months. Johnson had been Irumagawa Air Field during the last war. Chris and I roomed together at Johnson, in the BOQ. It was both our home and office. But we

Don Kierston (left) and Irv Clark at Suwon in mid-1951. Irv was the General Electric Tech Rep for the J47 engine which powered the F-86. (Irv Clark)

John Henderson, North American Aviation Tech Rep for the 4th FIW, points out the intricacies of the leading edge slat mechanism on the F-86A to (Left to right) Lt. Andy Anderson, Capt. Dick Becker, and Capt. Nick Farrell. Capt. Becker learned well and became the second jet ace in Korea on 9 September 1951. (NAA)

335th Squadron ground crews replace a tire at Taegu in March 1951. The PSP runway and taxiways at K-2 destroyed tires as the PSP would 'roll up' and puncture the tire. And the high pressure tires used on the F-86 were not easy to come by in the Far East. Taegu's PSP chewed up nineteen tires in the month or so of operations by Sabres. (Author)

were rarely there together as we traded work locations every three months after the squadrons deployed to Korea, one of us with the units in combat, the other back at Johnson. Normally there is only one Tech Rep assigned to a unit. In Korea the 4th had two and could have used three. When the Air Force did not request additional technical support, North American did the next best thing by providing three-man maintenance teams to help advise and support the crew chiefs and maintenance personnel – in addition to the tech reps.

The 336th FIS had arrived in Japan several days before we arrived aboard the Cape Esperance. Their aircraft had also suffered from salt spray damage, but not as greatly as those aboard the jeep carrier. Some of the trailing edges needed only to be cleaned and a protective coating applied, and they were ready to fly. They could have the corrosion fixed at the next periodic inspection. Others were badly corroded and had to have the area reworked by chemical treatment, or have the part replaced, before the aircraft was ready to fly. The first seven F-86As were ready by 13 December, and Lt.Col. Bruce Hinton took the aircraft to Kimpo AB, about twenty-five miles northwest of Seoul.

On the night of 15 December 1950, I was flown into K-14 (Kimpo AB) in a C-54 full of 120 gallon Sabre drop tanks. On the flightline were seven F-86As – Detachment A of the 4th FIG. It was cold and snowy, nothing unusual I was to find out. The Sabres had already flown one mission, an orientation flight. The next day would be the first combat mission to the area

It's summer at Suwon and the 'air conditioning' is on at Suwon's 'tent city' (they opened the tent flaps!). The tech reps lived in the same tents as the combat pilots at Suwon. (Irv Clark)

known as "MiG Alley." But snow blanketed the field that day, and the first two missions were flown on the 17th. The rest is history that was made by Lt.Col. Bruce Hinton.

Back at Kimpo we received only the necessary support equipment to operate, which didn't include much of the heavy equipment needed to maintain a wing of Sabres. And there were probably only about 100 crew chiefs and technicians to maintain the aircraft. We had only two spare J47 engines, and used them both. At the time I didn't keep a daily in-commission record. I should have, for no other reason than as a commendation to the airmen that dug holes in the frozen ground for shelter, and were privileged to suffer nearly frost-bitten fingers working out in the open in constant contact with freezing metal. But our in-commission rate was good in spite of the sub-zero

Ground crews remove the J47 from a 335th Squadron F-86A at Suwon in April 1951. The B-29 in the background was battle damaged and landed at K-13. Not being able to leave, the ground crews put a tarp over the wing and used the B-29 as an improvised engine 'shop' throughout the Summer of 1951. Hey, it kept out the dust and rain. (Irv Clark)

weather and lack of required equipment during this initial effort in Korea.

The weather came as somewhat of a surprise to all of us that first day in the Land of Chosin. All of us had carefully read the Movement Orders that read in part, "... will proceed from stations indicated to a theater of <u>temperate climate</u> for a ..." Temperate my butt! It certainly isn't temperate when the water bucket freezes eight feet from the tent stove, which was always going full blast!

Everything about that initial effort was in the crudest of conditions. We had to share space and housing with the 8th and 51st Fighter Group. We had major difficulties in servicing and rearming the airplanes at Kimpo, that were intensified by the deep-freeze temperatures and very little shelter for the ground crews. There were numerous frost bitten fingers, chapped lips, and drippy noses. And that didn't include what was laughingly called the food menu.

Jet fuel was delivered to us in fifty-five gallon drums, and we had to hand pump the fuel into the Sabre fuel tanks with a rotary hand pump. How long does it take to fill a Sabres fuel tanks? Too damn long! There were 435 gallons internal, with a pair of 120 gallon underwing drop tanks. Oil and hydraulic fluid was poured from the cans, being careful to minimize contamination as much as possible, even though we had no cheesecloth or chamois to strain the liquids through. We took additional precaution during the pre-flight, by draining the fuel sumps longer to eliminate water contamination. We did this even after we finally had the services of a couple of fuel trucks.

Drop tanks were a new and constant problem in those early days in Korea. The built-up drop tanks were readied on the base cradle from the boxes they were shipped in to Korea. But they were stored out in the open, amidst the mud, debris, and weather. However, we were fortunate. Even though we hadn't perfected the expertise it takes to assure drop tank release at a 100% figure, our release rate during the first twenty-one days of combat was satisfactory considering the conditions we were working under.

Jim Jackson, tech rep for the Sperry gun sight, operates the gun sight test stand as Sgt Don Parker works the switches in the cockpit of Col. Eagleston's F-86A. Every company that built a major part of the Sabre, sent a tech rep to Korea – engine, radar, gun sight, and of course, North American Aviation had at least two on base at all times. (USAF)

There were two major problems with drop tanks in Korea – 'hung tanks' and never enough tanks. FEAF authorized the use of modified F-80 drop tanks, called Misawa tanks, for use by the F-86 in March 1951. Built by Beech, the 165 gallon tank had new fins and mounting lugs for carriage by the F-86. (via David Menard)

This is how you checked for foreign objects in the intake at Suwon. During the night, the local 'friendlies' would sneak up and throw objects into the intake which would damage the engine as soon as it was started. The crew chief was responsible for checking the intake every morning. (Bob Hulteen)

Within a week after landing in Japan, the 4th FIG had 32 F-86As operational at Kimpo. We had to maintain them right out on the open ramp without revetments. Of course, we didn't even think about revetments in those days. We already had control of the air, and Bedcheck Charlie hadn't made an appearance as yet. But revetments would have created a windbreak for the mechanics. As it was, we had to fashion work windbreaks from tent sections to protect the crew chiefs from the sub-zero winds blowing in from Manchuria.

There were several minor problems that kept cropping up in Korea. One of these were the poppet valves that boosted the flight control hydraulic operation. The F-86A had two of these valves, one in the aileron system, the other in the elevator system. The elevator system valve was easy to change. But the aileron valve was a real ball-buster. It was bolted to the wing center spar, and very difficult to get to.

Guess which one was the problem? Of course! Murphy's Law always prevails in combat, and the aileron boost valve was the one that gave us problems. We had two valves fail, and we had one crew help the other crew make the repairs. This resulted in the replacement time being cut to a minimum, almost record time despite the horrendous working conditions. Still, changing this valve in sub-zero weather guaranteed frost bitten fingers.

One of the major complaints of the pilots was the constant icing of the rear canopy glass, which made the pilots visibility to the rear almost non-existent. Not a good thing in MiG Alley. I tried to make a quick fix by 'borrowing' some aluminum tubing out of a wrecked F-80 that was junked behind the Kimpo municipal building. I bent it by hand until it fit into the rear canopy, then hand-drilled eighty thousandth size holes into it before hooking it up to the F-86 cockpit heating system. It helped slightly, but certainly wasn't a cure for the problem. When I reported the problem to the factory, I was happy to learn (and report to the pilots) that Engineering had already made a change in the design and the later aircraft would have it installed.

During the twenty-one days of combat in December, we had three birds hit by MiG gunfire. Lt. Larry Bach was shot down on 22 December. The other two aircraft were hit in the

Sgt Ed Hill, crew chief on Capt. Dave Fitton's Sabre, ducks as sniper fire is heard on the flightline at K-13 in the summer of 1951. North Korean and Chinese infiltrators often penetrated the base defenses to harass the ground crews working on the airplanes. (Troy White)

Mr John Henderson, North American Aviation Tech Rep, shows 1Lt. Dick Becker and 1Lt. Andy Anderson on the 'how and why' of 'ratting the tailpipe" by bending the tabs on the plate just inside the exhaust. "Ratting the tailpipe" increased the exhaust temperature, thus increasing thrust and speed. It also overheated the engine. (Dick Becker)

Sgt Charles Moore refills the main fuselage tank of Lt. Jim Leatherbee's 334th Squadron F-86A with 435 gallons of JP jet fuel at Suwon in early March 1951. When the 334th moved back into Suwon, they brought fuel trucks with them. At least at Suwon, the men didn't have to hand pump the fuel from fifty-five gallon drums. (USAF)

tail section at the base of the vertical fin. This was the area where both the normal and alternate hydraulic lines for the horizontal stabilizer were located. In both cases, only one of the systems was shot away, and the remaining system was only partially ruptured. It only leaked when the system was actually in use, and both airplanes returned to Kimpo.

But a little this way or that, and both systems would have been taken out with disastrous results. Again I went to the junk F-80. I hacksawed a piece of armor plate, and had it installed between the two systems hydraulic lines. It worked and we did this to several of the aircraft. The later F-86Fs had an armor plate similar to the one we jury-rigged, added at the factory.

Another problem was inaccurate tail pipe temperature readings. This would cause one aircraft to inadvertently burn more fuel trying to stay with his leaders airplane. This wasn't really a failure of a part. It was something that occurred with the change in temperatures and locales. We didn't really solve this problem until we went back to Johnson AB following the 'Bug-Out From Kimpo' in January 1951. A simple re-calibration to the closest allowable tolerance was all that was needed to cure this.

One problem that simply never went away due to over-aggressiveness on the part of the pilots, was turbine wheel blade tip erosion. We started to find this following the first twenty-one days of combat. Our F-86A-5s had the early J47 (the -7 and -13 engine) engines that had a couple of adjustable tabs installed in the tailpipe. They were called 'mice' or 'rats' By bending these tabs, it varied the size and raised the temperature of the tailpipe, thus increasing the thrust. And increased thrust meant more speed.

Anyone with a wrench could adjust these tabs, commonly known as 'ratting the tailpipe'. And all the hot pilots wanted as much of an advantage as possible. So they had their crew chiefs make the proper adjustments. But since we were already setting the thrust output at over 100%, 'ratting the tailpipe' often caused excessive heat erosion of the turbine blade tips. It was just something that we learned to live with as we all wanted our guys to have the best chance against the MiGs.

Following the 'bug-out from Kimpo' on 2 January 1951, when the Chinese Reds overran the base, the Wing re-grouped back at Johnson. It was actually a blessing in disguise as we now had a little time to do some of the repairs right. And there was lots to be done in preparation for the return to Korea. The

Capt. Don Stuck, Engineering Officer for the 336th Squadron, and a combat pilot, designed and built this water supply from two F-80 drop tanks, to supply water to the Headquarters tent at Suwon in May 1951. Capt. Stuck received the Legion of Merit for his outstanding engineering accomplishments at Suwon in May 1951. (Bruce Hinton)

Heavy work was done with the aid of an Army M32 Sherman tank retriever vehicle. The men of the 4th used this type of equipment to move crashed or 'Class 26d' aircraft from one place to another at Suwon in June 1951. (Irv Clark)

Right: Jet engine test stand at Tachikawa AB, Japan in Summer 1951. Tachikawa remained the rear echelon support facility for the 4th Wing throughout the Summer of 1951 until FEAF activated the Tsuiki REMCO facility. The engine is surrounded by a concrete blast pen. (Irv Clark)

"Lightning Bug", a 336th Squadron F-86A at Johnson AB in early Summer 1951. The 'Bug' has the open style gun blast panel installed that replaced the older panel with the automatic gun doors. All the F-86As in Korea either had the doors wired open or replaced. (Jack White)

336th Squadron crew chiefs work on the J47 in the open air engine 'shop' at Kimpo in late Summer 1951. Even after moving to Kimpo, most of the work was accomplished while the engine hung on the chain hoist. Note Royal Australian Meteors in the background. (Irv Clark)

4th Maintenance Squadron worked with the crew chiefs in the combat squadrons to investigate and troubleshoot the more elusive problems.

The 4th returned to Korea in February, when the 334th began flying missions out of Taegu, down on the end of the peninsula, about 180 miles southeast of Kimpo and much too far to be able to get at the MiGs. Never the less, the 334th was flying daily missions. It was Chris' turn and he went with the 334th to Taegu, and later back to Suwon, while I stayed at Johnson.

In early March, our ground guys re-took the base at Suwon, and the 334th Squadron moved in almost before the last shots were fired. Once again, the Sabre was within range of the MiG bases in northwest Korea. But Suwon had been ravaged by the war, and needed much improvement before we could operate as a combat wing again. When retaken, there were no parking ramps or taxiways. However, in a matter of days, a limited parking capability and a tent camp were available.

As the base improved, the 4th sent more aircraft and personnel to Suwon. The personnel, air and ground, were billeted in tents on both sides of the runway. Everything was done in a tent at Suwon. The aircraft were all parked on one side of the runway. This arrangement would become very significant one night in June when Bedcheck Charlie came to visit.

Below: Army camouflage netting covers Lt. Simpson Evans' "The Bearded Clam" on the Suwon ramp in June 1951. The netting was very cumbersome to put on and take off. It was supposed to 'hide' the Sabre from prowling enemy aircraft, which rarely appeared anyway. Lt. Evans was a Navy pilot 'on loan' to the 336th Squadron. (John Henderson)

September 1951. Suwon epitomized what the Air Force called 'bare base conditions' – dirt ramps, PSP taxiways (when they finally got taxiways!) and open air maintenance. Here is "Minimum Effort", certainly one of the most photographed F-86As in Korea, with the engine removed. The J47 had to be changed every 100 hours of flight. (USAF)

In early June, Lt.Col. Glenn Eagleston got into a hell of a scrap with a very good MiG pilot, whom we all referred to as "Casey Jones." Well, Ol' Case shot the hell out of Eagle's F-86, and he had to belly it in. The airplane was a total loss so we stripped it of everything usable, then stuck it on top of some barrels at the distant, unused area off the end of the runway. Unfortunately, it was right in line with the rest of the parked Sabres – and our tent complex.

The idea was for Eagle's scrapped Sabre to draw fire from Bedcheck Charlie. On 17 June 1951, Bedcheck Charlie came calling shortly after 2 AM. The idea worked, but Charlie's aim wasn't the best. Bedcheck Charlie was a two-seat Po-2 bi-plane, with the rear gunner dropping small bomblets over the side. He did bomb Eagle's junk Sabre, but he missed. And his second bomb hit the tent complex. His third bomb was a direct hit on Lt. Phil Janney's Sabre, #49-1334, destroying it completely.

The first bomb was the only warning we had of the attack. As we dashed out of our tents to the nearby foxholes, the second bomb went off, spraying shrapnel into the ditches. Two people were hit by the shrapnel – Capt. Julius E. 'Jig-Easy' Smith and Leo Fournier, the GE ranging radar tech rep. By the time I got across the runway, the airplane fire was out.

Irv Clark, the GE engine rep, and I helped Leo as the medics took him to the MASH hospital at Yongdopo. Both men were evacuated back to the States, and recovered. Leo returned to work and the Air Force awarded him the Purple Heart, which hangs beside the chunk of Russian scrap metal that the medics removed from his liver.

The 1951-1952 Sabre Parts Problems

In late March 1951, the 4th moved its second squadron back to Suwon (K-13). Now the birds were again within range of MiG Alley, and the missions started almost immediately. Overall, the maintenance and working conditions were better at Suwon as it at least had a paved runway. And 5th AF made the 4th Group responsible for continued base improvements. Taegu had a PSP runway, which tore the hell out of the tires. But Suwon had almost no parking area for the airplanes. And no taxiways. It was a World War II relic that was only 200' wide. The airplanes landed on one side of the runway and taxiied up the other side as other Sabres were landing. Talk about hairy!

The fighting in MiG Alley wasn't always in favor of the Sabre pilots. The Soviet flyers could be very good, just ask Col. Eagleston, Jim Jabara, or Lt. Chuck Loyd, who stands in the hole in the flap made by a 37mm cannon shell. Lt. Loyd flew with the 334th Squadron and scored one MiG kill. (Bob Makinney)

There was only a few feet, between six and ten, between the wingtips of landing airplanes and those taxiing back to parking spots!

But the maintenance crews were outstanding. They worked tirelessly around the clock trying to keep as many airplane in commission as possible. But the pacing problem was one of parts availability. Towards the middle of the year, the aircraft-out-of-commission-for-parts (AOCP) became a growing concern. Chris and I reported the AOCP and indicated percentage totals (less than 60%) to the North American office in LA on a weekly status and activity report.

A tech rep's job is to communicate with the company and the user to keep the rear command aware of what's going on in the front lines. Bear in mind that my focus was on Sabres needing repairs or maintenance and getting them back in the air. The company knew early on about the problems we were having, and took remedial actions within their limits as prime contractor, to help maintain a high in-commission rate and low AOCP. But if the parts aren't being purchased by the government as requested by the command structure, then it's out of our hands on the ramp at Suwon.

The earliest problem that persisted was that of 'hung drop tanks'. It was a constant problem caused by poor maintenance facilities (the tanks were stored in the open and often were uncovered), the weather, which was either cold and wet or wet and cold, and a minor problem with the design of the tank release mechanism, which worked great back in the States, but suffered unlocking problems in combat situations. When Captain Jim Jabara made 'ace' on 20 May 1951 after his right drop tank failed to release, it got the attention of the higher command guys.

At North American, when John Casey, Manager of Field Service Department the Sabre, heard about the incident, then heard about the other 'hung tanks' in Korea, he dispatched a

Sgt Melvin Clapp makes adjustments to the ejector seat of a Sabre at Suwon in May 1951. Although not often called on for use by the pilots in Korea, the ejector seat was the single most important accessory in the Sabre. (USAF)

"Rebel IV", a 335th Squadron Sabre, in the junk yard at K-14 in the Fall of 1951. If battle damage was extensive, the airplane was 'class 26d' and cannibalized of every salvageable part for use on flyable Sabres. The parts shortage of late 1951 became so critical that Col. Harry Thyng informed the Pentagon that he could not longer guarantee air superiority in Korea! (Bob Makinney)

Left: Two 336th Squadron crew chiefs wipe the smoke residue off the gun panel of F-86A #48-260, one of the STOVEPIPE aircraft. The crew chief would liberally apply a coat of grease to the area, which would absorb the smoke residue and make it easier to clean off after a mission. (Arthur O'Neill)

flightline technician to work with us to correct the problem. Art Smith was sent to Korea to give the pilots in the 4th a better tank release reliability, and became known as the 'tank tech rep'.

The first thing Art did was to set up a production line concept of tank construction with water proofed shackles, and to train the crew chiefs in better tank installation preparation procedures. He had the air base group at Suwon construct a wooden building to both build-up the tanks and store them out of the weather. Doesn't sound too difficult until you realize that Korea didn't haven't a whole lot of building material to work with. They used old drop tank crates and whatever else wasn't already nailed down, to put up the crude but effective structure.

The most recurring problems for 'hung tanks' were traced to loose ground wires on the electrical connection, and moisture freezing the tank shackle release mechanism after being cold soaked at altitude enroute to the Yalu. The loose wire was relatively easy to correct – just tighten the connection before the tank was installed. The freezing of the shackle inflight took a little bit of ingenuity on our part. By the time we got to the 'hung tank', the ice had melted and the tank released on the first try!

To keep moisture out of the release mechanism, we rewrapped the shackle assembly after filling the release housing with a new Dow compound. The special oil paper wrap was then tightly sealed. It worked! And hung drop tank problems dropped to a minimum. North American armament engineer Paul Peterson re-designed the mechanical mechanism that locked the tank shackle to a post under the wing, and the electrical release control and the era of the 'hung tank' was eliminated. But the new tanks with the redesigned release shackles, didn't arrive for some months.

4th Fighter Group personnel man-handle a crated J47 for loading into the open cargo bay of an Air Force C-124A Globemaster at K-14 in late 1951. The C-124 will deliver the engine and other equipment needing repair, to the maintenance depot at Tachikawa. Note the 'tail stand' which kept the C-124 from dragging its tail. (Irv Clark)

The other problem with drop tanks was that at times they were in short supply. Remember, every time the pilots sighted MiGs along the Yalu, the first thing they did was to drop their tanks. That's two per airplane, with up to forty and fifty Sabres per mission, usually two missions per day. If MiG activity increased, it wasn't unusual to lose 1000-1500 tanks in a week!

All it took, no matter how hard the GIs labored to stay ahead of demand, was for the MiGs to come up and force the Sabres to drop tanks on back-to-back missions and the tank supply went right to zero! Then, in December 1951, the 51st

In January 1952, FEAMCOM opened a Rear Echelon Combined Operation (REMCO) facility at Tsuiki AB, at which all major maintenance for the F-86s of both the 4th and 51st FIGs (and later the 8th and 18th FBGs) was performed. Bill Grover was the North American Tech Rep assigned to the Tsuiki REMCO. (Bill Grover)

Wing went operational in F-86E Sabres, literally doubling the amount of drop tanks needed!

The problem with drop tanks never was completely solved. As demands increased, other manufacturers started building them, including one in Japan. FEAMCOM even got in the act by modifying large numbers of the so-called 'Misawa drop tanks', originally built to extend the range of the Lockheed F-80 Shooting Star. The tanks had angled fins and new shackle mounts added so they could be carried by the F-86s.

The Japanese-built drop tanks were identical to the Pastushion Aviation Corp. built 120 gallon combat tanks. But for some reason, the Japanese tanks never had the flight characteristics of the original design, and often would simply curl 'up' over the wing leading edge, and travel down the wing causing damage to the leading edge, the slats, or taking off the pitot boom. This problem became so acute that in late 1952, FEAMCOM ordered that all the Japanese-built tanks be painted olive drab so that the pilots knew what kind of tanks he was carrying, and could take certain maneuvers if he had to drop the tanks.

Just how many tanks were dropped in the war is hard to estimate. A 4th FIW report to FEAF for the period of January through June 1953 boggles the mind. During that six month period, the 4th FIW alone, dropped 18,315 120 gallon drop tanks, with April being the highest month with 3,847. And their were three other fighter wings flying the F-86 in Korea at the time!

There were many other spare parts shortages for the crews in Korea. Many items were already on back order when we left for Korea! And the parts supply line just never caught up to us in that first year. Then, during the summer of 1951 the F-86E arrived, which just made the problem greater. When the 51st FIG began training to fly combat with the F-86E, the draw-down of parts and equipment that was common to both models, created a supply procurement 'race' between the two wings operating in Korea.

The problems with AOCP rates being too high, and the increase in the number of MiGs based across the Yalu – some fifty odd Sabres from the 4th were facing over 500 MiG-15s in the summer of 1951 – caused the new CO of the 4th FIW to send a chilling message to Washington. Colonel Harry Thyng, an ace in World War II, took over command of the 4th FIW on 1 November 1951. His own operations officers were telling him that they couldn't keep the MiGs from breaking through the Sabre screen and hitting the B-29s and fighter bombers. There simply weren't enough airplanes available!

M/Sgt Fred Posey was the NCOIC of the 4th Group Radar & Gunsight Shop at K-14 in 51-52. (Dave Eldridge)

FEAF already had answered at least part of the dilemma by making the 51st FIG the second Sabre-equipped wing in Korea. But that still left Thyng with the high AOCP rate for the 4th. Colonel Thyng sent the following message to the Air Force Chief of Staff, General Hoyt Vandenberg: "Personal to Vandenberg from Thyng. I can no longer be responsible for air superiority in northwest Korea!" That got everyone's attention – including my bosses at North American. I was later told that the Chief of Staff immediately got a Air Force team together to go to Korea and make a list of required parts.

When 'Dutch' Kindelberger, President of North American Aviation, learned that the Air Force was sending a team to Japan and Korea to compile a list of all items needed by the combat squadrons, he directed Field Service to send a North American team to do the same thing – except to do it NOW and do it faster! It was known as Project PETER RABBIT.

I had completed my tour, returning to Los Amgeles by Christmas 1951. It was just in time to learn that a North Ameri-

Kimpo, Spring 1952. When MiG activity was at its highest, the Group would fly two and three missions per day. The crew chiefs didn't have time to go to the mess halls, so food was brought to them on the flightline in this 'canteen truck', a converted Army communications truck. (Irv Clark)

can survey team would be sent to Korea to determine what the spare parts needs were. By contacting all the units, both flying and support such as the 6408th MS at Tachikawa, the most comprehensive list could be compiled. The North American team wasn't dispatched to preempt the Air Force investigation in any way. 'Dutch' wanted to be working on as many of the known shortages as possible before the Air Force even contacted the company with their list.

The North American team consisted of Fred Prill, F-86 Project Engineer; Jack Shropshire, Supervisor of the Spares group; and myself representing Field Service. I was sent because I already knew the personnel and the bases. We made the trip in February 1952, returning to LA in about sixteen days. For their part, the Air Force gave us outstanding support by putting a C-47 and crew at our disposal so that we could travel to all the bases in the least amount of time. After all, both Air Force and North American were simply trying to get the parts the combat crews needed the fastest way possible, whether it was an Air Force or North American project.

In 1951, Far East Air Material Command (FEAMCOM) Headquarters was just beginning to establish a new concept in maintenance – the Rear Echelon Maintenance Combined Operation or REMCO. The idea was to combine the needs of all the units that flew the same type of airplane, at a single maintenance facility instead of by the individual squadron maintenance people. In this case, Tsuiki AB, Japan, was to be the site of the F-86 REMCO, and it would serve both the 4th and 51st Fighter Wings maintenance needs.

In January 1952, FEAMCOM moved both the 4th and 51st Maintenance Squadrons to Tsuiki and set up shop. This was a vital stop in our tour as most of the major maintenance would be performed here. Battle damage repair, engine overhaul and repair, machine shop, sheet metal and wood milling shops, and the production line maintenance (PLM) were just a part of the total activity provided at the Tsuiki REMCO.

In early 1952, General Vandenberg came to 'Dutch' Kindelberger with the Air Force list of needed parts. But 'Dutch' already had North American hard at work to provide those items for which they had the authority to procure. A complete support requirement came from the combined lists of Air Force and North American, which aided the support of additional squadrons posted later to 5th Air Force (the 18th and 8th Fighter Bomber Wings).

Even before the PETER RABBIT operation, Chris and I had made a list of peculiar small cost items that were in short supply. Individually, the items cost very little, but as a total, the cost was not small. Upon receipt of the list, North American provided over $50,000.00 worth of spare hardware to the Air Force at no additional cost on the contract.

When Penny Bowen came over to relieve me in the late summer of 1951 (he was F-86E trained), he personally brought about half of the required items along with the first of the three-man On the Spot Maintenance (OSM) Teams. Although these items were only part of what we needed, it did help reduce the AOCP during the months prior to implementation of the PETER RABBIT program.

Kimpo, April 1952. A/2C Earle Vickery, a 336th Squadron maintenance specialist, makes adjustments to the ejector seat in Capt. Brooks Liles F-86A "Sweetie Pie." Liles final score is shown on the gun bay door – four destroyed, three probably destroyed, and two damaged. (USAF)

The 'drop tank farm' at Kimpo in 1952, showing maintenance personnel attaching pylons and sway braces to modified Misawa 165 gallon tanks. Drop tanks were shipped in by the dozens, and made ready right on the flight line. If MiG activity was high, it was not unusual for the pilots to drop 1500 tanks in a week!. (NAA)

Following the end of the PETER RABBIT operation, I returned to the U.S. to work in the Field Service offices supporting both the 4th and 51st Wing programs in Korea. But that year I spent in Korea was one of the most gratifying of my life. It was a fine group of enlisted men that the 4th Fighter Wing took to Korea that first year. The crew chiefs and line maintenance personnel were very capable and knew every portion of their jobs to the Nth degree.

But crewing an airplane in a locale such as Korea, with less control of living and working conditions, was a far cry from their last stateside base conditions. And the change from ConUS operations to Korea took place very rapidly. It took awhile for the troops to adjust to the primitive working conditions. And the change from a base in the U.S. to a foreign combat zone necessitated a change in attitude for getting the job done.

Maj. J.E. Collins of FEAMCOM, holds a conference with 4th and 51st Group armament and radar technicians at the Consolidated Radar-Sight Shop at Kimpo in 1952. (J.E. Collins)

Albert N. "Norm" Kalow
Crew Chief, 335th FIS, K-13 1951

Norm Kalow was a crew chief in the 335th Squadron. He'd been with the 4th Fighter Wing before Korea, and came over with the STRAWBOSS gang in December 1950. Norm is the typical crew chief that John Henderson raves about. Just the regular crew chief that did his job, day after day, night after night, in temperatures that ranged as low as -40°F on the open ramp at Kimpo and Suwon. This is how he viewed the war and the F-86 Sabre.

Norm Kalow: It's spring in Korea. Korean nights are cool, great for sleeping when Bedcheck Charlie lets you sleep. Or you weren't up all night making some type of repair so the aircraft would be ready to fly the morning mission. The crew chiefs sleep in a 10 man tent just off the flightline at K-13. I get up and splash water on my face out of my helmet.

Our house boy Cha Chin, makes up the cot. He also sweeps up, fills our canteens, and just generally keeps busy in the tent. He's only fourteen and always smiling. We don't know anything about his family, or even if he still has one. But he's a good kid, and we all try and bring him something when we go on R&R.

Right after breakfast we begin pre-flighting the airplanes for the morning mission. Most days when the weather holds, the pilots fly two missions to MiG Alley. The first thing we do is remove the camouflage netting that covers all the Sabres on the flightline. Doesn't make much sense though. The airplanes are silver with large black and white stripes. And camouflaging them with the dark colored nets just makes them stand out all the more against the white of the concrete runway at K-13.

Right: You didn't have time or energy to run to the bathroom when you worked on the flight line at Kimpo. (Arthur O'Neil)

Anyway, I do my acrobatics for the day as I slide the net down off the fuselage and wings. Check the oxygen, fuel tanks, oil levels in all the tanks – then you do it all over again. The bird looks good, and there's still some time left for coffee that the cooks send over to the flightline. Sometimes there's even leftover baked goods for us. They're playing records over the P.A. system this morning – "China Night", "Tokyo Boogie Woogie", all played by Japanese bands. The new stuff from the states is totally unfamiliar to us.

'Herr' Schultz, the armorer, pulls open the gun bay doors and checks the six .50 caliber machine guns that are mounted on each side of the pilot. He bums a cigarette from me. He's always bumming them from me. Says he left his on the piano. But that was six weeks ago! Schultz got his nickname by serving in bombers during the big war. He was shot down over Germany, and became a POW. So the title 'Herr Schultz' was tacked on to him. He doesn't mind.

Tuno comes by and checks out the radio. It's the most important piece of equipment in the airplane. if a pilot can't hear one of his guys call a MiG on his tail, he could get shot down. Tuno takes extra care with the radio. He calls the tower and I hear him say – "Roger dodger, you old codger. I read you five by five over Easy channel." The radio works fine.

Julian Sprague stands by the sign denoting the headquarters of the refueling gang at Kimpo in 1952. (Vern Sprague)

The pilots are just now coming down the flightline. Hope I don't get the 'abort king'. Most of the pilots have an airplane assigned to them. But some don't, and some have to take another airplane when there's is down for some reason. But this guy is well-known for flying across the bomb line to get credit for a mission (they have to fly 100 missions before rotating home), then dreams up an imaginary problem with the airplane and brings it back home. We've checked his airplanes again

Sgt Dave Eldredge, the Skoshi 'Honcho' of the Radar-Gunsight shop at Kimpo, about to climb into 1Lt. Ira Porter's F-86F, #51-12941, at K-14 in October 1952. Within weeks, the Sabre would be assigned to 'The Mayor Of Sabre City', Col. James K Johnson, CO of the 4th Wing. (Dave Eldredge)

and again, nothing wrong. Finally the CO has the Engineering Officer check out his airplane after every mission. He finally shapes up.

But this afternoon I'm in luck. My pilot is Captain Ralph D. 'Hoot' Gibson. Hoot is known to be wherever the MiGs are. I re-check the airplane a third time and tell 'Hoot' the airplane is OK. He nods and smiles. He knows my airplane will be OK. He climbs into 'my' F-86A, FU-311, the "Blazing Buckeye", and straps himself in.

The crew chiefs help each other with the auxiliary power units (APU) used to start the big J47 engine. There still aren't enough of them to have one plugged into each Sabre, so we have to manhandle them from one airplane to the next. They're clumsy but necessary. The J47 requires so much power to start that external help is always needed. The APU is a big yellow box with wheels. Inside the box is a small air-cooled light plane engine coupled to a generator. A pair of heavy black cables run from the APU and plug into the side of the Sabre. We're ready.

'Hoot' starts the engine. We unplug the APU and move to the next F-86. Soon all the Sabres are started and taxiing down the side of the runway to takeoff position. It's quite hairy as the airplanes taxi down one side of the same runway they have to take off from. But no one has ever had an accident – yet. Two by two, the turn onto the runway, push full power up and begin their takeoff roll. The thick black smoke streams from the J47s as they slowly move down the runway. Once airborne, 'Hoot' pulls the gear handle and the landing gear retracts smoothly.

The Sabres head north, climbing the entire time. North toward the region of Korea known as "MiG Alley." As soon as the airplanes are out of sight, we begin to get ready for them when they return. If they tangle with the MiGs, there'll be drop tanks to hang for the afternoon mission. There's a C-119 waiting at the end of the runway. The ground crews are already unloading more boxes of drop tanks.

The tanks come in crates, and we have to put fins and fittings on them. We better uncrate and build up a bunch of tanks in case our guys get in a scrap up on the Yalu. MiG Alley must be paved with them. I heard that a set of drop tanks cost as much as a new Ford. Sometimes I have to hang two sets in one day. And if the tanks fail to drop, we lose a stripe. That's what we call 'negative incentive'.

After about an hour and a half, everybody starts to turn and look north. The Sabres are returning. We squint and check each airplane for tell-tale signs that they'd been in a fight. No drop tanks! They saw MiGs! How many have smoked gun ports? Some of the airplanes have obvious damage, but it doesn't look like anything serious. My bird is OK as 'Hoot' taxies back to the parking spot. But 'Hoot' apologizes to me for not getting a MiG. What a great guy.

What's all the excitement about. There's a crowd starting to form around the airplane about two down from mine. That's Joe Menden's airplane, FU-319. His pilot is Captain Jim Jabara. Everyone is shouting because he had just shot down his 5th and 6th MiGs, making him the first jet ace in history. A couple of his buddies, looks like Captain Roberts and Lt. Kemp, hoist him up on their shoulders as the photos keep clicking away. Captain Jabara lights up another cigar. It's his signature – he's never without one. I'm either too young, too immature, or too busy for the significance of the event to sink in.

Crew chiefs from the 334th Squadron sweat out a mission in a Kimpo revetment in late 1952. Sgt Sam Day relaxes in a 'armchair' made from ammunition boxes. (Curt Francom)

Sgt Ernie Stewart stands on one of the big refueling trucks at Johnson AB, Japan in January 1951. When the squadrons moved back into Suwon in March 1951, they brought refueling trucks with them. Each truck held 6000 gallons of JP-1 jet fuel. (Ernie Stewart)

As the PR guys and the rest of the pilots gather around Captain Jabara to hear the story of the fight, the rest of us crew chiefs get busy making the airplanes ready for the next morning. Hang new drop tanks, fill the oxygen system, fill the airplane with almost 600 gallons of JP jet fuel, check the oil, wipe the canopy glass, and check the airplane over one more time. It's fine. 'Hoot' did fire the guns, so here comes 'Herr' Schultz to perform his magic and share a joke or two. About this time we break for dinner.

As soon as the afternoon mission lands, we get the birds ready for the next morning. Then cover them up with the nets and go to supper. But the day still isn't done. If there's some kind of problem that you feel you can fix, you go at it after chow. Everyone pitches in to try and get one more Sabre ready for the next morning. If there's nothing going on on the flightline, we might have a brief training session conducted by the North American Tech Rep, Mr. John Henderson. No matter how many of these sessions we have on the heating and pressurization systems, they remain a mystery. Luckily, problems are few, and help is plentiful.

If there's no flightline problem to fix, and no training session, we adjourn to the outdoor movie theater. You grab a field jacket because the night air is really cool even in summer, find an empty crate to sit on, and enjoy last years film which you've probably already seen at least half a dozen times. Then it's back to the tent to relax a bit.

It was so cold on the flightline in Korea, whether you were at Suwon or Kimpo, that large portable heaters were used to pump warm air into the engine to get the oil flowing freely. Temperatures in the winter of 50-51 reached as low as -40°! (Author)

Tonight we're going to have a little extra fun at the expense of a new First Balloon (First Lieutenant). He's been pulling a 'bed check' of all things. Where's he think we're gonna go – Tokyo for the weekend! We don't like anyone coming into the tent after 'lights out', as there've been a couple of instances where guerrillas were sneaking in and cutting one of the guys' throats. So we've been rigging mess kits over the tent flaps. Anyone comes in, the kits drop and make a ton of racket.

Sure enough, after about a hour, one of the mess kits drops and wakes everybody up. Well we'd had this planned for about a week. We knew it would be the First Balloon checking beds. As soon as the kit hits the floor, we grab for our weapons – carbines, .38s, Colt .45s. Sgt. 'Arigato' Smith, who planned the whole deal, shouts – "A guerrilla, kill the son of a bitch!" The tent comes alive with the sound of bolts slamming shut on loaded weapons, and hammers being cocked.

The 'bed checker' shines his flashlight on his totally white face, scared out of his wits, and yells out – "Don't shoot, don't shoot! It's me!" And with that, he's gone in a flash. The tent breaks out in gales of laughter. And there were no more bed checks ever again.

We lay back down on our cots, still chuckling and trying to get a little sleep before the real 'bed check' comes to visit. This is a far more serious bed check to concern ourselves with. And one that doesn't run off very easily. He's known as "Bedcheck Charlie", and he is a North Korean two-winged trainer that waits until the middle of the night to come calling.

He comes over about 2 am, dropping small bombs on us. He usually doesn't hit anything, just makes enough noise to wake everybody up and then he's gone again. But in June he did get a lucky hit on one of the Sabres parked on the flightline. It caught fire and was destroyed. Several other birds had shrapnel damage. And one of the pilots and the GE Gunsight Tech Rep, Mr. Leo Fournier, were wounded.

Wahhhhhhhhh. Damn, the air raid siren goes off again tonight. We jump up and run to a nearby dug-in tank that serves as part of the base perimeter defense. We crawl under the tank, and listen as the tank commander keeps us informed over the hand set attached to the rear.

Here comes Charlie! K-13 is lit up from tracers coming from the quad .50s and 40mm anti-aircraft guns. It's so bright I can read a newspaper. Even the tank gets in on the action and opens up with that big cannon. The noise is deafening. The gunfire stops and someone says "They got him!" Well maybe. But at least it's over for tonight and we all climb out from under the tank and go back to our tent. Sleep comes hard, but it does come. And the rest of the night, whatever is left, is uneventful. I close my eyes and rest, ready to repeat the whole thing again tomorrow. And the next day, And the next.

A/1C Dave Eldridge
4th FIG Consolidated Radar & Gunsight Shop

I was in the Consolidated Radar & Gunsight Shop at Kimpo, as a Line Chief. The OIC was 1Lt. Warren Morgan, a true officer and gentleman. We worked 16-18 hours a day, almost every day of the week. Never before (or since) has a year gone by so fast. No one seemed to work very hard, but the job always got done and done right. Everyone knew everyone else, and we all knew that men's lives were at stake.

We lived in eight-man tents, sleeping on the old army standby, the folding cot. There was a small space heater fed by an oil line from a fifty-five gallon drum of kerosene outside the tent. At times, it got so cold (the actual temperature was classified info!) that the line would freeze and the fire would go out. That necessitated someone, usually the youngest guy in the tent, to get up and go thaw out the line. Which could be interesting using a fire to thaw out a kerosene line.

The latrine was the usual "twelve holer", with half of a fifty-five gallon drum under each hole. The sides of the latrine building had hinged panels that could be lifted to remove the 'receptacles', with the contents dumped into the 'honey wagon'. We usually farmed this out to the local Koreans. The 'honey wagon' was a large cart carrying 8-10 fifty-five gallon drums, and pulled by an ox. Needless to say, you knew well in advance when the 'honey wagon' was coming down the road. And when it was time to empty the cans, it was time! I was sitting on the throne one morning, with the outside temperature hovering near zero, when I felt a sudden blast of sub-zero air. As I looked down, the half drum beneath me was whisked away to be emptied. Surprise! Surprise!

Blackouts were fairly common, but anti-aircraft fire was not. During the blackouts, we were all supposed to be in the slit trenches that were dug between the tents. But no one that I knew ever went there. During one blackout, I was sitting on the edge of my bunk, glancing out the small window in the back door of the tent. Just then the nearest AA battery opened

In the early Summer of 1952, major overhaul work at Kimpo was still being performed on the open ramp, including engine replacement. Note that at this time, June 1952, the aircraft were in the process of having the new yellow and black bands applied to the fuselage, tail and wings in accordance with FEAF directives. (Irv Clark)

up!. It looked like those tracers were coming down instead of going up. I tried to dive under the bunk next to mine just as the occupant was scrambling out of it to do the same thing. I got kicked right in the head, but I never received a Purple Heart.

On another occasion, I walked from our shop down to the flightline one very dark night. Then realized that I'd forgotten something and turned around. Imagine my surprise to find the ground that I had just covered, littered with propaganda leaflets. There had been no air raid siren, no blackout, no AA, nothing. And not the faintest sound of an airplane passing overhead. But there they were! Old 'Charlie' must have cut his engine and glided across the field that night. It sure gave me a strange feeling.

One of the stories that came out of Korea concerned the AF Form 1, which was used by the pilots to write up problems, and then by the crew chiefs and maintenance personnel to indicate their solution to said problems. As the story goes, this particular pilot, not being able to find anything really wrong with his Sabre, wrote – "Bird-shit on the windshield!" As a solution, his crew chief calmly wrote on the Form 1 – "Windshield cleaned – bird severely reprimanded – will not happen again!" And so it went in the Land of the Morning Calm.

A/1C Curt Francom
Armorer, 335th Squadron, Kimpo 1952

One of the first things I noticed in Korea was that many items that made life a little easier, like soap and toothpaste, were a little hard to come by. All water had to be trucked in. If we showered, you turned the water on just long enough to get wet, soaped yourself down, then turned the water back on just long enough to rinse off. Drinking water was located at stations around the base in lister bags, a canvas bag that held maybe twenty-five gallons. It had a spigot on the bottom and we drank from paper cups. It was usually cold, but tasted lousy.

At night, we were visited from time to time by "Bedcheck Charlie", a North Korean biplane that would drop small grenades or bombs, sometimes leaflets, on the base. The sirens would wail and the searchlights would probe the night sky. But since he never laid any eggs, we soon started to ignore him since we knew he was just there to harass us and interrupt our sleep.

But on 13 December 1952, 'Charlie' changed his pattern. It looked like it was going to be more of the same, so we tried to ignore him. I had just gotten into bed (we didn't even go to the trenches anymore), when all hell broke loose. There were explosions and heavy guns firing. Someone threw open the tent door and all I could see was a sky full of tracers. I couldn't tell if they were incoming or outgoing. But it sure didn't take me long to leave my nice warm bed and scramble into the foxhole. In fact, I didn't even take time to grab my fatigues, and was dressed only in shorts and a t-shirt. And of course, the foxhole had about a foot of water in it. There I stood, in the freezing water in that foxhole, in only my skivvies and bare feet.

Once the firing stopped, we didn't stay long in the holes. The next day we worked on the foxholes, and that night we started sleeping in our clothes. Later that month, following the 'real' Bedcheck Charlie raid, I went with Sgts. Bill O'Dowd and Manuel Ruiz down to the front of the main hanger. We hung a pod under the wing of one of the Mosquitoes (T-6 Texans modified for Forward Air Control). They were going to try and use it against old 'Charlie' as everything else had failed up to that point. I later heard that it didn't work either, and that Marine Corsairs were found to be the best for the job of getting 'Bedcheck Charlie'.

By 1953, Col. Johnson had seen that his mechanics at least had cover over their heads while performing major maintenance at Kimpo. He had a large open-sided shed built as an engine shop. Everything was performed using man power and the mechanics had to physically move the engine crane back to replace the engine in an F-86. (Don Miller)

It takes eighteen personnel (and one dog) to get and keep one F-86 in the air. Lt. Robert Carter – pilot; (1) crew chief is A1C Gus Bouldry, (2) A1C George Vaught – armorer; (3) Maj. Stephen Bettinger – Operations Officer; (4) Capt. Harry Wade – Chaplin; (5) A1C Al Baumler – radar technician; (6) A1C Berkley Underwood – clerk; (7) A3C Jim Mckinney – air police; (8) A1C Gerald O'Neil – radio; (9) CPL Marty Karkula – anti-aircraft gunner; (10, 18 and 19) A1C Paul Bailey, A3C Joe Hollins and John Hicks – firemen; (11) A1C Dick Carls – supply; (12) A1C Bob Snoplip – gun camera; (13) A1C Merwood West – cook; (14 and 15) A1C Jack O'Brien and A1C Paul Sieck – fuelers; (16 and 17) A3C Jim Clarke and Ross Bartlett – medics. (Don Miller)

In the Spring of 1953, I was transferred to 'E Flight', as the armorer on F-86E #52-2855, one of the Canadian-built Sabres. I was really happy as now I got my name painted on one of these great airplanes. The Sabre was an armorers dream, very easy to work on. We pulled two week duty on the boresight range, working at night under lights, zeroing the guns in to 1000 feet. All the birds were rotated through on a regular interval, unless a pilot complained of the accuracy.

It was while I was working with the boresight crew that one of the guys told me that my airplane had been shot up by a MiG. The pilot had made it back, but the airplane was a mess. I jumped in the jeep and drove straight to the flightline to check on 'my airplane'. There was a very large, 37mm cannon shell hole up through the right wing, and several 23mm holes through the rear fuselage near the speed brake doors. The pilot was lucky that he made it back, but I never saw the airplane again.

One day, a bunch of the flightline guys had climbed up on top of the sand bag revetments to watch the Sabres return from MiG Alley. Looking up we saw a flight make their pitch-up for the landing. They were at a steep angle, parallel to the runway. As we watched, the pilot of the third Sabre, not watching his airspeed close enough (the Sabre was very unforgiving if the speed dropped below what was necessary to maintain flight), just fell out of the sky. The Sabre dropped like a rock. In the blink of an eye, a pilot was dead. A huge black smoke ring drifted up slowly southeast of the base, and stayed in the sky for the longest time to remind others that were still coming home. Life was very fragile in Korea, here one minute, gone the next.

A1C Tom Neilson, 4th FIG Refueling Specialist Kimpo AB, 1952-53

I was eighteen years old when I got to the 4th at Kimpo. It was April 1952. I was a low level Air Force equivalent of a 'grunt' in the next war. Because I had been through Supply School in the States, I was assigned to 'POL' – Petroleum, Oil, Lubricants. Everything was shipped in drums by rail, from Inchon – 440 barrels to the car load, including jet fuel. However, we did have a camouflaged storage tank for jet fuel, that was hooked by pipeline to the storage facilities at Inchon.

The guy I replaced, told me that because of breakage, theft, etc., I should show about 10% breakage in the records. I figured, what the hell, why just 10%? So I 'broke' about 50% of every shipment. As a result, we kept the Army engineers busy making sand bag revetments around all the extra fuel. But we never ran out of fuel at K-14. And by the time Winter came in 1952, I had several thousand gallons of DF #2 (diesel fuel #2) on hand for the coming winter. Everything at K-14 was run on DF #2 – trucks, tanks, half-tracks, and especially our tent-warmers, the proverbial pot-bellied stove.

But in the early part of the Winter, everyone, or rather everyone else had run out of DF #2. Thanks to the POL officer at K-14, I pretty much got to do things my way. So when Winter came and people were having trouble finding the elusive DF #2 to keep warm and vehicles moving, they came to me. I got lots of visits from people as far away as Chorwon, home of the Army 3rd Division, to get supplies of the 'non-existent' fuel that I had on hand. You did what you had to do to stay ahead of the bureaucrats. Otherwise, the combat troops would suffer. But not at K-14.

Captain Charles R. 'Dick' Volk
335th Fighter Interceptor Squadron Intelligence Officer, Kimpo 1953

I was the 335th FIS Intelligence Officer from June of 1952 to June of 1953. We briefed and debriefed every mission, handled the gun camera film, established Escape & Evasion training, plus conducting schools on aircraft recognition. Being 'long termers' (those that had to stay a full year), we even had charge of the official whiskey ration and all the accumulated dirty songs. We had the best job in the whole place – we saw and heard it all.

As I said, we kept the official whiskey ration. The Air Force in all its bureaucratic majesty, allotted two ounces of whiskey for every sortie. It was passed out to any pilot requesting it at the debriefing to calm them down. Our guys were having so much fun that no such sedative was called for. We duly kept records of every mission, forwarding them to 5th AF. Within days, back would come bottles of VO or Canadian Club whiskey. In the good weather months, we'd often accumulate two or three bottles per day. We just locked it up. And every so often, Col. Baker, 4th Group CO, would ask, "Dick, how much whiskey do we have?" When he felt there was enough, we'd empty the locker except for one bottle, and he'd host a 'pilots only' party at the O-Club.

In the whole eleven months I was there, I only know of one pilot who took his allotted ration. He was a Marine on loan to us from MAG 33, Major Rocky Gillis. He had flamed out over the west coast above the bomb line, way behind the front lines. He ejected OK, but banged up his arms on the way out of the airplane. He landed safely in the Yellow Sea, with a strong wind and sea running.

To get out of the chute in those days, you had to squeeze a release on the harness. But you didn't want to do that because the dinghy and survival kit were also attached to the harness. Rocky was in a real dilemma. His sore hands were too weak to squeeze the release. And if he did release the harness, he lost his major ocean survival equipment. The wind was so strong that it kept the chute inflated, dragging him along and smacking him from wave top to wave top. He figured he went at least three miles, getting more scared and exhausted with each wave.

Fortunately, the ResCAP (Rescue Combat Air Patrol) guys had spotted him and a chopper arrived just in time. He dropped the whole harness then, and was promptly picked up by the whirlybird. They brought him straight back to Kimpo. He jumped down out of the helicopter very wet, very cold and shaking, and very shook up. I took one quick look at him and said, "Major, how about a double of VO?" That resulted in a smiling jarhead and the only two shots we ever dispensed.

six

The End of 1951

Aces and More Aces

July 1951 saw the 4th still at Suwon. The runways were too short and there were no taxiways to speak of. But Kimpo was needed for F-80 operations. The fully loaded Shooting Stars needed the longer takeoff roll, and Kimpo was about 3000 feet longer than Suwon at this time. But FEAF was working on lengthening the Suwon runway. Not for use by the Sabres, but to be able to exchange bases with the F-80s. This would allow another five minutes patrol time for the F-86s on station in MiG Alley.

Operations during the first week lacked results as the MiGs were reluctant to fight. Flight after flight went to the Yalu, only to see the MiGs patrolling on their side of the river, making no attempt to cross and mix it up with the Sabres. But at the beginning of the second week, the situation changed.

On 8 July, the group flew their best mission of the war to date, at least as far as results were concerned. Over the area YD 4027 (Sinanju), the MiGs crossed the river at high altitude, and dove down on the anxiously waiting Sabre pilots. When the fight was over, there were six less MiGs to contend with the next day. Lt.Col. Francis 'Gabby' Gabreski, recently arrived from the US, got his first MiG. Major Franklin Fisher got a MiG, as did Capt. Milton Nelson. Bruce Hinton got a Damaged. And Lt. Dick Becker shot one MiG down and damaged another.

On the 9th of July, Milton Nelson shot another MiG down. And on the 11th, Nelson and 'Hoot' Gibson each got a MiG. And these MiGs were a little different as they ventured deeper into North Korea than previous MiGs had. Gibson and Nelson's victories came just north of the North Korean capitol city of Pyongyang.

But that was the end of MiG activity for July, as bad weather between the 16th and the 28th either kept the 4th on the ground at Suwon, or the MiGs on the ground at Antung. However, the weather cooperated on the 29th and both the MiGs and the F-86s were in place for a fight. This time the MiGs won.

The MiGs came across the Yalu much higher than the Sabres this day. And even though the F-86 pilots saw them coming, the MiG pilots were both aggressive and good. Diving through the Sabre formation with relative impunity, the MiGs shot the hell out of F-86A #49-1098, with 23mm cannon fire taking both the rudder and elevators off the Sabre in one pass. The airplane however, continued to fly, and the pilot brought it back over 100 miles, before ejecting 13,000 feet over the base. The pilot was uninjured.

Operation Stovepipe

One of the more interesting missions flown by the wing was Operation STOVEPIPE. STOVEPIPE was a weather reconnaissance and communications relay flight. In the Summer of 1951, three old '48 model F-86As were modified for the STOVEPIPE mission. The three aircraft had additional radio equipment installed, and were camouflaged with olive drab paint. The camouflage was needed to hide the low-flying STOVEPIPE aircraft from MiG interceptors.

A STOVEPIPE Sabre would usually launch at least an hour prior to mission takeoff time. Their initial mission was a last minute weather recon in MiG Alley. But bad weather in MiG Alley didn't always mean a canceled mission. The weather in Korea was freakish, clear one minute and stormy the next. The

A flight of four Sabres in close diamond formation make a pass over Suwon in June 1951. The diamond formation is quite unusual in the combat theater and was done as a show for the visit of 5th AF Commander, Lt.Gen. George Stratemeyer. With Suwon in UN hands for over four months, the base now had PSP taxiways and ramps. (USAF)

weather fronts seemed to all come straight down the Korean Peninsula. So a STOVEPIPE Sabre would check the weather, which would give the mission planners some idea of what it was like at the moment.

Another mission assigned to the STOVEPIPE aircraft, was that of communications relay between the radar site on Chodo Island and the Sabres on patrol in MiG Alley. If any of the radar sites picked up any unidentified aircraft either north or south of the Yalu, they would immediately contact the STOVEPIPE pilot flying near Pyongyang. He, in turn, would relay the alert to the flight commanders patrolling the Yalu.

At times, the STOVEPIPE aircraft were also used as airborne mission controller aircraft, with one of the commanders personally directing the battle. He would oversee the entire battle area, watching for MiGs trying to make a sneak attack on the Sabres. He could also call for help for any Sabre pilot that was under attack. And of course, the STOVEPIPE pilots could also verify a MiG claim by a lone Sabre pilot. (You needed both film and a second pair of eyes to get a MiG claim verified in Korea.)

Later on, the STOVEPIPE mission was flown by 4th Group T-33 aircraft, and also by RF-80 Shooting Stars from the 67th

A STOVEPIPE pilot taxies for takeoff during the early afternoon of 5 October 1951. This Sabre, F-86A #48-260, has olive drab paint applied to the upper surfaces of the fuselage and wings to 'hide it' from the high flying MiGs. All the paint did was cut 20mph off the top speed. This Sabre is now in the Smithsonian Museum. (Arthur O'Neill)

Five 335th Squadron Sabres on the new PSP ramp at Suwon AB in June 1951. The area beyond the end of the PSP is where the runway is being lengthened with new parking ramps. F-86A FU-276 was shot down on 22 June 1951, while FU-236 went down on 24 October 1951. (USAF)

Each flight was housed in their own tent, with a sign denoting the occupants and their prowess as MiG hunters. (Left) Awning Able Flight (335th FIS), the: "Antung Annihilators" was Capt. 'Hoot' Gibson's flight. He has three stars by his name, Jim Heckman has one. (Right) The "Wheel House" was the home of 'C' Flight in the 335th Squadron. Lt.Col. Ben Emmert has one victory and one probable on the sign, Capt. Milton Nelson has four MiGs confirmed. Maj. W. W. 'Bones' Marshall has yet to score, but he'll be an ace before the year is over. (Lon Walter)

TacReconWing, stationed just across the runway at Kimpo. Both the 4th and 51st Wings had aircraft for the STOVEPIPE mission, although the call sign for the 51st was different from the 4th.

It was during the month of July that the first pilots began to rotate back to the US. The replacement pilots were a mix of veterans and brand new pilots straight out of advanced fighter school. Some of the veterans had notable names like Lt.Col. 'Gabby' Gabreski and Major William Whisner, two World War II aces with over fifty victories between them.

The first of the new F-86E Sabres arrived at Suwon in July, The new F-86E had the top secret 'all-flying tail', a device that mechanically linked the movable horizontal stabilizer with the elevators. This increased the flight control area, and when combined with the new hydraulically actuated controls, gave the pilot much better control in the transonic speed range. It made the F-86 almost an entirely different airplane to fly in combat.

SAC had committed three RB-45C Tornado jet reconnaissance bombers to the Korean War in the Fall of 1950 as Detachment A of the 91st SRS. The RB-45Cs were a big boost to the capabilities of FEAFs reconnaissance forces. The RB-45C had four jet engines, and was the fastest jet bomber anywhere in the world at the time. But not fast enough. The MiGs were a full 100 mph faster than the Tornado bombers. On 4 December 1950, one of the Det A RB-45Cs was shot down by MiGs on a mission into the heart of MiG Alley.

It was apparent that the reconnaissance jet would have to have F-86 escort to be able to do its job correctly. The pilots of the 4th developed tactics for escorting the RB-45Cs. An RB-45 escort mission required a minimum of twelve aircraft. Since the RB-45C was reasonably fast, the MiGs could only attack from the rear. Therefore, the escort would have two flights of four directly over the bomber, with one flight lagging behind by 6000-8000 feet watching for MiGs attempting to attack from the rear. This approach worked well, and only that single aircraft was lost.

Escorting a force of B-29s was a completely different story. With a cruising speed of about 225 mph, the B-29 was much slower than the RB-45C. The F-86s had to keep air speed above .82 Mach to have any chance at all of catching the MiGs if they were attacked. This necessitated multiple rendezvous points to keep the B-29s covered throughout their bombing runs. The Sabres also had to fly either an elongated race track or figure eight pattern over the B-29 formation to keep from running away from them.

But the MiGs soon learned that an initial attack would draw the Sabre screen off, leaving the B-29s unprotected until the next flight of Sabres made the rendezvous. The problem was of course, the lack of F-86s in theater. In the Fall of 1951, only the 4th Wing was equipped with F-86s, about seventy-five aircraft if all were available. But this was during the great parts shortage era, and it was not unusual to have 50% of the Sabre force AOCP, meaning only about forty Sabres were available on any one mission. FEAF countered this by having F-84 Thunderjets fly close escort with the B-29s, with F-86s flying top cover for both. However, disaster struck on the 23 October 1951 mission to Namsi.

A force of ten B-29s left Kadena and rendezvoused with the F-84s over the Yellow Sea. The F-86 top cover met the strike force near the mouth of the Yalu River. A large force of MiGs was ready and waiting as the strike force flew toward Namsi. One hundred MiGs jumped on the thirty-four 4th Wing F-86s flying top cover. With the Sabres engaged, another force of fifty MiGs flew straight through the F-84 close escort and hit the B-29s hard – very hard!

Three of the B-29s and one F-84 were shot down immediately. When it was over, the attack on Namsi had been aborted. All seven remaining B-29s had been damaged so greatly that none flew again. It was the first time that U.S. Air Force bombers had been driven off a target by defending fighters. It cost the MiGs greatly as they lost six in the battle; two to F-86s, two to F-84s, and two to B-29 gunners. But the MiGs had finally won a battle. FEAF waas forced to abandon daylight precision bombing for night radar-directed bombing.

August began much as July had ended, with bad weather keeping contact to a minimum. On 9 August, the MiGs crossed the river again. But they just stayed high above the F-86s, which tried in vain to close on them. When the MiGs tired of the game, they simply turned around and flew home. The entry in the log read simply – "Sighted twenty-four MiGs, engaged none." Weather hampered operations again until the 17th. But again the MiGs just crossed the river and flew back home again.

On the 18th, the MiGs came down off their perch and fought. The results were the same as they had been since the beginning of the year. Two MiGs destroyed, Lts. Buford Hammond and Charles Loyd being credited with one MiG each; and Capt. Paul Bryce, Lt. Vassilias Tsufis, and Lt. Gill Garrett scored three damaged.

On the 19th, twenty-four F-86s were jumped by over fifty MiGs that crossed the river near Sinuiju. Major 'Bones' Marshall, Capts. Bert Gray and Bruce Cunningham, and Lt. Gill Garrett got one damaged each. But Capt. Dick Becker shot two MiGs down on this mission

On 23 August the group flew a mission into MiG Alley with negative results. But instead of landing back at Suwon, the group landed back at Kimpo. It would be the home of the 4th FIG for the remainder of the war. Both the 8th and 51st Fighter Groups took their F-80C Shooting Stars to Suwon, which had been lengthened to accommodate the heavily laden fighter bombers.

The first mission from recently renovated Kimpo brought instant results. The day after the 4th returned to Kimpo, the additional patrol time along the Yalu paid off. Col. Preston led twenty-three F-86As and Es that day. Near the end of the 'usual' patrol time, the MiGs attacked. But the F-86s had an additional

1Lt. Don Torres is about to start the engine for the morning STOVEPIPE flight. STOVEPIPE was the weather recon/radio relay flight that was flown in the Summer of 1951 to give an indication of the weather along the Yalu River. Three Sabres were used, and each was camouflaged on the upper surfaces with Army olive drab tank paint. (Don Torres)

"Miss Behaving" was the personal aircraft of Capt. Don Torres in the 336th Squadron. But as with literally every aircraft in Korea, if Torres wasn't scheduled to fly, the airplane would be flown by another pilot. Capt. Dick Becker shot down one of his five MiGs in "Miss Behaving." (Don Torres)

five minutes worth of fuel resulting from the shorter flight from Kimpo to MiG Alley. Col. Preston and Capt. Jack Robinson each shot down one of the MiGs. Weather and a lack of aggressiveness on the part of the MiGs kept the results for the rest of the month at zero.

But September was a different story. The MiGs were the most aggressive they had ever been. And it cost them dearly as the pilots of the 4th shot down a total of twelve MiGs. On the morning mission of 1 September, the Sabres sighted over twenty MiGs that were just entering MiG Alley as the F-86s were at 'Bingo' fuel and heading home. But the afternoon mission was better.

'Bones' Marshall was leading a section of eight F-86s from the 335th Squadron, when they were jumped by some fifty MiGs about fifteen miles west of Sinuiju. Marshall called for his flights to drop tanks, break into elements of two and engage the MiGs. 'Bones' and his wingman tacked onto a pair of MiGs that had passed through the F-86 formation. Closing to within 1000 feet, 'Bones' pulled the trigger for a short burst. When he left his finger off the trigger, nothing happened. The trigger was stuck in the firing position and the six .50s kept hammering.

Luckily, 'Bones' was in range of the MiGs and had good position on the last one. He just kept moving the nose of his airplane back and forth, hosing the MiG with continuous fire.

Squatting next to his Sabre, "Miss Behaving", 1Lt. Don Torres shows his crew chief, Sgt George Gabriel, the area from where he just returned following a mission in July 1951. Lt. Torres had several MiG probables and damaged to his credit. (USAF)

He scored hit after hit all over the MiG fuselage, canopy, and engine area, before the guns stopped firing with only 240 rounds left. The MiG erupted in smoke and fire, and the left side of the fuselage suddenly exploded and the MiG went down in flames. It was Major Marshall's first confirmed victory.

On 2 September, 'Bones' was again in the thick of the action. Col. 'Gabby' Gabreski led twenty-one F-86s to MiG

Alley, where they found twelve MiGs at YE 2000 (east of the Sui Ho Dam). With the MiGs not having numerical superiority, a rarity in MiG Alley, the F-86s took the fight to them. Major Marshall got his second victory in two days, and Capts. Richard Johns and 'Hoot' Gibson and Col. Gabreski each got one. The down side was that the group lost one this day, when 1Lt. Larry Layton (335th) was shot down.

The 9th of September was Ace Day in the 4th, when two aces were crowned in a single day. Capts. Dick 'MiG Wrecker' Becker and 'Hoot' Gibson got one MiG apiece making each of them an Ace. Becker got his MiG first, and thus became the second ace in Korea.

Dick Becker: "I was leading a flight of six to the Sinuiju area on the Yalu. Just after taking up our patrol track on the south side of the Yalu, I spotted about thirty MiGs, high above us on the north side of the river. I turned the flight towards the MiGs, dropped tanks and started to climb. Climbing through 39,000, I looked down and to the right. More MiGs! Twelve more to be exact!"

"These guys were in a good position and closing rapidly. I turned toward them and started to make a head-on pass. As soon as I started toward them and started to fire, the MiGs broke in all directions. I didn't have time to pull around on any of these guys. They just hit and run. When I looked around for the MiGs, I noticed that not only were the MiGs gone, so was the rest of my flight, including my wingman!"

"I was still sitting at 39,000, a good altitude to fight at. But without a wingman, it was a very precarious position to be in. So I started for home. Looking down, I spotted another batch of twelve MiGs about 3,000 feet below me. This time I had the advantage of speed and height. I dove down and watched the MiGs scatter. But with the speed I had built up, I had no problem chasing one of them down."

"I pulled in behind one of the MiGs, closed the range and fired. The six .50s walked all over his fuselage and the pilot suddenly bailed out. It was a good thing too, as the MiG blew up a few seconds later. The rest of the MiGs had time to regroup. And seeing one of their comrades explode under my guns, they were mad. But I still had plenty of speed built up, and started a run for home. They never caught up to me. When I landed at Kimpo, everyone was waiting for 'Hoot' and myself. We were officially the 2nd (me) and 3rd jet aces in history."

From that day through the end of the month, the MiGs came up and fought more frequently than they'd been doing in the previous months of the war. On the 10th, Lt.Col. George Jones, Lt. Booth Holker and 'Bones' Marshall each damaged one. On the 19th, the F-86s got another four damaged – Lt Otis Gordon hit two of the wily MiGs, while Capt. Richard Johns and Lt. John Honaker damaged one each. But the only destroyed that day was credited to Capt. Ken Sheen, an F-84 Thunderjet pilot in the 9th FBS! Lt. R.O. Barton got a damaged on the

An element of 336th Squadron Sabres taking off from Suwon past a 25th Squadron F-80C that's armed with a pair of 1,000 lb bombs. The F-86s are bound for MiG Alley in northwest Korea in the summer of 1951, while the F-80 will hit targets in support of the UN ground forces. (USAF)

Left: Mobile Control at Suwon was this converted Army 2 1/2 ton truck with a communications box and many antennas. Note the controller with his head out of the opening in the top, which could be covered by a 'liberated' B-26 bombardier nose cone during bad weather. (Irv Clark) Right: Ground Control Intercept radar truck at Suwon in the Summer of 1951. The GCI radar not only picked up inbound enemy aircraft, but also helped direct friendly pilots back to 'home plate'. (Leo Fournier)

21st, and Lt. Arthur O'Conner damaged another on the 22nd.

On the 25th of September, pilots of the 4th FIG scored five kills. Major Dick Creighton got his second victory, Lt. Booth Holker shot down two MiGs about fifteen miles north of Taechon, Lt. Charles Loyd got one about twenty miles north of Sinanju, and Lt. Paul Roach shared a MiG with his wingman Lt. Marshall Babb. The next day, Capt. Milton Nelson scored a probable, but the group lost one airplane. Col. Preston finished off the month by damaging another MiG on the 27th.

October was a good month with totals of twenty-six MiGs destroyed, three probables, and sixteen damaged. The big days were the 2nd and 16th. On the 2nd, the group shot down five MiGs with Col. Gabreski and Major Creighton getting one each. On the 16th, thirteen pilots from the 334th and 336th Squadrons shot down or damaged a total of twelve MiGs, with Col. Ben Preston getting his second, and Major Franklin Fisher getting two MiGs to bring his total to three. Lts. Cliff Brossart and Merlyn Hroch shared a MiG.

But the day was costly to the group also. With so many MiGs in the air, the fights seemed endless. And when the MiGs broke off, many pilots found themselves at or below 'Bingo' fuel. Some were far below 'Bingo'. Four Sabres flamed out during the return flight for lack of fuel. One Sabre crashed about twenty miles north of Kimpo, with the pilot safely ejecting. The other three made dead stick landings at K-14 without further incident.

November began with many of the pilots beginning transition training into the new F-86E. Many of the new E model Sabres had arrived by Navy carrier. The new Sabres were split between the veteran 4th FIG and the 51st FIG at Suwon, just beginning the transition from F-80 Shooting Stars to Sabres.

Many of the veteran pilots from the 4th were transferred into the 51st to give the group combat leadership and experience in fighting the elusive MiGs. At the same time, several of the pilots from the 51st were temporarily transferred into the 4th for combat training in the F-86. Col. 'Gabby' Gabreski was

Once off the base at Suwon, the carnage of war was evident wherever you looked. (left) A knocked out Chinese T-34 tank sits outside the main gate in the Suwon City Wall. (right)The remains of a bombed and burned out train near Suwon. (Bob Makinney and Irv Clark)

On 23 August 1951, the 4th Group flew another mission to MiG Alley. But instead of landing back at Suwon, the group landed at their new home – Kimpo AB, K-14. Kimpo was about thirty miles closer to the Yalu and had much better overall facilities for Sabre operations than Suwon. The nearest Sabre named "Gabby", is the F-86E flown by Lt.Col. Francis 'Gabby' Gabreski. (USAF)

transferred to the 51st to take over as Wing Commander. And he took several veterans with him including Lt.Col. George Jones, who took over as Group Commander, and Major Bill Whisner, who became CO of the 25th Squadron.

But missions were flown even as the transfers were in the mail. On the 2nd of November, Lt.Col. Jones and his wingman, Lt. Dick Pincoski shared a MiG. The shared MiG was the 100th MiG-15 shot down by 5th Air Force pilots since the MiG entered the war back in November of 1950. On the 4th of November, a pilot in the group scored another first. Captain William Guss, a Marine pilot on TDY with the 4th FIG, became the first Marine pilot to shoot down a MiG.

During mid-November, the Reds attempted to activate several air bases inside North Korea. The North Korean Air Force's 2nd Air Regiment moved into recently renovated Uiju Air Base on 7 November 1951. It was certainly a bold move on the part of the communists since 5th AF had air superiority over all of North Korea. They could, and eventually did, bring B-29 and fighter bomber attacks on Uiju at any time. The MiGs flew several missions from Uiju during the next ten days.

On the 18th of November, two F-86 pilots returning from MiG Alley, strafed the MiGs at Uiju. The pilots were Capt. Ken Chandler and Lt. Dayton Ragland. Lt. No Kum-Sok of the North Korean Air Force recalls that day: "About 10 am, I had just been relieved on Alert Duty. I knew the F-86s were in the area as we heard a dogfight over the radio."

"Suddenly, our regiment commander started waving his arms and screaming for us to get out of the way! I turned my eyes toward the sky over the northern end of the runway. There they were. Two jets speeding toward us at a high rate of speed, with that tell-tale smoke trail behind them. SABRES! The approaching Sabres were completely silent, like a supersonic whirlwind. The noses flashed as the pilots fired their .50 caliber guns. The bullets tore up the flight line full of MiGs, throwing streams of dirt into the air."

"I flung myself to the ground and pressed my face into the earth. Many of my fellow pilots were trapped in their airplanes. As quickly and silently as they came, the Sabres exited, with

The terminal building and control tower at Kimpo, showing the ravages of the fighting. Kimpo had been taken and retaken a total of four times in about a year. (NAA)

The original guard shack at the Kimpo main gate in September 1951. (Arthur O'Neill)

the scream of engines, the screams of men dying, and the explosions of airplanes destroying themselves in their wake." Twelve MiGs had been on the alert ramp at Uiju that day. With one pass, Chandler and Ragland had destroyed four MiGs, probably destroyed another, and damaged three more. The rest of the MiGs were evacuated from Uiju, and no further attempt was made to activate any air bases outside of Manchuria until after the end of the war in July 1953.

On 27 November, the 4th FIG crowned its fourth ace of the Korean War. Major Dick Creighton and Lt. William Dawson each shot down a MiG on this day. It was Creighton's 5th MiG. Major George Davis got two destroyed and one damaged. It was Davis' first confirmed victories, and the first of six multiple MiG days for Davis. Three days later Davis would become the 5th Ace in Korea.

The morning of the 30th dawned with the usual cold Korean haze. At first thought, it looked like a bad day for flying. But the weather cleared in time for the afternoon mission. It would be a mission to remember by everyone that participated. Intelligence had learned that the North Korean Air Force was going to plaster Cho-Do Island, a UN listening and rescue post about thirty-five miles off the coast of North Korea, and well behind the Main Line of Resistance.

On 9 September 1951, the second and third jet aces of the Korean War were crowned when Captains Dick 'MiG Wrecker' Becker and Ralph 'Hoot' Gibson shot down their fifth MiGs. Col. Francis Gabreski (then) 4th Group Commander shakes their hands following the mission. (USAF)

A few of the new F-86Es arrived in Korea in late July 1951. The E model Sabre featured the 'all-flying tail', which made the airplane controllable in the transonic speed ranges that were necessary to fight the MiGs at 40,000 feet over the Yalu. Most of the big hunters, got one of the new Es as soon as they were checked out in it. This Sabre, #50-673, was shot down on 28 November 1951. (Al Lukza)

One of the missions flown by 4th FIG pilots was escort of the RB-45C Tornado photo recon bomber. Even though the RB-45C was the fastest operational jet bomber in the world, it was still some 100 mph slower than the MiG-15. After the MiGs shot down one of the RB-45Cs in December 1950, all further missions to the Yalu (and beyond) required a fighter escort. (Author)

Cho-Do was the site of a Tactical Air Direction Center radar, which monitored the air space near the mouth of the Yalu River. Cho-Do was also the most forward of the FEAF air rescue stations, with detachments of SC-47 and SA-19 rescue airplanes, as well as H-5 and H-19 rescue helicopters. And it was a large pain in the neck to the communists. The Cho-Do GCI controllers could rapidly warn the Sabres patrolling along the Yalu, of any incoming MiG 'bandit trains' coming out of Antung, or any one of the other eight to ten MiG bases north of the Yalu.

In the early afternoon of the 30th, the North Korean Air Force dispatched a large formation of Tupolev Tu-2 propeller-driven light bombers, with an escort of Lavochkin LaGG-9 propeller fighters to attack Cho-Do's facilities. This formation of propeller aircraft was also escorted by about fifty MiG-15s. But 5th AF had been alerted to the attack and laid a trap for the bombers.

At 1532 local time, thirty one F-86s from the 4th FIG left Kimpo AB and headed north. When they returned one hour later, the NKAF bomber force had been decimated – eight of the twelve Tu-2s had been shot down, and three others received major damage; three of the sixteen LaGG-9s were shot down, and one of the escorting MiGs was shot down. The 4th FIG crowned two more aces that day – Major George Davis and Major Winton 'Bones' Marshall. The lone MiG-15 was shot down by Davis, his fourth kill of the day and the 100th MiG-15 shot down by pilots of the 4th.

The mission was Counter Air Patrol #0403. Major George Davis, CO of the 334th FIS, was leading Dignity Able Flight; Col. Harrison Thyng, CO of the 4th FIW led Dignity Baker Flight; while Col. Ben Preston led Red Flight and Major Winton Marshall was leading White Flight. Col. Preston made a feint to the northeast in the hopes of slipping past the MiG screen covering the bombers heading toward Cho Do. The feint worked, and the Sabres came back across the peninsula north of the MiG screen – right on the tail of the slow, propeller-driven Tu-2 bombers and sixteen LaGG-9s escorting the Tu-2 force. The LaGG-9 was roughly equivalent to the old P-47 Thunderbolt, and certainly no match for the Sabres.

Red and White flights got above and behind the MiGs that were patrolling about seventy-five miles north of the MLR, the two flights of Sabres suddenly turned west and dropped their tanks. At 1607 K, the Sabres sighted the bomber force. They were headed southwest at about 6,000 feet, and the LaGG-9s were flying above and behind them, with about sixteen MIGs flying high cover at about 35,000 feet.

Col. Preston started a high, head-on pass and opened fire. No hits. He turned, pulling up over the bomber flight, and came back down on one of the LaGG-9s. Again Preston opened fire. This time his six .50s found the mark and the LaGG-9 went into a sudden, uncontrollable dive, crashing into the mountains below.

White Flight arrived shortly after Red, with all four aircraft making a head-on pass against the bomber formation. Capt. Al Simmons, White Flight Lead, pulled up over the bombers, broke left and down and opened fire. After about twenty rounds, his guns quit. Lt. Bob Akin was flying as Simmons' wingman when his guns quit. Akin now took over the firing and let Simmons watch his tail. Akin picked out the fourth bomber in the last flight of four, pulled in behind him and fired, scoring multiple hits all over the bomber fuselage. The Tu-2 started down, on fire, and crashed.

Doug Evans and John Freeland were an extra flight within White Flight. Evans and Freeland came in from head-on, with

Col. Francis 'Gabby' Gabreski leans on the wing of an F-86A at Suwon in July 1951. 'Gabby' was assigned to 4th Wing Headquarters and scored two MiGs in July and September 1951, before taking over the 51st Wing in November, which had recently equipped with new F-86Es and moved to Suwon. (USAF)

(Left to right) Capt. Milton Nelson is congratulated by his wingman, 1Lt. Mose Gordon, following his third MiG kill of the war. Capt. Nelson, a 335th Squadron pilot, would end with four MiG victories to his credit. Gordon would transfer to the 51st Wing and get a MiG in January 1952. (USAF)

Evans' bullets finding the mark. The Tu-2 was on fire from one of the engines and wing, and Evans watched as the bomber crashed into the sea. Evans and Freeland then turned their attention to the other LaGG-9s and Tu-2s, made several firing passes with no results, then turned for home.

Major George Davis entered the area at 10,000 feet, turned north and started toward the Yalu. There they were, a large gaggle of Tu-2s heading south toward Cho Do. Davis went high above the bomber force, made a quick 180° turn, and came back down behind the Tu-2s. As he pulled within range, Davis opened fire and watched his bullets cross over the bomber from one wing to the other. The bomber slowed and dropped out of formation, but didn't crash. Major Davis and his wingman, Lt. Merlyn Hroch, turned back around and set up another pursuit curve on one of the other bombers. Davis fired, hitting the bomber in the fuel tanks. The wing exploded into flames and the Tu-2 went straight down into the sea.

About this time, Hroch and Davis became separated. Major Davis was turning his Sabre so tightly that Hroch couldn't stay with him. Finding himself alone in a sky full of MiGs, Hroch made a hasty retreat and joined up with some other Sabres for the flight back to Kimpo. Major Davis should have done the same thing, as standing orders were that if you became separated from your wingman, you were to proceed out of the area and head for home.

But that wasn't the way George Davis flew. (Major Davis had seven Japanese victories in World War II) Davis made another 180, and pulled in behind another of the bombers. With the Tu-2s flying at about 180 knots, Davis closed very rapidly from the 6 o'clock position. Davis fired and the bomber exploded, with the crew bailing out seconds before the airplane crashed into the sea. Still Davis wasn't through. He turned again, and again pulled in behind a Tu-2, He fired, the bomber exploded and crashed into the sea with no parachutes.

Col. Herman Schmid, 4th Wing Commander, laughs at something Lt.Gen. George Stratemeyer said during a visit from the Commander of FEAF. You always laugh at something a general says. (Leon Williams)

Davis was now at Bingo fuel status, and started for home, joining on the wing of Col. Preston. But as they started for home, Davis heard a distress call from one of his flight that was in trouble. It was Lt. Ray Barton. Davis turned his F-86 around and started north again. Looking down, he spotted a swept wing aircraft at about 3,000 feet heading north. He called

336th Squadron crew chiefs and armorers make last minute adjustments and top off the fuel tanks of the F-86As as the pilots are walking to the airplanes for the morning mission in October 1951. No crew chief wanted his Sabre to return with drop tanks and clean gun ports. That meant no MiGs were sighted. (USAF)

Maj. Dick Creighton brings the nose off the Kimpo runway as he heads towards MiG Alley in November 1951. Maj. Creighton would be the fourth jet ace of the war, when he shot down his fifth MiG on 27 November. (USAF)

Barton and told him to turn first left, then right. The swept wing aircraft in front of him did neither. It was a MiG.

Davis pulled in from six o'clock high. The MiG never saw him until it was too late. Davis fired, scoring good hits all over the fuselage and wing. The MiG crashed into the sea. Davis then saw three additional Tu-2s that were running for home. But he had only 80 gallons of fuel remaining, barely enough to get him back home. Davis turned for home, climbed for some altitude and started a glide for Kimpo. He flamed out on final approach but brought the '86 in for a same landing.

Davis score for the day was three Tu-2s destroyed, one MiG-15 destroyed, and one Tu-2 damaged. Amazingly, Davis had shot down four enemy aircraft and damaged one more, using only 1200 rounds of .50 caliber to do it. And he was flying one of the older F-86As, #49-1184, with the old Mark

(Left to right) Majors George Davis Jr. and Dick Creighton at Kimpo on 27 November 1950. Creighton has just shot down his fifth MiG to make ace, while Davis has just shot down his first two MiGs of the war. Three days later, Major Davis would shoot down four enemy aircraft to become the fifth jet ace in Korea. (NAA)

Left: 1Lt. Don Jabusch inspects what is left of his canopy after a MiG cannon shell exploded next to it. The MiG cannon fire blew off Jabusch's helmet and oxygen mask, put a large hole in the left wing and fuel tank. But Jabusch regained control of the heavily damaged Sabre, evaded the MiG, and brought the airplane home to Kimpo. (USAF)

30 November 1951, and the 4th FIG has a maximum effort mission to stop a force of North Korean Tu-2 bombers that are going to strike the radar station at Chodo Island. The 4th group put up thirty-one F-86s against the force of twelve Tu-2s, sixteen LaGG-9 fighters, and fifty MiGs. It was a slaughter! (USAF)

18 gun sight. It was the beginning of the legend of George Davis and his use of "Kentucky Windage."

The totals made Major George Davis the 5th Jet Ace of war. Major Winton Marshall became the 6th Ace when he shot down one Tu-2 and a LaGG-9. Totals for the day included eight of the twelve Tu-2s shot down, three of the LaGG-9s, and the lone MiG-15. Besides Davis and Marshall, Tu-2 victories went to Lt. Bob Akin, Capt. Ray Barton, Lt. John Burke, and Lt. Doug Evans, The LaGG-9s were credited to Col. Ben Preston, Lt. John Honaker, and Major Marshall.

The following day, 1 December, Lt.Gen. O.P. Weyland, commanding Far East Air Force, sent the following TWX to Col. Harrison Thyng, CO of the 4th: "Results yesterdays encounter F-86 with enemy Tu-2s, LaGG-9s and MiG-15s highly gratifying. Should teach the commies a lesson. And might even suggest to them the advantages of armistice. Congratulations on a fine days work. Signed Weyland."

The message from Gen. Weyland was the highlight of the day, as the patrolling Sabres sighted some eighty MiGs during the morning and afternoon patrols. But the MiGs were evidently stunned by the previous days action, as they stayed way above the patrolling Sabres, making no attempt to start a fight.

The following day, the MiGs came to fight. The afternoon mission found MiGs waiting for them just above Pyongyang. Maj. Zane Amell, Group Operations Officer was leading the flights. The MiGs were at 32,000 feet and evidently didn't see the F-86s until it was too late. Amell's flight was already in position and closing on the MiGs from 1500 feet when the MiGs started climbing to escape the pursuing Sabres. Amell closed to within 1000 feet and opened fire. The MiG exploded. Scratch one.

(Left to right) Representing a total of 29 1/2 MiGs are Major George Davis, Jr., (14), Maj. W.W. 'Bones' Marshall (6 1/2), Col. Ben Preston (4), and Maj. Dick Creighton (5). Col. Preston was the 4th Group Commander, while the three Majors each commanded a squadron. ('Bones' Marshall)

Maj. James Martin, 334th Squadron Exec, closed to 500 feet on a MiG near Sunan before firing. His .50 calibers scored heavy on the fuselage and right wing root, and the MiG exploded and burned. Martin had to break hard right to avoid colliding with the pieces. Scratch two. Martin also damaged another MiG near Chungsan.

Capt. Nelton Wilson got the third MiG near Kiyang-ni. Wilson closed on the MiG and fired, watching his strikes tear up the MiG's tail assembly, engine bay, and wing root. The MiG slowed and started to smoke, but didn't blow up. Other MiGs drove Wilson off before he and his wingman could confirm the MiG. But Col. Harrison Thyng, watched the MiG crash.

Capt. Mike Novak took his flight of four into a melee of MiGs and F-86s. Novak saw an element of Sabres trying to

Maj. George Davis, Jr, stands next to Dick Creighton's airplane following the slaughter of 30 November 1951, when Davis shot down three Tu-2 bombers and one MiG-15 to bring his score to six, becoming the fifth jet ace of the Korean War. The five victory stars on the Sabre, F-86A #49-1225, belong to Dick Creighton. (NAA)

evade a lone MiG that had gotten into a good firing position. As the MiG was firing on the Sabres, Novak and his wingman moved into a seven o'clock position. Novak opened fire, moved into the six o'clock and started to fire again. Novak's guns scored heavily on the left wing root and fuselage, and the MiG started to burn. Novak and his wingman watched the MiG go straight in. Scratch four.

On the 3rd of December, the group flew three missions. But although over 70 MiGs were sighted, they made no attempt to engage the patrolling F-86s. The next day Lt. Dick Pincoski got a damaged when his element got behind a couple of MiGs and he started to fire. Pincoski hit both wings, and the MiG started trailing a thin line of smoke or fuel. But it easily made it back across the river.

On the 5th of December, Maj. George Davis had another of his patented double-victory days. Leading the 334th Squadron, Davis found a pair of MiGs heading southeast near Sinanju, closed and fired. The MiG burst into flames and the pilot ejected. He got his second of the day a few minutes later during the return flight to Kimpo. A lone MiG was chasing an F-86 near the mouth of the Chong-Chon River. Davis closed in and fired. The MiG went into a violent spin and the pilot bailed out.

'Bones' Marshall was leading his 335th Squadron as top cover for an F-84 fighter-bomber strike near Sinanju, when he spotted several MiGs attempting to break up the F-84s. Marshall dove on the MiGs and fired, scoring several hits. But although the MiG was smoking, it was still flying and flew back across the Yalu. Marshall went back to covering the F-84s only to find more MiGs attacking the Thunderjet fighter-bombers. This MiG didn't get away. 'Bones' closed and fired, watching his .50 calibers walk through the fuselage and cockpit areas. The MiG suddenly exploded and Marshall had to fly through the debris, covering his windscreen with oil and jet fuel. His F-86 suffered minor damage from MiG pieces hitting the wings and tail assembly.

Lts. Gerald Beck and Ernest Neubert shared a MiG over Sukchon. Beck saw the MiG firing on the F-84s and he and Neubert immediately dove on him. Beck fired and the MiG started taking violent evasive action. Beck followed and con-

Opposite: On 30 November 1951, the 4th caught a flight of twelve Tu-2 bombers attempting to attack the radar station on Chodo Island, off the coast of North Korea. When the fight was over, 4th Group pilots had shot down eight of the bombers, damaged three, shot down three LaGG-9 fighters, and a MiG-15. (Left to right) Major George Davis shot down three Tu-2s and the lone MiG, Col. Ben Preston got one of the LaGG-9 fighters, and Major W.W. 'Bones' Marshall shot down a Tu-2 and a LaGG-9. Both Davis and Marshall made ace. (USAF)

Maj. W.W. 'Bones' Marshall's Sabre was "Mr. Bones V", F-86E #50-625, when he commanded the 335th Squadron at K-14 in 1952. Maj. Marshall's scoreboard shows seven red victory stars, one probable, and five damaged. ('Bones' Marshall)

336th Squadron mechanics begin pulling the aft section from F-86E #50-686 at Kimpo in November 1951. The F-86E began to make an even bigger impression with the pilots on both sides of the Yalu River. The E was only moderately faster than the A model Sabre, but the pilots had complete control, even when the airplane went supersonic – something the MiG could not do. And the MiG was almost uncontrollable at very high Mach speeds. (Al Lukza)

2Lt. A.C. Foster flew "Hot Spook", one of the oldest F-86As in the 336th Squadron. It was one of the very first Sabres delivered to the 4th FG on 27 May 1949, and was still flying combat in late 1951. (W. Gibson)

Another 'oldie but goodie' was 48-246, which was delivered to Andrews on 11 October 1949. It would have a much different history in late 1951 when it was converted from fighter to reconnaissance aircraft, and transferred to the 67th TRW across the field at Kimpo. (via David Menard)

Three aces that flew with both the 4th and 51st Groups in Korea. (Left to right) Col. 'Gabby' Gabreski, Commander of the 51st Group at Suwon had 6 1/2 MiGs (two with the 4th Wing); Capt. William Whisner had 5 1/2 MiGs (two with the 4th); and Lt.Col. George Jones had 6 1/2 MiGs (4 1/2 with the 4th Wing). All three transferred from the 4th to the 51st in November 1951. (William Whisner)

Major George A. Davis gives the 'V' sign, which actually indicates two MiGs destroyed. Major Davis, Commander of 334th Squadron, got his MiGs two at a time, for a total of fourteen. He was shot down and killed in action on 10 February 1952, after scoring his fourteenth victory and was awarded the Medal of Honor. (USAF)

tinued firing, scoring more hits. Suddenly the MiG made a violent turn, directly in front of Neubert, who immediately fired a long burst into the MiG. Neubert's fire hit the MiG all over the fuselage and wings, and it burst into flames, crashing near Sukchon. Capt. Ken Chandler got a Probable, and Capts. Conrad Mattson and Frank Mathews each scored a Damaged.

On the 6th, Lt. Charles Christinson, flying #4 in a four ship flight, got a MiG near Anju, a rather unusual occurrence for a #4 man. Capt. Ray Barton and Lt. Al Dymock got damages. The MiGs stayed away from the Sabres until the 11th, when Maj. Al Simmons and Lt. Don Griffith each got credit for a confirmed destroyed.

The 13th of December was another big day. Major George Davis got four this day, two on the morning mission, and another two in the afternoon. The two kills he scored on the morning mission made ten. He was the first double ace of the Korean War.

But Davis wasn't the only one to score this day. Capt. Ted Coberly also got two on the morning mission. And Col. Ben Preston, and Lts. Al Dymock, John Green, John Honaker, Claude Mitson, and Dick Pincoski each scored one confirmed victory. Mitson and Col. Preston each added another damaged on the 14th, to go with Col. Thyng's confirmed victory. Col. Thyng used only 150 rounds in destroying his MiG.

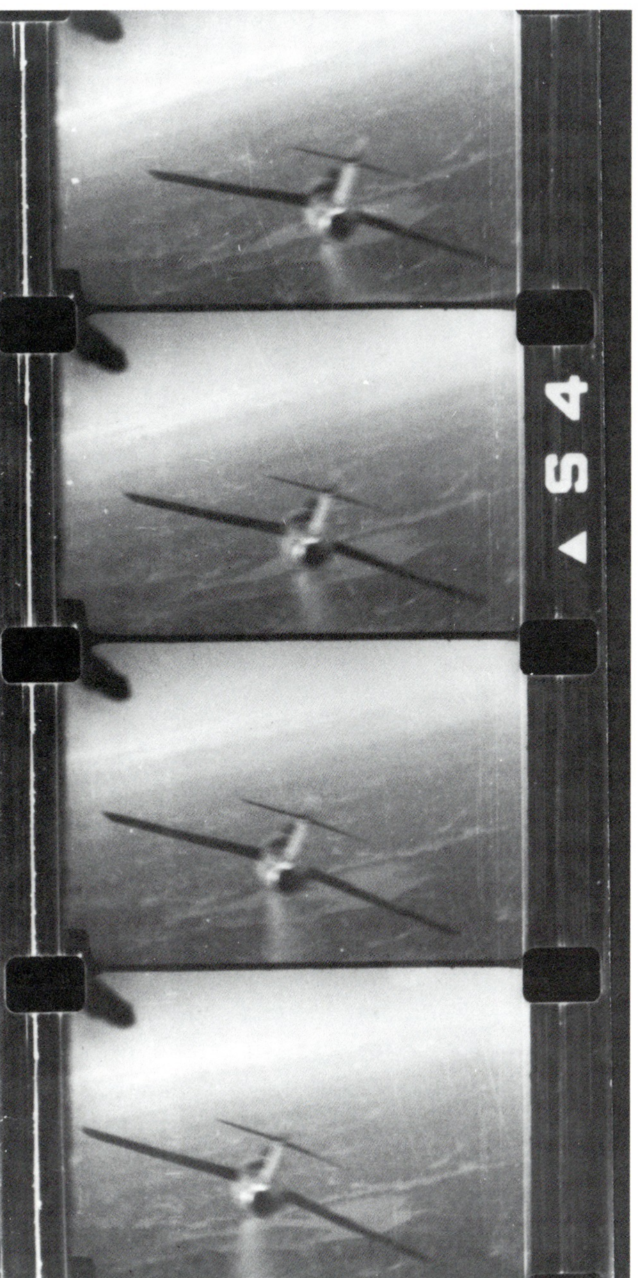

MiG kill by Maj. George Davis, Jr. (USAF)

Everyone's favorite sight after a long afternoon on the Yalu River was the mountain at the end of the runway at Kimpo, known variously as the "Witches Tit" and "Mt. Useless." The pilots had a saying – "If you can see Mt. Useless in the morning, you were flying!" (Irv Clark)

seven

1952-1953

The Era of Harry Thyng, "The Bloody Great Wheel"

New Years Day 1952 saw the beginning of the end for the MiG forces operating across the Yalu River. First was the emergence of the 51st Fighter Interceptor Wing at Suwon, as a operational combat unit. Colonel Francis 'Gabby' Gabreski, who transferred from the 4th in November, became the CO of the 51st as they transitioned into new F-86E Sabres. 'Gabby' took several veteran pilots with him, including Major Bill Whisner and Lt.Col. George Jones. The 51st flew their first combat mission on 1 December. 5th Air Force could now put up a force of some eighty Sabres – when the conditions were right.

Both the 4th and 51st were equipped with the new F-86E Sabre, which had the 'all-flying tail' that offered greater control in the transonic speed ranges. And the E models were slightly faster and longer ranged than the As were. But, while the 51st was equipped solely with the F-86E, the 4th Wing still had a large number of F-86As in their inventory. The mix of types hampered operations slightly as the Es with their greater performance could leave a wingman in an A model behind. This could be alleviated somewhat by 'ratting the tailpipe' in the A, giving the airplane more thrust and speed; or by pairing two E models in an element. This was rarely done since the veteran MiG killers all wanted the newer F-86Es. But more Es were on the way, as was the brand new F-86F with even greater performance.

And the 4th Wing had a new commander – Colonel Harrison R. 'Harry' Thyng, known to the crews at Kimpo as "The Bloody Great Wheel." Col. Thyng was a World War II ace, with six victories in North Africa. He took over command of the 4th Wing on 1 November 1951. The 4th Group Commander remained Col. Ben Preston. That same month, 5th AF moved the 335th FIS from Johnson AB, Japan, to Kimpo, giving the 4th a full three squadrons for the first time in the war. But the new wing commander found out rather quickly that three squadrons on paper do not necessarily mean they were available for combat.

When Col. Thyng took over, the AOCP (Aircraft Out Of Commission for Parts) rate was very high. Unacceptably high. The 4th had been a TDY unit until late spring 1951, and were on the very tail end of the Sabre parts supply line – the very end! This in spite of the fact that they were flying combat almost every day! Between those that were AOCP, and those that were out of commission from combat damage, or lost to the MiGs, it wasn't unusual for the in-commission rate to fall below 50% of authorized strength, which was about eighty aircraft. The parts supply problems weren't getting any better in spite of the wing being assigned permanently to 5th AF. And the MiG forces were getting bigger and better, with up to 500+ MiGs facing the Sabres in late 1951.

Gordon Beem was an NCO working in the 4th FIW Message Center in late 1951, and relates what happened next: "I joined the 4th in early September 1951 when Col. Herman Schmid was Wing CO. I was assigned as Chief Clerk of the Message Center."

"Col. Thyng arrived at Kimpo in early November, and assumed command of the Wing as he was senior to Col. Gabreski. Gabby then transferred to the 51st at Suwon. He'd already transitioned the 56th Fighter Wing to F-86s at Selfridge, and that was probably in his favor as the 51st was also transitioning from F-80s to F-86Es. There was quite a bit of a hassle over the pilots and senior officers that Gabby took with him from the 4th to Suwon."

"I was promoted to sergeant on 17 November, and placed in charge of the Classified Files Section. The 4th had been suffering from an unusually high, over 50%, AOCP ever since I arrived at K-14. It got so bad that Col. Thyng authorized Lt.Col. George Ola, the 4th M&S (Maintenance & Supply) Group CO, to obtain 4x4 trucks for most of the line and crew chiefs to go 'scrounging' around Korea for parts to bring down the AOCP rate."

"You know the 4th was an Eastern Air Defense Force (EADF) unit, that was TDY to FEAF, on detached service with 5th AF. Trying to get F-86 parts through normal channels was a nightmare. When we went to OCAMA (Oklahoma Air Material Area), primary supplier of F-86 parts, they told us to go to FEAMCOM (Far East Air Material Command). FEAMCOM then told us to go to OCAMA. In the meantime, whenever we had to put up a maximum effort, which was frequently, we'd have less than half of our '86s in commission. This situation continued for several weeks, and didn't get any better."

"We had three squadrons. Each squadron was assigned twenty-five aircraft, with a 10% augmentation 'for war conditions'. Thus the 4th had some 80+ Sabres to carry out the mission of 'maintaining air superiority in northwest Korea'. From the classified message traffic that I handled, I believe that Col. Thyng and his staff did everything humanly possible to solve the problem of an unacceptably high AOCP rate. But any 'max effort' called for in the 'frag orders' and the 4th would be hard pressed to put more than forty Sabres over MiG Alley."

"I had known Col. Harry Thyng to be an air warrior of high physical courage. He led the 4th personally and with great valor. But I also know that he was possessed of a character trait not as frequently seen – he had the moral courage to do what he knew to be right, even though there might be high personal cost involved. Harry was clearly headed for 'stars', and a message like the one that would come from his hand, and which went over the heads of four generals totaling at least a dozen stars, could well have cost him any chance to be a general himself. Yet he believed that the men whose lives he was responsible for, were at a disadvantage in MiG Alley due to the AOCP problem. After exhausting all other avenues, he took his career in his hands and sent a message that he knew was the right thing to do – no matter what the cost to him personally or professionally."

"I came to work one December morning and Maj. John Ross, 4th FIW Adjutant, called me and said, "The old Man has an Ops Immediate message he wants to get out right away." Maj. Ross handed me a folder with a hand-written draft message in it, which I took to my cubicle and read. It was a TOP SECRET, OPERATIONS IMMEDIATE message written in Col. Thyng's hand-writing. It was addressed to Gen. Hoyt Vandenberg, Chief of Staff, Air Force – with copies to Commanding General (CG) 5th AF, CG of FEAF, CG of Air Defense Command, and CG of EADF."

These six 4th Wing pilots contributed a great many of the wings 306 MiG victories in the first year of combat in Korea. (Left to right) Maj. W.W. Marshall, Col. Ben Preston, Maj. George Davis Jr., Maj. Dick Creighton, Col. Harrison Thyng, and Capt. Bob Love. (USAF)

"The first line read, "PERSONAL TO VANDENBERG FROM THYNG. I CAN NO LONGER BE RESPONSIBLE FOR AIR SUPERIORITY IN NORTHWEST KOREA!" The message then detailed the AOCP problems, the situation with FEAMCOM and OCAMA, the actions taken so far to resolve the matter, and the lack of success on all levels. Col. Thyng then went into detail about his concerns of taking the available aircraft and pilots into combat against the MiGs, which outnumbered the '86s up to 10-1."

During the first part of 1952, the men of the 4th constructed protective sandbag revetments at Kimpo. The destruction caused by 'Bedcheck Charlie' raids, plus the AOCP rate, dropped the in-commission rate to as high as 56% in October 1951, which was totally unacceptable. Note the mix of F-86As and Es. (Author)

"After I read the message, and before I prepared it for transmission, I asked Maj. Ross – "Is the Old Man really going to send this?" He replied that he'd asked him a similar question and that the Colonel had nearly bitten his head off in replying to the affirmative. I said that "it's sure going to kick up a storm." And Maj. Ross replied – "Well, you've know the Old Man for some time, why don't YOU ask him after you get the message typed and ready for his signature?""

"I went back to my desk and typed up the TWX, classified it, and got it ready for Col. Thyng's signature. After Maj. Ross signed off, I took it to Col. Thyng, who was in his office putting on his flight suit. I told him that the TS/OI message was ready, and then asked him – "Are you really going to send it?" He looked at me and replied – "Yes! There are too many lives at stake not to." I said – "All hell will break loose when the message gets to 5th, FEAF, ADC, and EADF!" He simply told me – "Tell Maj. Ross to tell anyone who calls, that I've gone on the morning mission." With that he signed the TWX form and handed it to me, picked up his helmet, and walked out to his jeep to drive down to his F-86."

"I took the TWX over to Communications and it was on its way. A typical mission took about 1 1/2 hours to complete. Before Col. Thyng was back, there was a call from Lt.Gen Frank Everest's office at 5th AF saying that the general wanted to see Col. Thyng "ASAP!", followed shortly by a message

On 1 November 1951, Col. Harry Thyng took over as Commander of the 4th Wing. Col. Thyng had 5 victories in Spitfires with the 31st FG in World War II. Known as "The Bloody Great Wheel", Col. Thyng would claim five MiGs during the time when he commanded the 4th Wing in Korea. (Harry Thyng)

A 334th Squadron F-86E has just been uncovered for the morning mission at Kimpo in March 1952. In early Spring 1952, FEAF ordered that all F-86 units in Korea adopt the black and yellow bands for air to air identification. (NAA)

Kimpo, February 1952. A/3C Miller was the crew chief on Capt. Robert Latshaw's F-86A, one of the first Sabres to fly 100 missions without an abort for any reason. Capt. Latshaw scored two of his five victories in 49-1142. (Irv Clark)

A pair of 335th Squadron Sabres on two minute alert at K-14 in April 1952. On the left is 1Lt. Martin Bambrick's F-86A, #49-1272, while the Sabre on the right was the F-86E flown by Capt. Bob Love, who would score six victories before going home in April 1952. Love's F-86E was named "Bernie's Bo." (Martin Bambrick)

from Gen. O.P. Weyland's office at FEAF with the same message. As I recall, there were messages later that day and the next, from both ADC and EADF CGs, asking for explanations from Col. Thyng."

"Since Gen. Weyland had four stars and out-ranked the 5th AF Commander, Col. Thyng hopped in the T-33 and headed to FEAF Hqtrs. But before he got back from Tokyo, we had a TS/OI from Washington. It was from Gen. Vandenberg, The first line read "PERSONAL FROM VANDENBERG TO THYNG." Copies were indicated to the CGs at FEAF, 5th AF, ADC, and EADF."

"The message began – "I was not aware of your problem. I have directed OCAMA and FEAMCOM to honor immediately all requisitions for parts from 4th FIW. Further I have directed that OCAMA airlift the parts requisitioned by 4th FIW to you with least practical delay. Further, I am assured you will receive parts within seventy-two to ninety six hours." And we got those parts! And the F-86s of the 4th FIW (and the 51st) maintained 'air superiority over northwest Korea."

The parts problems began to be alleviated almost immediately as Mr. Penney Bowen, the new North American Tech Rep to the 4th, arrived in mid-December. He brought with him almost $26,000.00 worth of spare parts paid for by North American Aviation themselves. It seems that John Henderson and Chris Chistopherson of North American, had the same trepidations as Col. Thyng. They expressed their feelings to 'Dutch' Kindelberger, President of North American, who immediately implemented Project PETER RABBIT, which got the parts and supplies rolling to Korea.

With the AOCP slowly but surely starting to come down, the 4th started putting up more aircraft for every mission. It began to look better the very first day of the new year, as the 4th was able to put up three missions. The morning mission saw thirty-two Sabres go north. They encountered over fifty MiGs. But the MiGs didn't want to come down off their perch. The first of two afternoon missions saw twenty 4th Wing F-86s engage 60+ MiGs. Col. Thyng got heavy strikes on two of the MiGs, but neither was seen to crash. The second mission of the afternoon sent eleven F-86s on an RF-80 photo recce mission to Namsi-Dong.

Three more missions were flown on the 3rd and the 5th of January. By the end of the month, in spite of the increase in aircraft availability, the MiG claims actually decreased. Most of the missions encountered MiG aircraft, which remained at altitudes above the Sabres, and refused to engage the F-86s. The totals for January were eight damaged and five destroyed – Captains Nelton Wilson, Robert Latshaw, Freeland Mathews, 1Lt. Conrad Nystrum, and Col. James Raebel, Deputy Group CO.

In February, the MiGs were very aggressive. But disaster struck, taking the life of the top scoring ace in Korea at the time. By the end of the month, 4th Wing pilots had scored eleven

Capt. James Horowitz climbs into the cockpit of his F-86E, which has the name "Slow Boat To China" done in flag symbols. Capt. Horowitz, using the pen name 'James Salter', would later write a novel about Korea named "The Hunters", which was later made into a film starring Robert Mitchum and Robert Wagner. (Karl Dittmer)

1Lt. Billy Dobbs was a pilot in the 335th Squadron at Kimpo in April 1952. He flew "Miss Sheeny", F-86A #49-1070, and had four MiG kills and three damaged. (USAF)

damaged, one probable, and six destroyed – Maj. Zane Amell, 1Lt. Russ Miller, 1Lt. Billy Dobbs, and Capt. Brooks Liles each got one. Maj. George Davis got two MiGs on the 10th to bring his total to fourteen. But it also cost him his life.

1Lt. Bill Littlefield was Major Davis' wingman on that fatal mission: "It was a MiG Sweep. We took off on the morning mission, 10 February 1952. Major Davis was leading the 334th Squadron. We were John Able Flight, with Major Davis as Lead. I was flying #4. Shortly after arriving at the Yalu, the element leader, John Able 3, developed oxygen problems. John Able 2, Major Davis' wingman, had previously reported a pressurization problem, so Major Davis ordered both #2 and #3 to return to base. I then moved up and became George's wingman."

"In the meantime, we'd broken away from the rest of the group, and began a northeast to southwest patrol along the south side of the Yalu. We were at 38,000 feet. As we completed a right turn and began heading back northeast, George spotted three flights of MiGs heading south across the river and well below us. They were in close fingertip formation, with flights in trail – twelve MiGs total."

"We came down on them and made our pass from their right rear and high. George opened fire on the #4 MiG in the last flight. I saw the MiG start smoking and fall out of formation. George then pulled out to the right, pulled up high, deployed his speed brakes, reversed, and started back in for another pass. He asked me if I saw the first one go down and I confirmed that I'd seen it. We were still at about 28,000-30,000 feet."

"By the time we were coming in for our second pass, we had overshot the last two flights and were lined up on the lead MiG flight. That left seven MiGs at our rear during this pass! He again selected the #4 MiG in the first flight and began firing. By now the MiGs behind us were firing. I saw George's target start smoking and it too, fell out of formation."

Easter Sunday, 1952. The men of the 4th Fighter Wing attend Easter services on the ramp at Kimpo, with Lt.Gen. Frank Everest, 5th AF Commander, in attendance. Following the services, the pilots climbed into their F-86s and went MiG-hunting. Note that some over zealous censor has removed the 334th FIS emblem from the gun bay door. (USAF)

"But at almost that same instant I saw George's aircraft begin smoking. The landing gear came down and I thought I heard a mike button depress for what might have been an attempted transmission. I have always thought that it was George trying to say something, but nothing came out."

"His aircraft then rolled over, did a 'split S', and headed for the ground, obviously out of control. I stayed with him through these 'falling leaf' maneuvers, calling several times over the radio with no response. In the meantime, several MiGs had departed formation and were chasing us. I noted several bursts of cannon fire. But my concentration was always trying to keep George's aircraft in sight and staying with him as long as possible."

"At one point, a MiG crossed directly in front of me and I took a quick 'snap shot' at him. I thought I got some hits, but the film disclosed nothing. I continued following George, and by this time I was getting some radio traffic from Col. Ben Preston, 4th Group Commander. I confirmed that George had been hit and was going down, giving my location and that I intended to stay with Major Davis as long as possible."

"Col. Preston proceeded to our area to attempt a rendezvous, but never succeeded. As Major Davis' aircraft approached the ground, it had assumed a nearly wings level diving atti-

Following the disastrous Bedcheck Charlie raids in mid-1951, sandbagged trenches were dug between most of the tents and living quarters. This is the 4th Communications Squadron area at Kimpo. (Don Prouty)

Right: (Left to right) Capt. Jim Horowitz, 1Lt. Jim Low, 1Lt. Al Smiley, 1Lt. Coy Austin, and Capt. Phil Coleman, MiG killers in the 335th Squadron, clown for the camera in June 1952. Coleman holds one of the new 'Mach Rider' patches designed for the pilots in D Flight. (Martin Bambrick)

"Joanne" was the name carried on the right side of Horowitz's F-86E. Markings on the right side of the aircraft reflect the name applied by the crew chief, while the red star 'kill markings' are those credited to the airplane, no matter who the pilot was. Many of the kills painted on the right gun bay door belong to Maj. 'Bones' Marshall. (Vern Sprague)

tude. The airplane smashed into the side of a small knoll in generally, a northerly direction. I again called Col. Preston, gave him my position and asked if he'd seen the black smoke and fire. He replied to the negative."

"I then pulled up, turned south, and started home as I was at 'Bingo' fuel. I'd actually called to Major Davis that I was at 'Bingo' before we first spotted any of the MiGs. As I was climbing up from the crash, I checked for MiGs around and to my rear, but saw none."

"At the debriefing, I told everyone that I was 99% certain that Major Davis had not ejected from his crippled Sabre. There was a slight chance that he'd ejected during the instant that I was checking on the MiGs behind us. But I don't think so. I think he was injured, or possibly even killed when his aircraft took the hits that knocked him out of the sky."

"Col. Preston told me that he felt that Major Davis was too overconfident. He had developed an attitude that the MiG pilots were incompetent, and that there wasn't a MiG pilot in the sky that could touch him. Had he retained a little more respect for the MiG pilots (there were a lot of really good ones that were flying at that time), he probably wouldn't have pulled up, deployed his speed brakes and thereby losing valuable air speed, and came back down on the first flight of MiGs with seven of them sitting behind us and firing."

Major George Davis was awarded the Medal Of Honor for actions on that day. At the time of his death he was the top scoring ace in Korea – and the only Double Ace. His score for the war was eleven MiGs and three Tu-2 bombers destroyed, one probable and two damaged, all in the space of thirty-one missions. He shot down MiGs two at a time on four different missions, getting four on 13 December 1951, two in the morning and two more in the afternoon. Had he lived, there is little doubt in anyone's minds that he would have been the top scorer of the war.

'Mach Rider' patch designed for members of 'D' Flight, 335th Squadron. The caricature is of Capt. Phil Colman, 'D' Flight Leader. 'D' Flight was the highest scoring flight in Korea, with 24 victories.

The month of March saw a great increase in MiG activity. And with it an increase in MiG claims by 4th pilots. The MiGs came down to play on eleven days in March. And the total claims for the month were twenty-nine damaged, eight probables, and twenty-six destroyed. But 5th AF only allowed 6 of the claims to be confirmed as victories. The rest were either down-graded or disallowed entirely for lack of verification.

MiG claims could only be verified by gun camera film, or by a second pilot that saw the MiG destroyed. If the gun camera film showed the MiG exploding or crash, or the pilot ejecting from the aircraft – that was a CONFIRMED victory. It could also be verified by a signed statement from another airman,

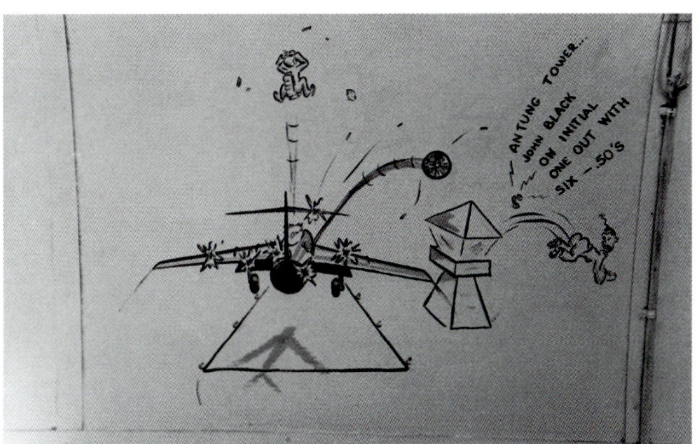

Cartoons on the wall in the O-Club at Kimpo. (Karl Dittmer)

i.e. bomber crew, recce pilot, etc., that witnessed the combat. Anything not meeting those two criteria and the claim was not allowed. It was tough to get victories in Korea!

May 1952 was a very memorable month for the men of the 4th – but a bittersweet one. Colonel Walker 'Bud' Mahurin, another of the renowned World War II aces from the 56th Fighter Group was appointed Group Commander on 18 March. 'Bud' Mahurin had twenty-one victories over the German Luftwaffe, plus another when he commanded the 3rd Air Commando Group in the Pacific.

One of the first things that Col. Mahurin instituted was a dive bombing mission for the 4th – something quite out of context for the air superiority-minded pilots of the 4th. Except for the brief interlude of rocket missions in early 1951, the 4th had flown nothing but MiG sweeps and screens during the Korean War. Mahurin also gave the pilots permission to use all their remaining ammunition on ground targets of opportunity that they encountered on the flight home from MiG Alley.

Col. Mahurin personally led four dive bombing missions. The attacks were made at an altitude ranging from 6,000 to 13,000 feet. At this time, the 4th was equipped with F-86A and E aircraft, although a few of the new Fs were enroute. On the dive bombing missions, the drop tanks were removed and replaced with 500 lb. bombs. There were, however, a few missions flown on which the aircraft were configured with a single drop tank and single 500 lb. bomb to increase the range or 'loiter time' of the aircraft over the target. It wouldn't be until the arrival of the F-86F-5 that a Sabre would be able to carry a pair of 120 gallon drop tanks and a pair of 500 lb. bombs. But for these early missions, the pilots flew with either drop tanks or bombs.

Sadly, on 13 May, while leading the third dive bombing mission of the day, Col. Mahurin's F-86 was hit by ground fire

Harmonizing the guns of a 335th Squadron F-86A on the Kimpo ramp at night in the summer of 1952. The guns were harmonized to converge at 1200 feet. By the Summer of 1952, it was reasonably safe to work at night with lights on. (USAF)

Flight Lieutenant Wal Rivers, Royal Australian Air Force, unfastens his parachute harness following a mission in 1952. There were quite a few foreign air force pilots flying combat missions with the 4th in 1952. Flt.Lt. Rivers was flying Maj. Ted Coberly's F-86 with the 334th Squadron. (Australian War Memorial)

Left: Nose art began making an appearance on 4th Wing Sabres in the Summer of 1952. One of the featured 'artists' was Capt. Karl Dittmer, who painted such famous airplanes as Col. Walker Mahurin's "Honest John" and Capt. Cliff Jolley's "Jolley Roger." "Beep Val" was the aircraft of 1Lt. John Nolli. (Karl Dittmer)

One of the regular missions flown by the 4th Wing was escort of the unarmed photo reconnaissance RF-80As from the 15th TRS. The RF-80 pilot would fly to the target area at or beyond the Yalu River. He was a sitting duck, not being anywhere near as fast as the MiGs, and had an escort of at least four F-86s on every mission. (Bill Coffey)

and crashed north of the bomb line. Col. Mahurin, who had been shot down in World War II and evaded capture, was captured by the North Koreans. He would remain a POW until repatriated in 1953. Col. Mahurin had shot down 3 1/2 MiGs since his arrival in Korea, which brought his total victories to 25 1/2. Lt.Col. Ralph Kuhn assumed command of the Group on 14 May.

In May a large group of pilots reached the 100 mission plateau and were rotated home, leaving the Group short on experienced pilots. Although new pilots were constantly being assigned from stateside units and straight out of the Fighter School, the Group pilot strength remained at a low ebb. FEAF answered that need in mid-May by temporarily in-activating the 339th F(AW)S at Johnson AB, and transferring their pilots into the 4th FIW.

However, few of the pilots transferring from the 339th had any jet time at all, having been equipped with the North American F-82G Twin Mustang propeller-driven fighter aircraft. All these new pilots were sent through the new F-86 Mobile Training Detachment that had been set up at Tsuiki AB, Japan. At Tsuiki, the new pilots transitioned first to T-33s, before being checked out in F-86s and sent to Kimpo for assignment.

In May, one of the truly aggravating problems with F-86 combat operations was answered, at least to a small degree. The problem was the lack of drop tanks in the theater. Whenever MiGs were sighted, the F-86s would drop their tanks. If the 4th could put up fifty Sabres for a mission, and the MiGs came up to play, 100 drop tanks were scattered over North Korea. And often, the Group would put up two or three missions in a single day.

FEAF authorized a Japanese company to begin production of underwing drop tanks for the F-86. The new tanks looked very similar to the American-built tanks. But the differences could bring as many problems as they answered. The new tanks were smaller internally than the American tanks, being only 110 gallons as compared with the 120 gallons available with

Capt. Robert Latshaw pulls away from his parking spot at Kimpo in the Spring of 1952. Capt. Latshaw flew with the 335th Squadron and scored five MiG victories to become the fourteenth jet ace of the Korean War on 3 May 1952. (via Tom Brewer)

the American-built tanks. And they were less aerodynamic and quite crude in appearance which also caused more drag.

It was found that the different aerodynamics of the Japanese tanks, caused a totally different flight attitude when they were ejected. At times, the new tanks would roll up and ride down the wing leading edge, damaging the slats and carrying away the wingtip pitot boom. Other times the tanks would roll along the underside of the wing and damage the flaps, or worse, hit the horizontal stabilizer.

So hazardous were the flight characteristics of the Japanese tanks, that FEAF ordered that they all be painted Olive Drab so that a pilot would know at a glance which type of tanks he was carrying, and could take appropriate measures when the order came to "Drop tanks!" Officially, the 4th FIG history notes that "these tanks are undesirable and will be used in the future only when American made tanks are unavailable."

May 1952 ended as one of the greatest months in the history of jet operations in the Air Force. The 4th FIG set a new record for combat sorties, flying 3331; and in combat hours flown at 5315 hours. And even though the MiGs were more aggressive, and under the control of an improved ground control intercept system, the pilots of the 4th shot down twenty-five MiGs, with four probables, and fourteen damaged.

Three more aces were crowned in May – Captain Robert T. Latshaw Jr. got his fifth MiG on 3 May, 1Lt. Jim Kasler made ace on 15 May, and the 'Bloody Great Wheel" himself, Col. Harry Thyng got his fifth MiG on 20 May. A new name in the 4th FIG log books was added on 8 May, when 1Lt. Jim 'Dad' Low got his first MiG. One month later Jim Low would make ace. On the 20th, 1Lt. Coy Austin, 335th Squadron, got his second MiG kill – and the Group's 200th of the war.

Aces in the same day, 3 May 1952. Maj. Don Adams of the 16th Squadron at Suwon congratulates Capt. Robert Latshaw of the 335th Squadron on his fifth MiG kill in Korea. Adams became the thirteenth jet ace, while Latshaw was the 14th. (USAF)

Combat operations in June were greatly hampered by bad weather, and the Group flew only 1495 sorties to MiG Alley, less than half of Mays total. The MiGs did come up on several occasions for "Graduation Day" against the F-86s. These MiG pilots were quite aggressive, and many flew with improved skill and flight integrity. Never the less, the pilots of the 4th prevailed again, scoring fifteen destroyed, one probable, and

"Honest John" was an F-86E originally flown by Col. Walker Mahurin, whose nickname was Honest John, when he was Group Commander in the summer of 1952. Sitting in a Kimpo revetment in late summer of 1952, the badge of the 336th Squadron is only partially complete on the gun bay door. (Wm. K. Thomas)

Col. Walker Mahurin was assigned as the 4th Group CO at Kimpo on 18 March 1952. Col. Mahurin pioneered the low level strafing attacks on targets of opportunity during the flight home from MiG Alley. Col. Mahurin was shot down on 14 May 1952. (USAF)

six damaged. 1Lt. Jim Low was crowned the seventeenth jet ace of the war when he got his fifth MiG on 15 June. Colonel Royal N. 'King' Baker took over command of the Group on 1 June, bringing to Korea 3 1/2 victories from World War II.

In July, the bad weather continued. Mission totals were again down, dropping to 1267 sorties. Interestingly, the weather seemed to be worse over South Korea than North Korea. MiGs were encountered on only seven days during July. But radar indicated that large MiG formations were flying south of the Yalu River on several of the eight days that Kimpo was completely socked-in. On six of the remaining days, small flights of two and four aircraft were able to take off from Kimpo in an attempt to engage the MiGs. By the end of the month, 4th pilots had shot down eight MiGs, probably destroyed three more, and damaged a further eight.

One day that was an exception was the 4th of July. The Group was screening for a force of F-84 Thunderjets that were attacking the Suiho Dam complex. The MiGs decided to try and put a damper on the U.S. national holiday. They put up a large force and attempted to break through the Sabre screen to get at the fighter bombers. By the end of the day, seven MiGs were destroyed, with one probable and three damaged.

The totals for the day included Col. Baker's and Capt. Cliff Jolley's second MiGs, Jim Low's sixth, and Capt. James Horowitz scored his first. Capt. Horowitz would later write a fictional novel about his tour in Korea, called "The Hunters" under the pen name of James Salter.

The extremely bad weather through the summer of 1952, began taking its toll on the base conditions at Kimpo. Never even resembling one of the bases in either the ConUS or in Europe, most of Kimpo was covered by PSP (pierced steel plank) matting in the parking areas, with sandbag revetments protecting the aircraft from bomb and rocket attacks. The sandbag revetments began collapsing due to the constant rain of the summer monsoon, and all had to be rebuilt. This became a 'priority issue' since the group had already been warned of the impending arrival of Typhoon 'Karen'. 'Karen' was obliging and waited until 23 August to come ashore and pummel the base.

Some of the nose art was quite raunchy, such as "Temptation", which featured the Playboy Marilyn Monroe nude, and "Lady Luck", a 334th Squadron F-86A. Interestingly, the aircraft has a serial number on the tail (49-1129) that is different from the buzz number on the aft fuselage (FU-128). (Curt Francom)

Most of the rest of the month, the weather and the MiGs were cooperative. On the 1st of the month, the Group put up a major effort – two missions totaling eighty-five Sabres. Major Felix Asla Jr., CO of the 336th Squadron, led the flights. He had four MiGs and was looking forward to becoming the eighteenth jet ace of the war. It was his ninety-seventh mission.

Approaching the Yalu, Major Asla's flights encountered some 60+ MiGs, and immediately started to engage the swift little Red jets. Pulling in behind one of the MiGs, Major Asla was about to fire when another MiG got between Asla and his wingman, and right on Asla's tail. A short burst of accurate 23mm cannon fire from the MiG's guns, set Asla's F-86E on fire. Major Felix Asla was not able to eject and was killed. Two days later, Major Louis Green took over command of the 336th.

On 6 August, Capt. Bill Ryan, of the 334th Squadron, got a pair of MiGs – one of them the hard way. Pulling in behind a

In the Spring of 1952, the F-86F arrived in Korea. The F-86F had much more power than previous models, with 5950 lbs of thrust. This gave the Sabre pilots more speed at altitude. The MiG advantages were melting away. Later models of the F had the new '6-3' hard wing', which gave the Sabre pilot the ability to turn with the much lighter MiG. (Karl Dittmer)

Maj. Felix Asla, Commander of the 336th Squadron and his wingman take off from Kimpo in March 1952 bound for MiG Alley. Maj. Asla would score four victories in Korea before being shot down on 1 August 1952. (NAA)

"Scramble!" is the signal that sends these 335th Squadron F-86s into the air in late Spring 1952. Capt. Billy Dobbs is flying the second F-86, "Miss Sheeney", F-86A #49-1070. The lead Sabre, FU-180, was Lt.Col. Bruce Hinton's original aircraft. (via Tom Brewer)

MiG, Captain Ryan had just started to fire when another MiG slipped in behind his Sabre and opened up. Jinking this way and that, the MiG's cannon shells overshot Capt. Ryan's Sabre – right into the fuselage of the MiG that Ryan had staked out. The deadly MiG cannon fire exploded the MiG in front of Ryan. He then reversed and got on the tail of the MiG that had shot down his leader. He opened fire and the MiG started to smoke before going into an uncontrolled dive. Ryan was credited with both MiGs.

On 7 August, Captain Clifford D. Jolley shot down two MiGs to bring his total to four destroyed. He got his fifth the next afternoon, becoming the eighteenth jet ace in Korea. But he was almost listed on the enemy ledger of credits. On the big mission on the 4th of July, Captain Jolley shot down his second MiG. But a MiG also got behind Jolley, shooting big holes in his helmet and knocking the oxygen mask right off his face. Captain Jolley made it to the ocean, and bailed out into the Yellow Sea, where a 3rd RS 'Dumbo' flying boat picked him up and returned him to Kimpo. The incident was especially embarrassing as Jolley was flying Captain Bob Love's F-86E, "Bernie's Bo." It was Capt. Love's favorite Sabre, and the one he had scored his fifth victory in, becoming the twelfth jet ace.

Maj. Felix Asla's crew chief makes an adjustment to the control column in Maj. Asla's F-86E "The Chopper" in July 1952.. Maj. Asla's F-86E, #51-2767, shows four victories and four probables on the gun bay door, plus twelve knocked out trucks and one tank painted under the gun bay. (via Warren Thompson)

Above and right: Capt. Chuck Owens flew "Liza Gal/El Diablo", when he was assigned to the 336th Squadron in August 1952. Capt. Owens' Sabre shows eight MiG victories, fifteen trucks and one tank kill markings. The 336th 'Rocketeers' badge has not yet been completed. Capt. Owens' final confirmed count was two MiG kills and six probables. (W.K. Thomas and Charles Owens)

By the end of August, the Group had flown 1540 sorties, and encountered the wily MiG on sixteen of the thirty-one days. Group pilots claimed twenty-one destroyed, two probables, and twenty-eight damaged. The biggest day was the 6th when over 185 MiGs were encountered, with 4th pilots downing five and damaging four more. One Sabre was lost in addition to Major Asla. On 20 August, 1Lt. Norman Schmidt's F-86E ingested some MiG parts, and he was forced to step out of the airplane into the Korea Bay, where an HU-16 'Dumbo' was waiting to pick him out of the drink.

September saw the arrival of a new MiG squadron, the crowning of two more jet aces in the 4th, the arrival of the first batch of F-86Fs modified to combat the great rate of climb of the much lighter MiG-15.

By the end of the month, the Group had filed seventy-seven MiG claims – thirty-seven destroyed, four probables, and thirty-six damaged. With the weather cooperating, the Group was able to fly twenty-eight of the thirty days of the month. Total sorties for September was 1813 in 157 missions – fifty MiG sweeps, fifty-seven scramble intercepts, twenty-eight escort missions for the fighter-bombers and recon birds, seven weather recce missions, nine ResCAPs, and six interdiction (dive bomb) missions. 1Lt. Edgar Powell and Captain John Taylor shared a MiG on 7 September – the 335th Squadron's 100th MiG kill.

The MiGs came up in force on twenty of the thirty days in September. And the pilots were quick to observe that a large number of MiGs were painted dark green and blue, much different from the normal silver MiGs they'd been encountering. These green MiGs were crossing the Yalu at a very low altitude, to try and engage the F-84s operating in MiG Alley. On 4 September, eighty-nine MiGs engaged the 334th Squadron, which was being led by Major Frederick 'Boots' Blesse. The 334th pilots shot down eight of the MiGs, damaging two more. Major Blesse got one of the MiGs that day, which made him the nineteenth ace in Korea with four MiGs and an LaGG-9. On the 8th, Major Blesse would get two more MiGs. By 3 October he had ten MiGs, a 'Double Jet Ace'.

On the 21st, over 110 MiGs came across the River and engaged the Sabres. An hour later, 4th Group pilots had claimed four destroyed, one probable, and six damaged. Two of the 'destroyed' were shot down by Captain Robinson Risner of the 336th Squadron, making him the twentieth jet ace of the war. The Group claimed another four destroyed on the 28th, including two by a Marine pilot on loan to the 4th – Major Rocky Gillis, USMC.

Late in the month, the Group received three F-86Fs that had been modified at Tsuiki with an internal Jet Assisted Take-Off system. The JATO installation consisted of three 1000 LB thrust JATO bottles mounted below the engine, just behind the main gear bays. The fuselage was bulged in the area of the JATO, which effectively hid the installation. The JATO bottles had a thirty-eight second duration when fired with a two second burn overlap. All three aircraft were assigned to the 335th Squadron.

Captains Clifford Jolley and Karl Dittmer flew the JATO-equipped birds. Captain Jolley: "Eventually there were between four and six airplanes modified with the JATO units – half with slats and the rest were 'hard wings'. The aircraft were about 40 knots faster than a normal F-86F. You could fire the JATO all at once or in a sequence. There were six pilots in the 335th Squadron assigned to fly the JATO airplanes. All were very experienced, with lots of jet time and missions. We lost one airplane and pilot during the program. I got two MiGs flying the JATO birds, but I would have gotten them anyway, without using the JATO."

Captain Dittmer: "There were six birds – three with slats and three with the hard leading edge, the 'F' wing. The forward fuselage was slightly deeper just aft of the wing trailing edge. As you can see from the enclosed sketch, the JATO bottles were mounted internally below the J47. The nozzles exited on the belly just aft of the trailing edge of the wing. I have no idea how they recharged them. But they must have had a way or they would have had to pull the aft section off the airplane to replace the JATO units."

"They were a bitch to fly in that they wouldn't hold altitude. But they would do a very slow porpoise – like a small boat riding a series of very gentle swells. They were also cursed with an aft center of gravity, much like a P-51 with a full fuselage fuel tank. But at least the '51 would eat up the aft tank fuel before getting into combat. "

"The JATO bottles could be fired in train or simultaneously. There was a three position switch located just aft of the throttle, tucked up under the canopy rail, not on the console. They were

Maj. Dick Ayersman flew "Baby Linda" when he commanded the 334th Squadron at Kimpo in the Summer of 1952. The markings on the left side of a 4th Group Sabre told a story. The airplane name and/or art work was usually the pilots option, but not always. Red stars under the canopy were victories scored by the pilot, while those applied under the crew block were credited to the crew chief. "Baby Linda's" crew chief was A/1C Manual Reyes, and he has three confirmed victories and six damaged. (S/L Eric Smith)

a bit hard to get at in a hurry, but then it wasn't hard to overload my dumb head. We only fired them to try and overtake the MiGs that were a bit out of range."

"The JATO birds were a bit nasty because you couldn't hold altitude steady. Usually one would fly its 'up cycle' while the other was on its 'down cycle'. The cycle was of slow duration and took about 500 feet between the top and bottom of the oscillation. Once the JATO units were fired, the effect was a gentle acceleration. It took a few seconds to get the full effect. We preferred the 'salvo position', since 'in-train' was just too long to wait."

"I can relate what it was like with a mission I flew with Captain Cope. Cope spotted the MiGs, which automatically made him Flight Lead. He made his attack from behind and fired the JATO, which placed him about 1500 feet ahead of me. We had started out line abreast. After he fired most of his ammo at the MiG, I was back even with him. What happened next, illustrates the second problem we had with those birds."

"I'd been watching a MiG attempting to get into a firing position on Cope, and advised him that he had one "a ways back", and "to call the break when you're through shooting." To my surprise, he immediately called "Break left!" I was on his left, and a normal break would have been to the right, plac-

Capt. Cliff Jolley arrived at Kimpo in the late Spring of 1952. His first achievement was shooting down a MiG on 4 May. His second was being shot down in Capt. Bob Love's favorite Sabre, "Bernie's Bo." Here he is with A/2C Ernie Balasz at Kimpo in the Summer of 1952. (Cliff Jolley)

Right: Col. Thyng and Capt. Leonard 'Bill' Lilley listen and laugh as Capt. Alphonso Pena describes his MiG kill on 16 September 1952. It was Pena's 100th and last mission of the war. Bill Lilley also shot down his fourth MiG on this mission. Lilley would become the twenty-second ace two months later on 18 November. (USAF)

"Betty Boots" was the F-86E-6 that was flown by Capt. Karl Dittmer in the 335th Squadron. Besides being the renowned artist at Kimpo, Capt. Dittmer shot down two MiGs. The F-86E-6 was one of sixty Sabres built by Canadair Ltd., to bolster the inventories of the squadrons operating in Korea. (Karl Dittmer)

Capt. Cliff Jolley taxies past the camera bound for MiG Alley in late September 1952. Jolley's aircraft, "Jolley Roger", shows six victories on the nose. He would score his seventh and last victory on 11 October. (Cliff Jolley)

ing the MiG behind him in a position where I could take him. Obviously I was being attacked and didn't see it coming. So I snapped to the left and looked to my right just as a MiG overshot."

"I started to reverse, since this would have given me excellent position on the MiG. But Cope shouted – "No! No!, keep turning!" Another MiG overshot. However, by now my F-86 was buffeting with gusto in a high speed stall. I had to use considerable forward pressure on the stick. (With the JATO birds, you had stick force reversal due to the aft CG position). But before breaking the stall, I glanced back at the two guys behind me and immediately re-entered the stall. I guess they couldn't fall as fast as I fell, and they eventually broke off their attack."

"Cope and I rejoined and headed back north. At the Yalu, I swung left paralleling the river, and spotted two more MiGs crossing our path, with another pair following them. The second pair looked good to me (for an attack), and I was turning right to get behind them when I noticed a third pair behind the pair I had staked out. They would arrive at our position just as our turn was complete. I asked Cope if he had the third pair in sight. He replied "Roge!""

"Temptation", the F-86E-5 flown by Col. Ben Preston and Capt. Bill Lilley, to name just a few of her pilots, was damaged by a MiG in December 1952, and crashed at Kimpo, severely damaging the nose. The F-86E was airlifted back to the Tsuiki REMCO, where it was determined that she would never fly again. She was stripped and scrapped. (USAF)

Right: The Kimpo Base Chapel in 1952. (Dave Eldredge)

One of the 335th Squadron F-86Fs that had three JATO rockets installed in the fuselage under the J47 compressor section. When the pilot hit the switch, the aircraft easily accelerated to over 700 mph. But after the rocket fired, the pilot had to haul around over 600 lbs of extra weight, and a center of gravity that was much further aft than normal. (Cliff Jolley)

"A second later I flipped inverted to arrive directly over the leader of the third pair of MiGs. He elected to make a left break and I completed the roll to slide across his rear. But instead of hosing him right then, I attempted to get into a still better position, completely messing up the opportunity. I eventually got a few strikes on his aft end before he got me slowed sufficiently."

"At this point the MiG broke out of his turn and started to climb. I fired the JATO and began to catch the fleeing MiG. The JATO tended to interfere with your attack. I mean it was difficult to concentrate on an attack while fumbling for the switch to fire the JATO. At the same time I called Cope to see if he had me in sight. Firing the JATO unit made for easy identification. He didn't answer, so I broke off my attack and headed back to the general area of the start of the engagement. Numerous MiGs were circling, with several more at a lower altitude, much lower than the main bunch."

"I saw a pillar of smoke from the ground and possibly a second. From the sight, I assumed that Cope had collided with the MiG wingman. I tried a few more calls before starting for home. Cope was eventually listed as killed in action." The Group lost six F-86s in September – five to the MiGs, including Cope's JATO bird, and a second JATO bird that crashed at K-14.

In October, the personnel situation became critical, especially with maintenance people. The 'old heads' started rotating home, including many of the crew chiefs. New personnel were arriving daily, but they had to be trained to be able to maintain a 'combat airplane'. The situation was alleviated somewhat by retiring the last of the original F-86A Sabres from combat.

The MiGs came up about 50% of the time in October. By the end of the month, the Group had shot down thirteen MiGs,

Zany Betty Hutton brought her troop to Kimpo in the Fall of 1952 to entertain the troops. It was a helluva show! (Jack Moore)

Left: Squadron Leader Eric Smith, on loan from the RAF, flew with the 334th Squadron in the Summer of 1952. S/L Smith's F-86E-6 was #52-2875, and he flew with Bill Lilley. (Eric Smith) Right: 335th armorers assist A/3C S.A. Brown in re-arming Maj. William Thomas' F-86E-10 "Virginia Belle." The F-86 had three ammunition canisters on each side, each one holding 300 rounds of .50 caliber ammunition. However, normally only 275 rounds were carried to alleviate gun stoppage problems caused by jamming. (W.K. Thomas)

with one probable, and twenty damaged. Several significant victories were counted in October. On 3 October, Major 'Boots' Blesse shot down his ninth MiG, which, with his LaGG-9 kill, made him a double ace. His flight was patrolling the south side of the river when they spotted some MiGs. Blesse gave chase, but he couldn't close and the MiGs went back across the river.

At Bingo fuel, Blesse and his wingman, 1Lt. Eugene Faber, started for home. But a flight of MiGs jumped them on their withdrawal. "Boots" called the 'Break!', and the two Sabres split. Major Blesse pulled around behind one of the MiGs and poured fire into him. The MiG immediately caught fire and went into an uncontrolled dive. The other MiGs ran for home. But now Major Blesse was way below Bingo. He pointed his airplane south, and proceeded toward Paengnyong-Do, where he bailed out of his out of fuel Sabre. A waiting 'Dumbo' plucked him out of the water and returned him to Kimpo. 5th Air Force was taking no chances and rotated Boots' home on the 10th of October.

On 4 October, Major Richard Ayersman was leading a flight to the Yalu. On his wing was one of the new guys – Captain Manual J. 'Pete' Fernandez. It was Pete's tenth mission. Major Ayersman spotted four MiGs and pulled in behind to

Capt. Hank Crescibene stands in the cockpit of his F-86E on the Kimpo ramp in late August 1952. The artwork on Crescibene's 335th Squadron Sabre was done by Karl Dittmer. Capt. Crescibene scored one MiG kill on 4 August 1952. (Karl Dittmer)

take a shot – with Pete keeping his tail clear. Suddenly Pete looked back and saw a pair of MiGs pulling into position, high and immediately behind the two Sabres.

Fernandez called for Ayersman to "Break left!", which took them out of the sights of the MiGs temporarily. But Pete continued his turn, pulling in behind one of the MiGs. At 800 feet, Pete fired, scoring hits all over the fuselage. The MiG slowed and Pete closed the range still further. He fired again. The second burst set the MiG afire, and it fell off on the left wing, smoking and burning. Ayersman and Fernandez followed the burning MiG until it crashed. It was Captain Pete Fernandez's first victory. The next day, Pete was an Element Leader.

During the month of October, the Group received twenty-nine additional F-86Fs to replace the older F-86As that had been retired from combat. On the 25th of October, Lt.Col. Royal Baker shot down his third MiG. It was the Group's 300th victory in Korea. Colonel Charles King took over the 4th Wing on 2 October when Col. Harrison Thyng was rotated home.

November began with the removal of the remaining JATO-equipped F-86Fs from combat. The three remaining airplanes were ferried back to Tsuiki REMCO where the JATO modifications were reversed and the aircraft were returned to combat.

The weather over Korea was fair and cool during the first week of November. The MiGs came up often. But they usually

Ice cream came to the men of the fourth via Sikorsky H-5 helicopter from the USS Los Angeles, a Navy cruiser operating in the Yellow Sea. (Author)

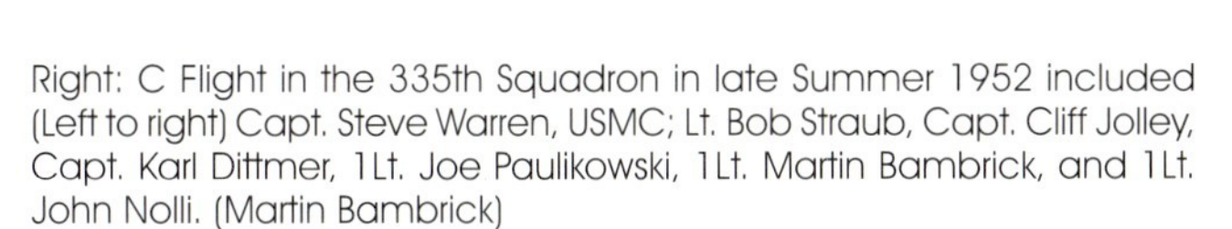

Right: C Flight in the 335th Squadron in late Summer 1952 included (Left to right) Capt. Steve Warren, USMC; Lt. Bob Straub, Capt. Cliff Jolley, Capt. Karl Dittmer, 1Lt. Joe Paulikowski, 1Lt. Martin Bambrick, and 1Lt. John Nolli. (Martin Bambrick)

The pilot of "Bonnie and Cuddles", a 334th Squadron F-86E, taxies to the takeoff spot for a mission in October 1952. The Sabre carries drop tanks manufactured in Japan. The Japanese tanks had some strange flight characteristics which was the reason they were painted olive green, and the pilot took evasive action so the tanks wouldn't roll along the underside of the airplane when dropped. (USAF)

Maj. William Thomas' "Virginia Belle", also carried the nose art "Gopher Patrol", a derogatory term toward the Chinese pilots. Maj. Thomas' Sabre has one MiG kill and two trains destroyed on the gun bay door. Only one drop tank is installed as Maj. Thomas was involved in some experimental bombing trials where the Sabre had one bomb and one drop tank. (via Ken Buchanen)

stayed up, high above the ceiling of the Sabres. Group pilots shot down two MiGs on the 1st, damaging four more, with two probables on the first two days. But then the MiGs started staying high 'on the perch', and no further contact was achieved until the 17th. The weather turned sour during the second week and remained lousy for the rest of the month.

But on the 17th, the MiGs came to fight. And when the day was finished, three MiGs had gone down to the guns of Major Bill Cosby, Col. Royal Baker, and Lt.Col. Chester Van Etten. It was Col. Baker's 5th MiG, making him the twenty-first jet ace in Korea. The next day, Captain Bill Lilley was Dog Flight Lead, with Pete Fernandez as his Element Lead.

Approaching the Chong Chong River, they spotted two MiGs engaged with a flight of Sabres about 5,000 feet below them. One of the MiGs broke away, and attempted to 'zoom-climb' out of the combat. But Lilley's flight was waiting for him. The MiG burst through in front of Dog Flight, and Bill Lilley got off a quick burst as the MiG went through their for-

Two 335th Squadron chiefs remove the tarps from an F-86F-10 on the Kimpo ramp in December 1952. The winter of 1952-53 was much warmer than either 50-51 or 51-52, with the temperature dropping to only -30°. (USAF)

mation. Lilley fired just thirty rounds from each gun, but that was enough. Strikes were observed on the fuselage of the MiG, and the MiG rolled straight in from 38,000 feet. Captain Bill Illey became the twenty-second jet ace with that victory.

November ended with only ten MiGs destroyed, four probables, and six damaged. A light month for victories. But the weather was lousy, offering only seventeen days of good flying for both the Sabres and the MiGs. On the 21st, Major James Hagerstrom shot down his first MiG. He would later become the only jet ace in Korea not assigned to either the 4th or 51st Fighter Wings, as he transferred to the 18th Fighter Bomber Group when that unit transitioned into new F-86F fighter bombers.

On the 17th of November, the 4th Fighter Wing got a new commander – Colonel James K. Johnson. And a new era began.

Below: By late 1952, large 6,000 gallon tankers brought fuel to the flightline. Fuel was brought to Korea by Navy tanker and offloaded at Inchon. Railroad tank cars then brought the fuel to Kimpo, Suwon, and the other bases. Bedcheck Charlie hit the fuel dump one night – it burned for almost a week! (Don Stewart)

eight

The Aces Talk

Captain Dick "MiG Wrecker" Becker, 334th FIS, 4th FIG, 24 March 1951
F-86A #49-1257

I had just returned to Korea following the 'bug-out from Kimpo' on 2 January. The GIs had just retaken Suwon (K-13) and we moved back in as soon as the runway was clear again. My squadron, the 334th FIS, was one of the two squadrons in Korea at the time. The 336th remained at Taegu for awhile longer.

My first victory was never confirmed. We were flying a MiG Sweep to the Yalu. It was my nineteenth mission. I was in Jim Jabara's flight. He was Eagle Red Lead and I was Eagle Red 3. As we entered the area known as MiG Alley in northwest Korea, we spotted a large gaggle of MiGs above us, at least twenty, maybe more. Jim ordered 'Drop tanks!" and the fight was on. But to my dismay, my left drop tank hung up. What to do. Standing orders were to get yourself home if you couldn't drop your tanks. I decided to fight the poor handling and stay with Jabara.

The MiGs broke down into us as we started climbing. We split their formation right in two. Jim's element took the ten MiGs to our left, my element took the ten MiGs to our right. The airplane was very heavy because of the hung left tank, but the MiGs weren't getting away! Wracking the Sabre back and forth trying to get one of the MiGs in my sights, I finally got one to hold still just long enough. I pulled in behind him and gave him a long burst. The MiG stopped, smoking heavily. Then he went into a flat spin at about 18,000 feet. I followed him down to about 14,000 then had to break off due to other MiGs that were plenty mad at me .

The MiG disappeared into the cloud deck at about 5,000 feet. Two other F-86 flights were coming down to help us and saw the MiG go into the cloud deck streaming smoke and obviously out of control. But no one saw him crash.

I wrote up the report claiming a victory, and shot it off the 5th Air Force Headquarters, confident that I would be awarded my first 'kill'. Wrong! A few days later the claim was returned from 5th AF – disallowed. It would go down as a 'Probable' since no one had followed it down to see it crash. Neither I, Jabara, nor anyone else that saw that MiG going down, had any doubts it was a goner. But ...

It was tough to get a confirmed victory in Korea.

Captain Dick 'MiG Wrecker' Becker, 334th FIS, 4th FIG, 9 September 1951
F-86A #49-1257

I was leading a flight of six F-86s as Eagle Blue Leader. Ray Barton and Bob Harper were leading the other elements. We were patrolling the Sinuiju/Anju area in northwest Korea – the heart of MiG Alley. Shortly after arriving in the area, I sighted a formation of about thirty MiGs sitting high on their perch above us.

I called my squadron CO and told him about the MiGs, then ordered my guys to drop tanks, all the while turning and climbing toward the MiG formation. As we were climbing to attack the first bunch of MiGs, I suddenly caught sight of another MiG formation that was diving on us – right through their own formation.!

I had my guys hold their positions as the MiGs started to bore in for the kill. Coming at us head-on, I waited until the last second before opening fire. The MiGs broke in all directions. And my flight followed. All three elements turned and started chasing the MiGs. Barton and Harper's elements went one way, I went another.

I rolled out at 39,000 feet and began looking around. I was alone! My wingman had gotten lost somewhere in the melee. I started to make a hasty retreat since I had no wingman to cover my tail. Then I noticed another twelve MiGs entering the area about 3,000 feet below me. Without even thinking about it, I pulled around to get a little advantage, and dove on the Russian formation.

One against twelve! Not too good of odds, I thought. But the MiGs were even more shook than I was by the way I jumped on them. They were probably thinking "What kind of maniac is this?" The MiGs broke in every direction, and no one was flying anyone's wing. I pulled in behind one of the MiGs that was all alone, lined him up with the pipper, and pulled the trigger. The MiG stopped suddenly, the pilot ejected, and the MiG exploded. Scratch One!

There were still plenty of MiGs around and I soon found another loner trying to get out of my way. I fired on him but missed. He dove away and headed north. I continued this pattern of jumping on any MiG in the area, squeeze off a few rounds, then break away. At about the same moment, both the MiGs and my fuel were gone.

I turned south, got as high as possible, and started for home. When I landed, there was a welcoming committee waiting for me. The kill was my 5th, making me the second ace in the Korean War. I learned later that day that Hoot (Capt. Ralph D. 'Hoot' Gibson) had also gotten his 5th. I'll never know why someone decided I was the second Ace and Hoot was the third. It's just as likely that Hoot was second and I third. It's tough enough to know where you are in a fight, who is with you, who is behind you, how much fuel you have left, how much ammo, etc. How is a pilot supposed to keep exact time when he scored that elusive 5th victory.

Capt. Dick Becker, known as "MiG Wrecker Becker", shows four fingers indicating his fourth victory, as he climbs out of his F-86A, #49-1257, at Kimpo on 18 August 1951. Capt. Becker was assigned to the 334th Squadron and had shot down two MiGs on this day. (Dick Becker)

Capt. Dick Becker is congratulated by his crew chief T/Sgt Robert Hulteen, on the date of his fifth victory in Korea – 9 September 1951. Capt. Becker and Capt. 'Hoot' Gibson, each shot down their fifth MiG on 9 September. Becker was declared the second jet ace in the Korean War. (Dick Becker)

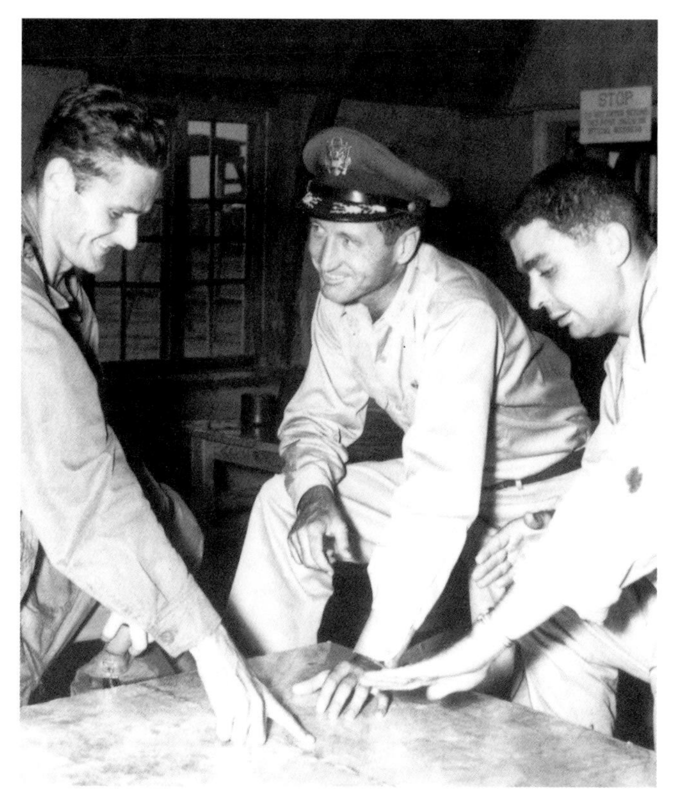

Left: Capt. Hoot Gibson shows Col. Herman Schmid, 4th Wing Commander, where in North Korea he was when he shot down his fifth MiG of the war. Watching is Capt. Dick Becker who also scored his fifth victory on this same day, 9 September 1951. (Dick Becker)

My final 'score' was five victories, one probable, and two damaged, not bad for only 82 missions. Within an hour after both Hoot and I landed at K-14, we received telegrams grounding us from any further combat. We were ordered back to the states. "But I still have eighteen missions to fly!", I complained. And Jabara had flown almost 125! Didn't matter. Hoot and I were on our way home two days later. I was back in the States on 23 September, and ended up assigned to the 5th FIS at McGuire AFB flying F-94Bs!

Capt. Dick Becker gives a demonstration at 5th AF Headquarters in Seoul, how he shot down his fifth MIG, making him the second jet ace in Korea. As soon as Captains Becker and Gibson landed following the fifth victories, they were grounded from further combat and rotated back to the United States. (Dick Becker)

Colonel Ben Preston, 4th Fighter Interceptor Group Commander, July 1951 through 18 March 1952

I was the commander of the 4th Fighter Interceptor Group from mid-July 1951 through mid-March 1952 when Colonel Walker Mahurin took over. It was the toughest era in regards to the prevailing conditions in Korea. We were short of almost everything, except MiGs of course. Base conditions were abominable, both for the men and the airplanes. Parts and supplies to keep 'em flying were scarce. And like the Vietnam War ten years hence, no one at home seemed to care what was going on.

But the morale of the men, both pilots and ground crews, was superb. The ground crews did everything asked of them, and then some. And the pilots were always flying the airplanes beyond the design limits. They had to, the MiG was a much better performing airplane in Korea.

When I took over the Group, I only had two squadrons available for combat – the 334th and 335th FIS. The 336th was still back at Johnson AB, Japan for air defense duties. The 4th FIG was based at Suwon, which we had retaken back in February. The runway itself wasn't too bad, a single, narrow strip that was reasonably smooth. We shared the strip with the 51st Group, who were flying F-80 Shooting Stars.

The Suwon runway had only one taxi strip entrance, which made recovery after a mission very hairy indeed. We landed on one side of the runway, swung around at the end, and taxiied back up the other side. All the while, other returning aircraft kept coming in to land. Our wing tip clearance was maybe ten feet, but I doubt it. Six would be closer to the truth.

It really became interesting when aircraft returned with battle damage and barely under control, many close to zero fuel and some with no fuel, dead-sticking in with no chance for a go-around. The new pilots fresh from the States couldn't

Right: Always the thought at Kimpo. (Larry Hendle)

believe their eyes as they watched us recover at Suwon. But you can get used to almost anything after awhile.

One of the things I noticed right away after taking over the Group was how beat the pilots looked, and how dirty the airplanes were. But after a very short period of time, the planes started looking great, and the pilots looked perfectly normal and healthy. By then, I guess I was as baggy-eyed as the rest of the crews, and didn't notice.

Towards the end of August 1951, we moved the Group to Kimpo. Kimpo had a longer, wider concrete runway, accessible from either end. There were a few shot up brick and masonry buildings at Kimpo that we repaired, and we got a portable power plant operating to provide electricity. Now we had asphalt parking ramps and taxiways, which alleviated the traffic control problems that Suwon had.

At the same time, 5th AF released my third squadron for duty in Korea. The 336th FIS flew in from Johnson in late August. Now we could put up a pretty fair show for the first time. An average day's group effort started running about 25-30 Sabres, and we started getting into some real nasty fights.

It became obvious that the Russian-Chinese training program had gotten into high gear. It was very cyclical. Contact would be very sporadic with the MiGs seemingly avoiding tangling with us. Then as time passed, they would be a little more willing to mix it up. And then for about a week or so, they would turn out 100-200 MiGs and seek active combat.

This whole cycle would cover a period of maybe six weeks. 'Graduation Day' was always hairy. After the first 'break' in combat (as in a pool game), things would rapidly break down to the minimum of pairs, called an element – one guy and his wingman. The MiGs would usually attack in loose formations, never with flight integrity or in pairs as with our pilots.

In those early days, before the 51st Group transitioned to Sabres, I credit four factors as reasons that we weren't shot out of the air, and run out of Korea; 1.) We had better pilots. 2.) The MiG-15 was unstable laterally at high mach, and therefore a poor gun platform. 3.) Because of their sheer weight in numbers, the MiGs simply could not get at us while trying to fly a pursuit curve. 4.) We started replacing the F-86A manually-controlled Sabre with F-86Es, which had hydraulic controls. We could almost always escape at "Bingo" fuel, by going into a full throttle vertical dive, which the MiG could not follow.

Regarding crossing the Yalu River. During my tenure as CO, my orders were very strict in observing the Yalu River sanctuary line. There would be no 'hot pursuit' across that line – period! I heard after I was back in the states that Gabby Gabreski pioneered the 'hot pursuit' operation after he took over the 51st FIG. But that's just hearsay. I think that after the 51st came up to strength, the powers that be tacitly OK'd that kind of aggressive operation. Whereas in July '51, I was told to keep losses to a minimum. By the summer of '52 it was a whole new ballgame, i.e. plenty of spares, twice as many aircraft and pilots, etc.

Regarding MiG kills – MiGs were shot down in every conceivable flight attitude and situation. Actually, the hairiest missions of all never resulted in a kill. Whereas the downing of a MiG was at times as simple as making a practice gunnery pass at a towed target.

Col. Ben Preston, Commanding 4th Group, flew "Lil' Punkin'", F-86E #51-2747. The gun bay door on Col. Preston's Sabre shows his entire score, four kills, three damaged. (via Marty Isham)

1Lt. 'Ralph 'Hoot' Gibson marks his third MiG kill on the score board at Suwon 18 July 1951, as 1Lt. Larry Layton, his wingman, looks on. 'Hoot' would make captain in August and shoot down his fifth MiG on 9 September 1951, becoming the third jet ace in the Korean War. (USAF)

Major Winton W. 'Bones' Marshall, Commander, 335th FIS, 1951-1952
F-86E #50-525

Maj. W.W. 'Bones' Marshall, was the CO of the 335th Squadron at Kimpo in late 1951. 'Bones' Marshall shot down his first MiG on 1 September 1951, and shot down a LaGG-9 and a Tu-2 in the slaughter that took place on 30 November 1951. He was crowned the sixth jet ace in the Korean War. (USAF)

Milk Run To MiG Alley

We had thirty-two F-86 Sabres from all three squadrons this day. We were climbing to altitude in the weather, going to MiG Alley in northwest Korea. Suddenly, we broke out of the overcast, and into the clear at about 20,000 feet.

Our mission this morning was to provide top cover for the fighter bombers flying a close support mission. However, during the mission briefing, we had been told that the weather over North Korea would be socked in, from the deck all the way to combat altitudes – above 35,000 feet. Further that the weather at Sinanju and in MiG Alley was also bad. So the MiGs wouldn't be flying.

The weather in the fighter bomber target area was touch and go, so the weather recce aircraft had been directed to make a visual check of the area. He reported back that the weather was marginal at best, but the mission could be flown. Weather doesn't affect the troops on the ground, who were involved in one hell of a fight. So 5th Air Force issued the order – the mission was a 'go'.

For us in the Sabres, this meant that we would be flying in the weather all the way to MiG Alley. On arrival, we would try to find enough open space between the clouds to set up our combat air patrol long enough for the fighter bombers to complete their mission. With the MiGs not flying, it would be a lousy 'milk run'.

Once the word was out, most of the 'hot shot fighter jocks' quickly came up with some excuse, like a cold or a sore toe, so they could be taken off the mission. The 'big hunters' didn't want to waste even one valuable combat sortie. All assigned combat pilots at both the headquarters and the combat squadrons were required to fly 100 combat sorties, no more and no less, before rotating home. So you tried to outguess the weather and the MiGs, and only fly on the best air-fighting days – the days when you had a good chance the MiGs would come up.

I was leading the 335th Squadron, and was disappointed to be flying and wasting one of my missions on a 'milk run'. However, as the squadron commander, I had to do my share of the bad with the good. Further, even on a 'milk run', you had the additional responsibility of leading your formation into a combat zone, with a great many pilots of lesser combat fighting capabilities. They weren't all bad, just inexperienced. I had one such pilot on my wing for this mission.

Maj. 'Bones' Marshall flew F-86E-5 #50-625, appropriately named "Mr. Bones V." This photo taken in the Spring of 1951, shows Marshall's complete score – 7 1/2 victories, although he was officially credited with only 6 1/2, and 5 damaged. ('Bones' Marshall)

These pilots came in several categories. The worst was the weak pilot, one that never saw a MiG first, and couldn't hit the side of a barn if he did see them. And he couldn't or wouldn't hold a 'high G' turn in combat, something very basic to any good pilot. This guy should have been transferred out of the 4th. But it was Air Force policy that once he was assigned to a group, we had to see them through the 100 missions. So we tried to only schedule them on 'milk run' missions.

Then there is the 'new guy' who has less than ten sorties under his belt, is still learning, and is still not sure where MiG Alley is! Some of these guys have twenty missions and are still considered 'new guys'. They've never been in a fight nor even seen a MiG.

Then there are the staff weenies from Headquarters. Their minds are more on their paper work than fighting the MiGs. So even after fifty missions, they still haven't been in a fight. And the nearest MiGs they've seen are the far off contrails heading back north. These guys are a greater menace to themselves, as well as the formation. Again, their minds are just not in the game. To protect the innocent, we got in the habit of calling them all 'new guys', until they got into their first really big fight.

I have almost been shot down several times with a 'weenie' on my wing, versus the new pilot who is so excited that he keeps shouting "MiGs!" every time one of our own F-86s crosses over behind us. I love the young wingman who keeps calling out "MiGs!", right or wrong. With him I'll never get my butt shot off as against the 'dead ass' who is so lazy or unsure of himself that he never says anything until you're under fire. Which certainly made life interesting.

I am being less than kind when I say that once the word is out that mission was probably going to be a 'milk run', there is a great rush by these lesser pilots to get on the mission. We made every effort to train and improve the fighting capabilities of our weaker squadron pilots. However, one has to respect the Headquarters pilot, who has the courage to admit his own weaknesses in combat operations, and as a result, wants to fly on the safer 'milk runs'. In many cases, their bosses won't let them fly enough to gain and/or maintain their combat capability.

We had greater opportunities in the squadrons. We flew at least every third day, so our combat proficiency was continually being improved. Our combat pilots had great confidence in themselves and in the F-86. There were also many good combat pilots in Headquarters, who flew as often as we did.

But I was just as happy to have the weaker guys flying on days when there was a low probability of seeing the MiGs. The Air Force was rotating all of their fighter pilots through the combat in Korea, to build up combat experience. We had been told that the Soviets were doing the same thing – rotating

A good friend of Maj. Marshall, and the pilot named fifth jet ace in the Korean War on the same day that Marshall made 'ace', was Maj. George Davis, Jr. Maj. Davis, Commanding 334th Squadron, shot down 14 1/2 aircraft in Korea (plus seven Japanese aircraft in World War II), before being shot down on 10 February 1952. Maj. Davis was awarded the Medal Of Honor for the mission on which he was killed. (NAA)

entire squadrons through Antung, joining in the air battles against the American Sabres.

So we were seeing both the mediocre and the good MiG fighter units. There had been a period when the MiG kill ratio had surged in favor of the Sabres. We were told that as a result, the Soviets had brought in their best units to even the score. These MiG pilots were a hell of a lot more aggressive and we were having to fight and fly like hell to shake them off, or get into position to fire.

The wingman was one of the reasons that many Sabre pilots scored big. Every MiG killer in the Korean War will tell you that besides your own fighting skill and a great deal of luck, there was no factor more important to your success in fighting the MiGs than having a good wingman.

Our squadron wingmen were the best. In sighting the MiGs first, calling out attacks and sticking with their leaders through the most violent combat maneuvers. With a lesser experienced pilot on your wing, you'd lose him on the first hard break. 4th Group policy established that the minimum fighting element in the combat zone, i.e. MiG Alley, was two. So unless you were able to quickly rejoin formation with your wingman, or another lone aircraft to fly your wing, you were required to get the hell out of there – NOW! As a result, two badly needed F-86s, now flying singly, had become combat ineffective and lost to the entire mission.

I realize how lucky I have been to be involved in so many air battles. I was credited with twenty aircraft, either destroyed, probably destroyed, or damaged. In addition I had chased a lot of MiGs, but didn't hit anything. And I had been shot at myself at least 10-15 times, including once where the enemy pilot scored some really good hits and badly damaged my aircraft. And that was by a LaGG-9 propeller-driver aircraft! So out of 100 combat missions, I was probably involved in fifty or more actual air battles with enemy aircraft, most of the time being MiG-15s. That's a hell of a lot of air fighting, considering the weather and the days when the MiGs didn't fly at all, i.e. the 'milk runs'. I will say again that my success throughout my 100 missions was entirely due to having the greatest wingmen in the business.

One of the most important people in the 334th Squadron was Sgt. Duck, in charge of the pilots personal equipment like parachutes, helmets, and oxygen masks. The pilots all treated him nice. (NAA)

"Casey Jones"

Someone in one of the other squadrons transmitted the call that "Casey Jones" was aboard. There he was, a single contrail sitting high above all the other MiG formations. "Casey Jones", the legendary trainman. A code name given to the MiG tactical commander, the guy that directed all the "bandit trains" out of Antung. He flew in a single MiG, well above all the MiG flights, directing the air battle. With him aboard we knew we could expect a hell of an air battle.

Prior to the advent of "Casey Jones", it had seemed that the MiGs had been making only individual attack runs, usually low and at the six o'clock position.

But with "Ol' Case' directing the fight, the MiGs put emphasis on a coordinated high side attack, in conjunction with their normal low six o'clock passes. While you were turning into the pair making the high angle attack, two more were coming up your tailpipe. They were attacking in groups of four to six aircraft, which was more than the two-ship F-86 element could cope with. Interestingly enough, with these increased tactics, we were still maintaining the kill ratio that we'd had from the beginning. But now we were having to do a hell of a lot more fighting than in the past.

Our three squadrons had entered MiG Alley in our basic combat formation of four ship flights, the 'finger four formation'. But when the fight began, we quickly broke down into elements of two, which was our best fighting posture. It was estimated that the number of MiG contrails overhead now exceeded 70+ MiGs. I would have been completely confident of success in the face of even those odds, with my own wingman. But given the situation, it was the bloody end if you had a wingman who couldn't hack it.

I'll remember this mission for all the days of my life. Never have I had to fight so hard to survive. And surprisingly, in the act of surviving, to fall into the lap of Lady Luck and destroy my antagonizer.

We had just rolled out from breaking into the two attacking MiGs, when almost immediately, my cockpit was surrounded by a hail of bright tracers from the cannons of the MiG on my tail. They looked the size of oranges as they went by the canopy. My wingman had said nothing. I jerked the stick back so hard that I easily exceeded the aircraft 'G' limits. The MiG went one direction and my wingman the other. I had lost them both.

Before I could take a breath, I was again the target of a stream of tracers, but a lot closer this time. There was a second MiG sitting right on my tail. Startled, I again slammed the stick back, trying to 'split S' out of there. It produced spectacular results. My Sabre did a neat snap roll, and I ended up in an inverted spin with zero air speed. This was a great evasive maneuver, I thought. No one could have stayed with me through that gyration.

Except, when I looked out through my canopy, there was a MiG. And we were both spinning down together, canopy to canopy. In seconds I made a quick spin recovery. But so did he. We had ended up in a flat spin, with very little air speed, in a nose-up attitude. Except that his nose was almost pointing at me. I expected him to start firing at any moment.

As an illustration of the great flight stability of the F-86, my aircraft completely responded when I again slammed the sloppy stick to one side, kicking the rudders as hard as I could. It worked! I was off in another spin, slower but more controllable this time.

Then the impossible happened. There was my MiG, also spinning down in the same air space with me. We were fast losing too much altitude, so I again made a spin recovery. The MiG recovered right beside me. Except this time, he was at my 12 o'clock position – directly in front of me. It was a simple task to open fire. I must have hit something vital as the MiG suddenly caught fire and exploded.

What a great fighter pilot that MiG guy was. I thought he was Ol' Casey Jones himself. Other Sabre pilots that had seen the fight, said that the MiG appeared to have stuck with me in my hard break, until we both snap-rolled and fell off in that first spin. That MiG driver proved to be one hell of wingman, when he stuck with me in a formation of sorts, as we both spun down the second time, with destination unknown. It was just Lady Luck riding with me, that he ended up in the dead center of my gunsight. Otherwise, I don't know. I was well below 'Bingo' fuel, and it was either then or I wouldn't have made it home.

That fight had probably lasted little more than five minutes, but it seemed like a lifetime. It seemed impossible that in so short a period of time, I had been shot at two times, continuously exceeded the aircraft 'G' limits with my maneuvers, and snap-rolled and spun the airplane twice. All the time being together with an enemy aircraft, until I recovered in a position to shoot him out of the sky. What an air battle!

As I headed home, about 200 miles away, I realized that I had concentrated so hard on that MiG and my survival, that I had heard no radio transmissions from any other Sabres in the area. I half regretted the loss of such a great pilot, even though he was on the other side. He certainly looked ten feet tall to me. I would have loved to have sat down for a beer or vodka, at the O-club with that guy, trading fighter pilot stories together.

What was different between his MiG and my Sabre, that he could stay with me through such high 'G' turns? Did he purposely fly into the snap roll and spin, to stay with me? Or was it an unexpected maneuver, as it had been for me? Why didn't he shoot at me when we both recovered from that first spin? And finally, was his fuel as low, his flying suit as wet, and his arm as tired as mine was in those last few seconds?

It had been one hell of a 'Milk Run' day. I am sure that my wingman will remember it for days to come. He probably pulled more 'Gs' that day than anytime in his life, as he survived several attacks by that bunch of MiGs. He could be proud that he did the best he could under those circumstances.

Colonel Harrison R. Thyng, 4th Fighter Interceptor Wing Commander
Kimpo AB 1952

The day was clear, still, and suspenseful. MiG Alley had been quiet for nearly a week as the MiG pilots wouldn't cross the Yalu to engage our guys. Each day my guys searched the skies across the river, taunting, threatening, even entreating the MiG pilots to come up and fight. Still they didn't accept our challenges.

Today just had to be the day we'd been waiting for. Excitement was running high. Flight leaders were deviously planning with the other members of their flight, not only on how the enemy was to be hit, but also how their flight could outfox

The "Bloody Great Wheel" himself – Col. Harrison R. Thyng, Commander of the 4th Wing at Kimpo throughout most of 1952. Col. Thyng scored 'only' five MiG victories in Korea (plus five German fighters in World War II), although all his wingmen and crew chiefs say he scored double that number. Thyng often gave the credit for a victory to his wingman. (Harrison Thyng)

the other flights and be the first to tangle with the wily MiGs. Competition was tremendously high in the 4th. It would be the flight leader with the greatest aggressiveness and ingenuity that scored.

After takeoff, we broke up the squadron formations into flights of four. Each flight criss-crossed and swept the skies over MiG Alley at different times, areas and altitudes to confuse the enemy radar. With their ground radar advantage, the enemy controllers would direct mass attacks on our formations. Each one coming at us at high Mach and usually with a high degree of surprise. Of course, we baited the MiGs with our small units. And it took a lot of guts to go up with only four birds, always on the attack, and engage an enemy 200 miles from our home base.

My guys grew more eager as the final details for the mission were ironed out. Takeoff times, areas, and patrol altitudes were settled. Weather details were laid on us, including the altitude of the contrail level, i.e. 'the Cons'. The 'cons', which were our best 'radar', would be between 39,000 and 41,000 feet today. Our flights would be just above and below that level. That way we could see the MiGs either going up to set up and attack, or diving down on us. It was like Mother Nature was protecting us against a surprise attack. The speed of jet fighter combat, and the vastness of the sky over northwest Korea did not give the human eye time to always spot an enemy aircraft until it was too late.

My flight was 'Blue Flight', and I briefed them myself. On my wing was Flt/Lt. J.M. 'Paddy' Nichols, an RAF exchange pilot, and, like myself, a World War II retread. I decided to patrol at 46,000 feet, beginning just south of the mouth of the Yalu. From here we could spot the hundreds of little silver MiGs on the fields at Antung, Ta Tung Kou, Takushan, and Fen Cheng, which were just a few miles away. I wanted to arrive in MiG Alley about fifteen minutes after our first flights. On the flight to the Alley, we conserved fuel in every possible manner, and maintained radio silence.

Our first flights arrived at the Yalu, but the MiGs ignored us again. You could hear our guys calling the MiGs over the radio, but to no avail. It wouldn't be long before our guys reached 'Bingo' fuel, and would be forced to return to Kimpo, vexed and frustrated.

We couldn't figure out why the MiGs didn't accept our challenge. They had all the advantages. The MiG was an excellent machine. It could outclimb the Sabre, and always had an altitude advantage. The MiG pilots were always over friendly territory in case they had to eject. They always outnumbered us, sometimes as high as 7:1. They even had the advantage of a sanctuary to hide in. If they got in trouble, they simply dove back across the Yalu, where our guys were forbidden to go. But even with all these advantages, today they were again reluctant to fight.

Col. Thyng shares a laugh with Lt.Gen. Glenn O. Barcus, Commander of 5th AF in Korea, in the Officers Mess at Kimpo. (Jim Low)

Our flights had been in the area about twenty minutes now, and most were at 'Bingo' fuel and departing the area. My element leader and his wingman had also returned to Kimpo with mechanical problems. All that was left high above the Yalu was Paddy and myself. Suddenly below us, across the river at Antung, we watched as two MiGs taxied out and lined up for takeoff. The MiGs rolled down the runway, and headed north! All we could hope for was that they'd turn south and cross the Yalu.

But they didn't. Bitterly antagonized by our restrictions regarding the Yalu 'border', I was determined to influence this

The date is 15 June 1952 and the 4th has reason to celebrate. First is a visit by Gen. Nathan Twining, Air Force Vice Chief of Staff, and Mr Ross Gilpatrick. Then to make the day right, 1Lt. Jim Low shot down his fifth MiG to make 'ace'. (Left to right) unknown, Gen Twining, Col. Thyng, Mr. Gilpatrick, and Lt. Low talking with Mr Gilpatrick. (Jim Low)

pair of MiG pilots. From our altitude, I told Paddy to dive down at well over Mach 1, cross the river and 'boom' Antung. The unexpected and shattering sonic 'booms' woke everybody up. We re-crossed the river and watched.

Our ruse worked and the MiGs veered and went across the river looking for us. With our terrific speed from the supersonic dive, we easily swung in behind the two MiGs. Radio silence was broken on both sides now. The Red ground controllers were warning the MiG pilots of our position (at their six o'clock and closing!). The two MiGs split and started back toward Antung. I yelled at Paddy: – "I'll take the leader! Blast the one on the left!"

I opened fire from directly behind the MiG, immediately scoring hits on the fuselage. Debris starting coming off the MiG, showering my Sabre with pieces. I knew I was sucking

Right: 1Lt. Jim Low was known as 'Dad' because he was the oldest pilot in his class at Nellis. 'Dad' Low became the seventeenth jet ace in Korea on 15 June 1952. He scored his sixth victory on 4 July before being rotated home, but returned in November and added to his score. (Jim Low)

Below: Four Aces – (Left to right) 1Lt. Jim Low (335th) – nine MiGs, Capt. Robinson Risner (336th) – eight MiGs, Col. Royal Baker (4th Group CO) – thirteen victories, and Capt. Bill Lilley (334th) – seven MiGs. (USAF)

MiG parts into my intake right into the engine. Would it last? The MiG crossed the Yalu, heading straight toward Antung. With his home field boundary in sight, he suddenly blew up in a mass of flames, with the wreckage scattering across Antung. No other MiGs attempted to takeoff.

Meanwhile Paddy was chasing the other MiG and hollering at me: – "The bloody bastard is starting to swing your way!" I broke left and there was Paddy blasting away, and chasing the MiG directly into my path. Needless to say, we both could've fired on this MiG. And neither of us realized that in the chase, we were inadvertently "slightly north" of the river. However, the chase was short, as the MiG disappeared in a smoking dive.

We were both at 'Bingo', and couldn't take the time to watch him crash. Thus Paddy lost credit for the second kill. We had to get home fast! We blasted back across Antung, throttles wide open, on the deck, dodging the flak, and then climbed to altitude to preserve what little fuel remained in our tanks. None of the MiGs at the other bases came after us, and all we had to worry about was the extremely heavy flak. We were finally able to coax the Sabres up to 40,000 feet. But we were still over eighty miles from Kimpo, and our fuel was desperate to put it mildly.

"Paddy, Let's shut 'em down and glide." He replied – "Right Chief. That was a bit of a go for a few minutes!" I don't think an Englishman ever gets excited. We shut down the engines and glided. It was very quiet, cold and tense. A few minutes, really alone, with only the Lord up there with the fighter pilot now.

Col. Thyng's jeep on the K-14 flightline in 1952. (Col. Jim Thyng)

Maj. Felix Asla, Jr, was the Commander of 336th squadron at Kimpo in Summer 1952. Maj. Asla shot down 4 MiGs in the Spring of 1952. He was shot down and killed on 1 August 1952 (Author)

The 335th Squadron alert ramp at K-14 in Spring 1952. Col. Thyng's F-86E, FU-623 named "Pretty Mary and the Js", was assigned to the 335th Squadron. In the Spring of 1952, FEAF ordered the 4th Wing to change their aircraft markings from black and white stripes to black and yellow stripes. (Charles Volk)

In November 1952, 1Lt. Jim Low returned to K-14 to add to his MiG kill score. The crew chief of his Sabre, F-86E #51-2870, congratulates Low on 18 December 1952, for his ninth and last victory. Note the telltale smoked gun ports on Low's Sabre. (Dave Eldredge)

Had we computed our glide distance right? Would we be lucky and get the J47 to restart? But there it was – Kimpo AB in the distance. Paddy and I both got a restart on the few, very few gallons we had saved for the landing. We'd made it! We landed and taxied into the revetments. Both us were elated at our success.

One of the intangibles was the attitude of the Reds. They couldn't help but be aroused by the insulting violation of his sanctuary. He couldn't be sure about his security any longer. They had to wonder, had the UN restrictions been lifted, or was it simply the men in the F-86s doing it on their own? Would the UN pilots now cross the Yalu to avenge any brother pilot that the MiGs had shot down – even against the restrictions? The Reds didn't know, and wouldn't. But their arrogant attitude ended. The challenge had been met.

Captain Leonard W. 'Bill' Lilley, 334th Fighter Interceptor Squadron

K-14 Fall-Winter, 1952

Much has been written on the subject of MiG pilots and tactics. During my tour, I saw virtually every formation that re-

The 335th Squadron scored its 100th victory in the Korean War on 7 September 1952, when Capt. John Taylor and 1Lt. Edgar Powell worked together to shoot down one MiG and damage another. (Left to right) Col. Royal Baker, 4th Group CO, Capt. Taylor, Capt. Cliff Jolley, Lt. Powell, and Lt.Col. Carroll McElroy, CO of the 335th Squadron. (USAF)

Capt. Cliff Jolley checks the assignment sheet as he gets ready to man the mobile control microphone at K-14 in September 1952. The mobile control vehicle at K-14 was a Dodge 3/4 ton truck with a tin sided box enclosing the radios. A B-26 nose cone sat atop the box for operations in bad weather. (Cliff Jolley)

portedly they flew – from the 'Lone Eagle' single to large gaggles. The largest formation I ever saw was forty-four MiGs. Eleven flights of four, climbing south across the Yalu. Not bad odds so Squadron Leader Eric Smith, RAF, and I attacked! Things didn't work out quite as we had planned and we went from potential heroes to definitely dumb in a heartbeat. In the blink of an eye, there were so many MiGs at our six o'clock, I was certain they would collide.

Now, our most effective defensive maneuver when wired at the six o'clock, was a diving high G tight spiral. It's very hard to hit a target under such conditions. When the MiGs did this to us, which they rarely did, we just stayed with them until they rolled out, then closed in for the kill. So that's exactly what we did – a tight spiral to the right with Eric below and inside of me, pulling maximum Gs, and yelling at me to pull it in tighter! There were MiGs firing just under our tailpipes!

Sooner or later we had to run out of altitude, and since these MiGs were veritable tigers (again something rare) and wouldn't let go, I knew what was ultimately in store for us. And I didn't like it. But suddenly, as if on command, all the MiGs broke off and headed back across the river. We leveled off at 10,000 feet, limp and exhausted – and mighty relieved. Col. Royal Baker, 4th group CO, was very displeased with our attempt to clear the skies all by ourselves. He met us at the revetment and admonished us accordingly. But we were so happy just to make it back that we scarcely heard anything he said. But I could tell he wasn't too happy with us.

MiG TACTICS – The MiGs practiced a number of bomber attack formations on us. On one mission, we had climbed to 40,000 feet, well above the cons. Imagine our surprise when four MiGs flying perfect line-abreast, dove down on us from about 50,000. All four opened fired simultaneously during the dive, pulling out just over our flight, then zoom-climbed back to 50,000 – still in perfect line-abreast formation. They probably 'fired out' (emptied their ammo bay) as they only had about seven seconds worth of ammo. But it seemed an eternity from the time we first spotted those four noses, all sparkling with cannon fire. Why none of us were hit was another miracle. I only experienced this thrill one time (and was glad of it too!).

I saw a number of eight ship flights flying modified V formation – a MiG leader with three ships echeloned to his left, and another four to his right. We usually tried to get the

Capt. Leonard W. 'Bill' Lilley, 334th Squadron, points to his fifth red star indicating that he is now a jet ace. The date is 18 November 1952. He would score twice more before going home in January 1953. (Bill Lilley)

Right: A2C Curt Francom was an armorer in the 334th Squadron and took care of the guns on a couple of Bill Lilley's Sabres, including his regular mount, F-86E #51-2764. Capt. Lilley's Sabre was heavily damaged in a fight with one of the MiG 'honchos' on Christmas Day 1952. (Robert V. Johnson)

RESTRICTED
Security Information

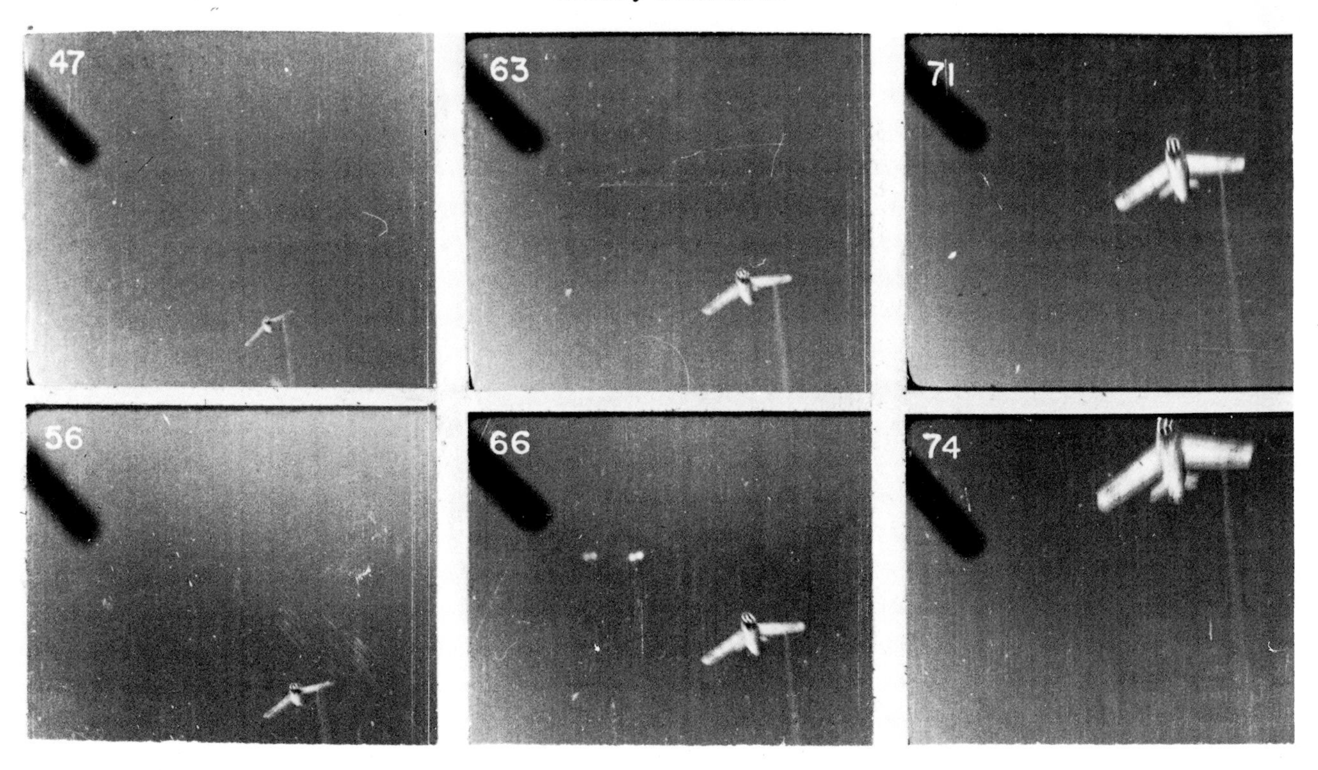

Plate I--Nose Attack Against MIG-15
(CAG 228-P074-1, range on frame 47, 900 ft.; azimuth 2°, elevation -26° off nose)

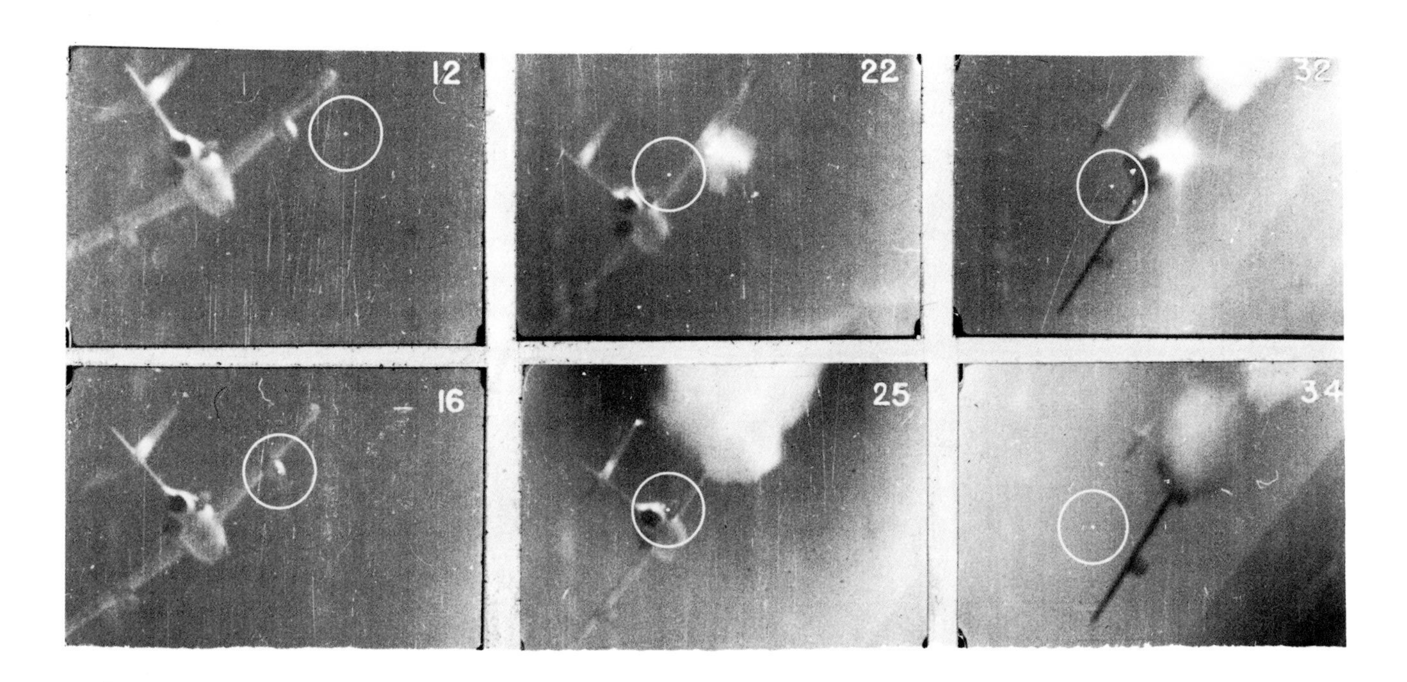

MiG kill by Capt. Bill Lilley. (USAF)

Aircraft were often shared by pilots due to Sabres being AOCP, pilots on R&R or not scheduled, or rotated home. Col. Thomas DeJarnette, Group Commander, sits in S/L Eric Smith's F-86E 6 at K-14 in 1953. S/L Smith was Capt. Bill Lilley's wingman on a number of flights. (Dick Keener)

Capt. Bill Lilley sits runway alert with Capt. Ryland Dewey and other 334th pilots at K-14 in October 1952. Capt. Lilley's flight are 'scramble alert' or one minute alert aircraft, meaning the pilots were in the cockpit and ready to go within one minute or less. (Drury Callahan)

leader before we were seen in the hopes that one or more of the wingmen would eject. In some MiG fights, this did happen, but never with me. Usually we were spotted and MiGs would split, one flight going high right and the other high or level left, in the hopes of suckering us into follow. Then the high flight would come down on us in perfect high six o'clock firing position. We rarely took the bait.

Another favorite MiG formation was the 'Daisey Chain', where several MiGs would form a wide circle high above our operating altitude. (They always had a 5,000 foot altitude advantage on us.) Occasionally, a 'Lone Eagle' would dive down and make a quick firing pass at us. If the MiG immediately zoom-climbed back up on his perch, there was little that we could do. However, if he stayed to press his attack, he invariably lost. And his friends on high rarely left the security of their perch to come to their comrade's aid.

Summing up, I believe their (the MiG pilots') air discipline wasn't anywhere near as good as ours, and it made a big difference. For instance, we noted many MiG solo flights in the combat area. By contrast, we were not allowed to remain in the Alley alone. If you became separated from your wingman or leader, you withdrew in great haste to rendezvous at some designated area outside of MiG Alley. We would return to the Alley only if we were able to rejoin with another flight or element, and had sufficient fuel to do so.

I don't have any accurate figures, but most of the pilots that I personally knew, and who were subsequently shot down, violated the above rule, staying in alone in an attempt to score. A fighter pilot, at least one that wants to score, is loathe to break off an engagement when he's starting to gain an advantage. But there is no way to clear yourself when concentrating on the gunnery problem in a high speed jet dog fight. It is the most vulnerable of all times. With no eyes to the rear clearing, disaster usually follows.

The proficiency of individual MiG pilots varied greatly. Overall, they probably had less total fighter time than our guys. And probably very little experience in 'rat-racing'. Most of our pilots 'rat-raced' a lot as soon as they got their wings. I know in my case it really paid off. My big problem was learning when not to fire in a really wild, hairy rat race.

But even against their best, such as the occasional Russian Air Regiment that rotated through Manchuria for combat experience, we excelled. We stayed together, i.e. flight integrity, as long as possible, working our elements in support of one another with great success. By and large, the MiG pilots didn't seem to understand the great value of working together.

18 November 1952, Kimpo AB. Col. James K. Johnson congratulates Col. Royal Baker (left) and Capt. Bill Lilley (right) on their victories in the previous two days. Col. Johnson took over as Wing Commander just seven days before. Col. Baker would score thirteen victories, while Col. Johnson had ten. (Bill Lilley)

Many times, when their formations broke up, they appeared confused, not knowing what to do except to run for the River and hope we wouldn't follow.

Captain Leonard W. 'Bill' Lilley, 334th FIS, 16 September 1952
F-86E #52-2833

On 16 September 1952, my flight was scrambled from K-14 by DENTIST Control, the GCI radar. Several trains of MiGs were up, and our guys were fully engaged. We were directed to go directly to the Yalu, just down river from the Suiho Dam. Arriving in the area, we began our patrol but saw no activity. My other element had to leave early when one of the aircraft experienced fuel sequencing problems. That left S/L Eric Smith and I to finish the patrol.

We were nearing 'Bingo' fuel when we spotted five MiGs taking off from Antung and heading northeast. We watched them and were slightly surprised when they turned south and crossed the River at a very low altitude. This was the first time I had seen MiGs stay low and cross the River. They usually climbed to altitude on their side of the River until they had an altitude advantage on us. Then they would race across the river and dive down on us. But these guys stayed low.

Eric and I commenced a dive, wide and to the side of the MiGs. We were still above them but closing very fast. The MiGs were in a valley, climbing slowly, with the lead element in close formation, followed by another pair some distance behind and the single much farther back. They were all stacked down be-

Capt. Bill Lilley taxies for takeoff position at K-14 early September 1952 in his regularly assigned F-86E-10, #51-2764. Capt. Lilley scored only twice in his 'regular' aircraft, once on 4 September and again on 14 September. (Phil Anderson)

low the lead MiG. The MiGs were all camouflaged with zig-zag brown and black stripes on the upper fuselage and wings; and the bottom was painted a robin's egg blue. Very pretty and very effective. I riveted my eyes on the lead element and began to slide over into the valley.

Then something distracted me. I can't remember exactly what, but I diverted my eyes for a fraction of a second. When I looked back at where I thought the MiGs should be, they weren't there. Like magic, they were gone. I called Eric to ask where they had gone. He didn't have them as he had been watching me and clearing both of our 6s.

I continued descending into the valley, heading toward where I thought the MiGs should be. Suddenly, popping up under my nose directly in front of me, was a MiG about 500 feet ahead. He had wing tanks on, which I had never seen on a MiG before. I glanced quickly to my right and the MiG wingman was there, almost in close formation with me and off my right wing. I yelled at Eric that I was 'padlocked', and fired a quick burst that hit the MiG leader in the engine. His engine exploded and all kinds of parts and debris came out of his tailpipe along with a long tongue of flame.

Just as all this was happening, a splash of his jet fuel hit my windscreen, leaving an oily film covering it, essentially blinding me at the most critical moment. Almost simultaneously, Eric called 'Break right! Now!" The other MiG element had moved in right behind us at our six o'clock and getting into firing position. Still blinded, with a very high 'pucker factor' at this point, I broke right – right into the MiG wingman. About that time, the windscreen started to clear and I could see the hills that we were below in the valley. After that, I never saw the MiG wingman or the other MiG element except briefly as we exited the area at high speed. The MiGs didn't pursue.

Eric and I watched the burning MiG leader in a shallow dive to the left. He impacted on the side of the hill in a big fireball. Neither of us saw any ejection or chute. And being very low on fuel at this point, we beat a hasty retreat. It was my forty-seventh mission and my fourth MiG kill. Two months

One of Capt. Bill Lilley's favorite wingman was Squadron Leader Eric Smith, an RAF exchange pilot assigned to the 334th Squadron to gain combat experience. S/L Smith flew this F-86E-6, one of sixty Sabres built by Canadair Ltd. (Eric Smith)

and twenty-five missions later I made 'ace'. A month later I had #6, and then almost bought the farm.

Captain Leonard W. 'Bill' Lilley, 334th FIS Christmas Day 1952

It was Christmas Day 1952. There are few holidays in war. But believe me, the hand of the Lord was certainly hard at work on this day. I was flying my regular Sabre, #51-2764, Capt. Ryland Dewey and I were at 39,000' over the Suiho Dam on a routine patrol. GCI called nothing out and I was very surprised when a lone MiG swept down from high above, firing all the way. He must have been just sitting up there waiting. But he overshot and we turned hard into him as he reversed and came back at us.

This scissors action continued three or four more turns and gradually we worked our way behind him. But we had to kill our air speed to accomplish it. As we rolled out behind him, I had to pop my speed brakes to keep from running right into him. This killed my speed for sure, and I had reduced throttle a bit as well. At a distance of less than 1000 feet, I pulled in the speed brakes and started forward on the throttle. Just as I was about to fire, a loud explosion nearly made my heart stop. The following thoughts all took place in a single second as my mind operated as supersonically as my airplane.

What the hell was that? Cannon fire from another MiG that Dewey hadn't seen and had let slip in behind me? Instinctively, my body jerked severely, so forceful that I pulled the stick back, causing the airplane to snap into a hard, right turn spin. Suddenly, I'm looking down at a very white, frozen and forbidding Sui Ho Reservoir. I was swirling like a top. I realized I had to stop that by stopping the spin, which I did, and I leveled out at about 20,000 – with the engine flamed out!

Dewey pulled in close and asked me what I was doing? I told him that I'd been hit and for him to check me over. He did and said there appeared to be no damage of any kind. I asked him if he'd seen any other MiGs while I was mixing it up with the #1 guy and he said "No." I was confused but started for the mouth of the Yalu River in case I had to eject. Coasting down the River toward the yellow Sea, I tried my first air start – no luck.

This continued to a point south of the mouth of the Yalu, descending at 250 knots, trying one air start after another. With not even a glimmer of a start. By now I'm at 10,000 feet and flak is bursting all around us as we reached the coast. I looked down at what was a very ugly sight. There were ice floes as far as I could see. I knew I wouldn't survive a minute in those waters if I had to bail out. (We hadn't been issued survival suits at that time.) So I had a long talk with the All Mighty and hit the start button one more time.

Capt. Cliff Jolley was "The Jolley Roger", when he flew with the 335th Squadron in the summer of 1952. Capt. Jolley scored seven victories between 4 May and 11 October 1952. His Sabre also carried the name "Jolley Roger" and the skull and crossbones. (Cliff Jolley)

I couldn't believe my eyes when the needles suddenly started to move. I felt as if I was watching a miracle, something that wasn't supposed to happen, in fact, something that couldn't really happen. I immediately converted the increase in air speed into altitude and headed toward K-14 with my heart pounding so hard that I could hear it. Gaining altitude, I set up a glide path directly for Kimpo and made a safe 'power on' landing. When I retarded the throttle on shutdown, the engine froze up stopped. The engineering types were all in agreement that it truly was a miracle that I was able to air start that engine. It was my ninety-third mission and the last time that I flew my beloved #764. I flew eight more missions before leaving Kimpo on 1 February 1953.

Lt.Col. Vermont Garrison, 335th FIS Squadron Commander
5 June 1953

First let me tell you about one that I didn't get and one that almost got me. We were patrolling at about 40,000 feet. My wingman and I got into a gaggle of MiGs on this day. I had MiGs in front of me, on which I was closing, and MiGs behind us at about 5 o'clock high. I had the not-so-bright idea that I could shoot down the MiG I was closing on, before the MiGs that were high and behind us could get a shot at us. I intended to open fire at about 1500 feet.

My wingman kept calling out the MiGs behind us and saying they were coming in and starting to get into position, which of course I knew. However, I misjudged the speed the MiG was closing on me and all at once he's in firing range and those big golf balls are ripping past my canopy. I thought to myself, 'Garrison, you stupid shit, you've blown it this time.'

With the MiG firing from about 200 feet, I could easily see the pilot. I yanked the stick over and went into a left turn as hard as the airplane could turn at that altitude. I turned so hard, the airplane began shuddering in a partial stall. My wingman was on the MiGs tail a few hundred feet back. I finally got the MiG low and behind me, but I didn't dare roll out as that would have given him a point blank tail shot.

My wingman called me and said the MiG was rolling out in the opposite direction. I told him, "You take him and I'll cover you!" He did, started firing and the last we saw of that MiG was when he went into a layer of low clouds trailing a heavy plume of black smoke. I always figured that the MiG pilot had 'fired out' (used all his ammunition) trying to get me. I don't know if there's a moral to this story or not. But if there is, it ought to be "Don't get too damned cocky and you'll live to fight another day."

"The Grey Eagle", Lt.Col. Vermont Garrison commanded the 335th Squadron in 1953. 'Gary' Garrison was a former member of the Eagle Squadron and the 4th Fighter Group in World War Two, scoring eleven German victories. He shot down ten MiGs during the Korean War. (USAF)

Kimpo AB, 5 June 1953. (L) Col. Johnson and (R) Maj. deJarnette congratulate Lt.Col. Garrison on scoring his 5th and 6th MiG kills, making him the 32nd jet ace in the Korean War. Garrison would score four more MiG victories to become one of nine 4th Wing pilots that made 'double ace' status. (Sylvia Johnson)

On the mission of 5 June 1953, it was the proverbial 'another day', and we were ready for a fight, even if the MiGs didn't want one. I had four Migs to my credit and wanted that fifth one. It was an afternoon mission, a typical MiG Sweep of the Yalu River area. We were Yellow Flight. I was Yellow Lead, Lt. Harry Jones was #2 on my wing, Captain Lonnie Moore was Yellow 3, and Lt. Bill Schrimsher was #4.

We proceeded north to the Yalu. No MiG activity on our side of the river. So, after turning off our IFF beacons (which could tell our own radar at Chodo which side of the river we were on!), I took the flight a little further north towards an airfield called Fengcheng that we knew the MiGs were using.

We arrived over Fengcheng at about 45,000. Looking down, I observed around 30-40 MiGs taking off from the field. This is too good to be true! I told my guys to 'Drop tanks!', and we peeled off and headed down towards the MiG base. As we passed through about 20,000 feet, I noticed about 15-20 MiGs that were orbiting over the field at our altitude. They were undoubtably there to provide cover for the MiGs that were taking off.

We continued on down at a very high rate of speed. I leveled off behind two of the MiGs at about 500 feet altitude, opening fire on the nearest MiG to me. Due to our speed, my closure rate was terrific. I fired a long burst, hitting the MiG the whole time. The MiG blew up right in my face.

I immediately picked out a second MiG farther ahead and opened fire. My speed continued to let me close at a high rate. I hit the second MiG all the way in. I pulled up over his right wing and watched as the MiG rollled over, crashed and exploded about 500 feet below me. I then observed a third MiG turning right, just ahead and low on the tree tops.

I figured I was about run out of ammunition so I told my wingman, Lt. Jones, "Take him Harry, I'll cover you." Harry opened fire hitting the MiG in the aft section. The Migs tail came off and it crashed in the hills. Meanwhile Lonnie and Bill Schrimser were also shooting. They destroyed two, one of which I saw crash and explode. Then, the roof fell in!

The MiGs we had gone through on our way down to get the guys in the traffic pattern, were now streaming down on top of us. I yelled for everyone to get out and take advantage of the few clouds that were around. With the speed we had built up in the dive and attack, we were able to shake off the MiGs before we got back to the Yalu. We, a flight of four, had destroyed five MiGs in less than two minutes. I received the only damage when some pieces from the first MiG I had shot down hit my aircraft. Nothing serious however and everyone made it back safely.

Totals for the mission - Garrison, two MiGs destroyed, Harry Jones, one destroyed, Lonnie Moore, one destroyed and a share of another with Bill Schrimser. Lt.Col. Vermont Garrison became the thirty-seconbd jet ace in the Korean War on this mission. Of course, as soon as they landed, the crew chief exposed the gun camera film since there were some strange objects like control towers and fuel trucks on it. UFOs I guess.

19 July 1953. No.10 for the 'Grey Eagle'. Lt.Col. Vermont Garrison taxiis into his parking spot with no tanks and dirty guns – MiGs were sighted, shot down same. Lt.Col. Garrison had 7 1/3 victories in World War II. (Don Miller)

nine

MiG Killers and Wingmen

In Korea, the fighter doctrine was the same as it had been during World War II. It worked against both the Luftwaffe and the Japanese Air Force, so why wouldn't it work against the MiGs in Korea. U.S. Air Force tactics evolved around a basic combat formation of two airplanes, called an element. A flight was made up of two elements. Within the element was a lead airplane and his wingman.

When MiGs were sighted, the flight leader would make the attack. If more than one MiG was involved, the flight broke down into two elements, with each element lead staking out a target MiG. The job of the lead aircraft was to attack the enemy aircraft. The job of his wingman was to watch his leaders tail for any other MiGs that might try and sneak in behind the attacking Sabres.

One of the favorite MiG tactics was to send a lone MiG into a sky full of Sabres, wait until one of the Sabre flights started to get into firing position, then zoom down out of the sun, pull in behind the attacking Sabres, and shoot one or both Sabres down. It was a good tactic unless you were the 'volunteer' that led the Sabres into the trap. It was the Sabre wingman that kept that from happening.

In the early days of the conflict, the role of the wingman was emphasized in the "Clobber College" sessions taught to all new guys prior to assignment to one of the combat units in Korea. Later, after the 4th Wing moved to Kimpo, the schools were held on base or during some routine flights far below MiG Alley.

It was the leader, and only the leader, that got to fire on a MiG that was staked out. The only time a wingman got to fire was if a MiG flew directly in front of him, or if his Lead 'fired out', i.e. used up all his ammunition, and he would tell the wingman to finish the job. In this case, the victory credit would be shared by both pilots.

In Korea, you 'flew the wing' until you were promoted to element lead. That was usually about 35+ mission. Of course, there were some pilots that made Lead right away. Guys like 2/Lt. Jim Low who shot down a MiG on his second mission, and made ace about five weeks and thirty missions later. But Low was the exception to the rule.

Some pilots never did get to fly Lead. It could be because they were unlucky, unaggressive, or simply a bad pilot. You had to be in the right spot at the right time to even see the MiGs. It was not uncommon for a pilot to fly his 100 missions and never see the MiGs. Or if he saw them they were far away, too far for any type of engagement to occur. Or he was stuck with an 'ace' pilot, i.e. someone that needed the victories to achieve acedom or better.

The wingman's role was usually tougher than his leader. While Lead would be watching the MiG he'd staked out, the wingman had to watch everywhere else. And had to fly right with his leader throughout the combat maneuvers, which were often quite violent and erratic. And you had to know when to call your leader off his attack due to impending danger from attack from another angle. If you called too soon, a possible victory was lost and your leader would be quite upset. If you called too late, it could end up in disaster for both you and your leader.

For every MiG victory scored in Korea, their was a wingman that did not score. But his leader always gave him proper credit. Some pilots gave their victories to their wingman in appreciation of their efforts. Col. Harrison Thyng is known to have given at least three MiG kills to his wingmen after he had made ace. These are the stories of the men that did not make ace. Some were MiG-killers, some were wingmen.

1/Lt. Robert Makinney, 334th Fighter Interceptor Squadron,
Suwon AB, 8 July 1951

During the early stages of the war, the 4th FIW had a dual mission – protect the fighter bombers by flying fighter sweeps between the target area and any MiGs attempting to intercept the friendlies; and escort of B-29 Superforts conducting daylight missions against targets throughout North Korea.

The afternoon mission for 8 July 1951 was a bomber escort to the Pyongyang area. I was scheduled for the mission. It was my fifth combat mission and I hadn't even seen an enemy airplane yet. The normal procedure for new guys like me, was the first mission was an orientation ride up the west coast to the mouth of the Yalu (called the Hot Spot), then fly eastward up the river to the Suiho Reservoir (the Mizu), then back south across the very center of North Korea back to our base at Suwon. Suwon (K-13) was Homeplate for the 4th FIG in the summer of 1951. Later that summer we moved back up to Kimpo (K-14).

Appropriate sign on 4th Group Operations at Kimpo in 1952. (O.C. Wilkinson)

From the Hot Spot, we could see the three major MiG bases at Antung, Ta Tung Kou, and at Takushan. It made me nervous as every base was covered with shiny silver MiG-15s. But for me, none had gotten airborne – YET! For this flight I would be flying the number two position in the lead flight. I was flying wing for one of the most famous fighter pilots of all time – Colonel Francis "Gabby" Gabreski, the World War II ace with something like thirty-four victories. He had recently arrived in Korea and was the 4th FIW Deputy Wing Commander.

An element of 335th Squadron Sabres enroute to MiG Alley in late 1952. The basic U.S. Air Force fighter formation is the element of two. The element leader is the offensive pilot that goes after the enemy aircraft. The wingman's mission is defensive, watching for enemy aircraft moving into position on the flight. (Karl Dittmer)

We took off from K-13 to the south, in elements of two, with all elements joining in squadron formation as we made a 180° turn back to the north just east of Homeplate. Their were sixteen aircraft, four flights of four. We were Dignity Mike Flight, and the Colonel was Dignity Mike Lead, Dig Mike for short. I was Dig Mike Two.

We climbed out on a northwest heading, crossed the Haeju Peninsula, and leveled off at 25,000 feet. We rendezvoused with the B-29s as they coasted in just north of Chinampo at the mouth of the Taedong River. They were in three three-ship vees. According to the ops plan, we crossed over the Superfort formation, setting up a race track pattern to the north of the bombers. Approaching the target, the radio chatter suddenly intensified. Flak was appearing everywhere, both above and below the bomber formation.

Suddenly the radio came alive as the Superfort flight commander called – "Dignity, this is Jakeman (the B-29 flight call sign). We are at 'Windy'" 'Windy' was the point five minutes from bomb release. This also was an advisory to the F-51 flights that were attacking the flak batteries, to get the hell out of the way!

As soon as the Superforts had crossed over the target and released their load of bombs, we initiated a turn to the south. Again, the radio was alive. It was the F-51 flight commander – "Dignity, this is Filter Leader (the F-51 call sign). We have bandits in the area!"

But our mission was to protect the bombers, and we continued our escort until the B-29s were well out of the area. Colonel Gabreski got on the radio and called the bomber commander – "Jakeman, this is Dig Mike Lead. We have you clear of the area. We'd like to break off and go back and help Filter." Jakeman replied – "Roger, and thanks for the cover."

Gabby made a hard turn back toward Pyongyang, and called "Dig Mike – drop your tanks and go to 100%!" With the increase in power, and having lost the drag of our underwing drop tanks, we accelerated immediately, and initiated a climb to altitude. Within minutes we were approaching Pyongyang from the southeast at over 30,000 feet, and going well over .92 Mach.

Without warning, Gabby suddenly dropped his nose and brought his power back almost to idle. It was obvious that he had sighted something. But try as I might, I couldn't see any-

Often the wingman will take the brunt of an enemy attack. 1Lt. Bob Makinney had the canopy shot off his F-86A in a fight with the MiGs. (Bob Makinney)

Right: 1Lt. Robert W Smith (335th) flew as a wingman for about forty mission before moving to Element Lead. His final score in Korea was two kills, one probable, and two damaged. Following Korea, (then) Maj. Smith flew the NF-104A to a World Altitude Record of 120,800 feet. (Bob Smith)

Left: 1Lt. Bob Smith and other 335th pilots enjoy themselves at Swig Alley, the O-Club at Kimpo. (Bob Smith) Right: 1Lt. Chuck Loyd stands in the hole where a MiG 37mm cannon shell almost took his left flap completely off. Loyd's Sabre was bracketed by the MiG pilot and suffered extensive damage to both flaps. Without flaps, Loyd's landing was exciting to say the least. (Bob Makinney)

thing. In the dive, we accelerated to about the F-86s maximum speed of Mach 1, as we descended below 20,000 feet. Gabby started firing at an extremely excessive range. I could see the smoke exiting his gun ports, blowing back over his fuselage. But I still didn't see what it was that he was shooting at.

I slid in closer to Gabby's tail as he fired a second burst. I was about fifty to sixty feet below and behind him, kind of like 'flying the slot' in an aerobatic team formation. Straining my eyes, I then saw what it was that he was firing at. A MiG! The first one I'd ever seen up close. And this MiG was in trouble. Gabby was lighting him up all along the trailing edge of his right wing with his .50 calibers. The MiG pulled up sharply, Gabby followed, firing again and scoring more hits on the MiG fuselage.

At this point, with his greater air speed, Gabby overshot the MiG, sliding past him and climbing a couple of hundred feet above the MiG. I maneuvered into position where the MiG was in my sights. I was sorely tempted to fire, but instinctively thought "It's Gabby's kill, not mine." More importantly, I was a wingman and my leader was out in front of me (and the MiG), and needed my eyes to keep him in the clear. Without another thought, I added power, slid past the MiG and rejoined Gabby, who was still in my peripheral sight.

As I flew past the MiG, he had rolled inverted, and was starting into an almost vertical dive. I was sure he had lost his engine and would ultimately crash. And with that thought, I rejoined Gabby, who was in a right turn already looking for more bandits.

I had just regained my proper wing position when Gabby again dove for the deck. This time the descent was much more orderly. As we leveled off around 6,000 feet, Gabby opened fire at a MiG at a range of about 1500 feet. I watched as numerous pieces of the MiG's tail started to come off as Gabby's rounds hit. The MiG pilot took no evasive action, just continued a slight descending flight. We watched as the MiG crossed the Taedong River and crashed into a hill on the south bank.

At this point we were at low altitude, and very close to Bingo fuel. The radio chatter had subsided to the point that it seemed to be about the right time to head for home. As we

Right: Maj. Frederick 'Boots' Blesse (334th) in the cockpit of his assigned aircraft in the Summer of 1952, F-86E #51-2821, following his 'ace mission' on 4 September 1952. Maj. Blesse would score another five MiGs in Korea, then write a tactics manual for air-to-air gunnery, "No Guts, No Glory", which is still used today. (USAF)

climbed back to altitude for the flight home, I asked Gabby – "Was that two?" He replied – "Negative." At the debriefing, Gabby explained that he had attacked a single MiG. When the MiG dove for the deck and leveled off at low altitude, the MiG pilot was probably hoping we'd lost him and he would be able to escape from the beating he'd sustained. It's highly unlikely that he'd have made it back the 100 miles to his base north of the Yalu. Gabby's second attack made sure of it! It was Colonel Gabreski's first kill in Korea. He would get one more in the 4th FIW, then add 4 1/2 MiGs to his total after he took over command of the 51st FIW in September 1951.

By 1953, the facilities at Kimpo were reasonably comfortable. This is the 336th Squadron alert hut showing the homemade lounge chairs made from drop tank crates and tent canvas. By this date, the alert pilots no longer had to sit in the cockpit. (Howard Weston)

Lt. Martin Bambrick (left) flew wing for Capt. Bob Love, eleventh jet ace of the war, in the 335th Squadron during the Spring of 1952. He moved to Element Lead in the Summer, flying with 1Lt. Henry Crescibene (right), and scoring a victory on 4 September 1952. (Martin Bambrick)

Lt. Don Jabusch, 335th Fighter Interceptor Squadron
9 September 1951

I was flying number two on the wing of Major 'Bones' Marshall, our squadron commander. The mission was a Combat Air Patrol, and we took off in the early afternoon of 9 September 1951. Today I had the pleasure of flying Colonel 'Gabby' Gabreski's personal F-86, which carried his nickname "Gabby" on the nose.

After patrolling for some time in the area between Sinuiju and Sinanju, Major Marshall and I became separated from the rest of the flight after making initial contact with the MiGs. At the time we were at 30,000'. We had just rolled out of a turn and I was on his left side moving back up to get in a good line abreast position, when I experienced a loud explosion in my cockpit.

Instantly all the plexiglass was gone from my canopy, as well as my helmet and oxygen mask. I immediately rolled my airplane inverted, assuming that I had been hit by a MiG, and pulled into a full throttle split-S. The wind was curling around the windscreen so I couldn't see to my rear. On the way down I made several abrupt jinking maneuvers in the event that the MiG was still back there.

1Lt. Martin Bambrick (335th) flew "Wham Bam", F-86E #51-2821, which carried some of Capt. Karl Dittmer's famous artwork, after Maj. 'Boots' Blesse got an F-86F. Bambrick flew one of the older A model Sabres, #49-1272, when he was on Bob Love's wing. (Karl Dittmer)

I leveled off at 1500 feet and noticed a stinging sensation in my left eyebrow. When I touched it with my finger, it came away bloody. It was then that I noticed my instrument panel was getting liberally speckled with the red stuff. About that time I checked my airspeed indicator and saw that I was still going about 560 knots. I had pulled out of my dive heading west, with the intent of getting out over the water in case I had to eject. Knowing that I couldn't make it back to Kimpo at 1500', I started to climb to over 10,000 feet to conserve fuel.

The flight back along the coast was uneventful. But it seemed to take forever since I'd throttled back to 230 knots to conserve fuel. I had some concern as I came by Inchon. We'd been told never to overfly the Inchon harbor area as our Navy would shoot at anything that flew over. But they either didn't see me, or they ignored me as nothing happened.

Above: Every bit as big a part of the MiG-killing flight as the pilot and his wingman, was the ground crew that kept the Sabres in tip-top condition. Lt.Col. William Cosby, 334th Squadron CO, waits for M/Sgt Rayburn to hit the starting switch on the type C-6 auxiliary power unit as his crew chief, A3C Wayne Dewey, stands by. Col. Cosby scored two MiG kills in "Funfrus", F-86F #51-2883. (USAF)

Right: 6 June 1952. Capt. Jere Lewis scored his 2nd victory flying with the 334th Squadron. June 6th was a bad day for the MiG forces as they lost eight aircraft, including four to 4th Wing pilots – Capt. Lewis, 1Lt. Jim Low, Maj. Felix Asla, and 1Lt. John Moore. (USAF)

Being low on fuel I came in from the north, rocking my wings so the tower would know that I had no radio. I was about to break for a landing when I noticed that I was head-on with a flight of Sabres that were just about to make the break. But they were landing to the north! And I was landing to the south! I throttled up, went over the top and fell in behind number four in the pattern. The landing was normal.

After getting parked I was able to see for the first time what had happened to my Sabre. I had taken one 23mm cannon shell in the left wing, just inboard and aft (less than a foot!) from my left wing fuel filler cap. It blew a hole in the fuel cell, so I was lucky it didn't flame right then. Undoubtedly shrapnel from the exploding cannon shell pierced the canopy, causing it to shatter. The flight surgeon fixed my eyebrow with four of his neatest whip stitches and I was good as new in a couple of days. The airplane took a little longer to fix.

Lt. Don Jabusch, 335th Fighter Interceptor Squadron 30 November 1951

Our friendly islands off the west coast of North Korea, i.e. Chodo Island, had been attacked frequently by aircraft including North Korean Air Force twin-engine bombers. Our spooks (CIA guys) by whatever means, had found out that the North Koreans were coming back in force to bomb the islands on the 30th of November. We were called into Combat Ops for a late briefing (for us), and went out to the airplanes for a 1600 hrs. takeoff.

We expected to find several bombers coming south at about the mouth of the Yalu, about thirty minutes after takeoff. On the way up to this turkey shoot, we flew east of the central ridge of mountains so as to confuse the enemy GCI radar as to our intentions. As we proceeded north, I was convinced that we were being set up for the grand kill. We were below the

A 335th Squadron crew chief takes a break on the alert ramp in the Summer of 1952, as a 15th TRS RF-80 taxies past. Alert aircraft were plugged in to the starter cart, with the crew chief on, in or under the aircraft at all times. The pilots could rest nearby as long as they were within running distance of the Sabre. (Drury Callahan)

1Lt. Don Jabusch was "The Jaybird" when he flew with the 335th Squadron in 1951. Lt. Jabusch flew with Maj. 'Bones' Marshall on several occasions. (Don Jabusch)

cons (contrails), so we weren't exposed very much. But the MiGs were up there, and they were coming south in great numbers.

We had other things in mind, the bombers, so we proceeded on as briefed. The other two squadrons were selected to make the first attacks on the bombers, later identified as Tu-2s, while my squadron flew top cover. The whole wing made a left turn as we neared the Yalu, and then all hell broke loose. One of the two Sabre squadrons attacking the bombers soon called that they were in on the bombers, and there was no apparent MiG support. So our squadron was given the Ok to come in for the attack.

We descended with lots of airspeed, and when we made our left turn in behind the bombers, we were going well over .9 Mach at least. Number 3 and I were on the inside of the turn so we got whipped off like a yo-yo as we started to engage. I shortly lost sight of my element leader and called to tell him so. There were so many F-86s rotating around the group of Tu-2s that I had no idea which one of these guys was my leader.

I continued my pass through the bomber formation, but was going so fast that I couldn't line up on anything. Since I'd lost my leader, I was supposed to go home. But I wanted to have one more try. I pulled up into something between a loop and a chandelle, and as I was inverted, flew right through a flight of MiGs heading south. I called out the bogies in a general call to anyone that might be interested, then continued my pass back toward the bombers. When you have flown wing all of your combat career, you really don't have a good idea of the shooting end of the action. I started to fire so early at that bomber, that an F-86 passed in front of me, shooting at the same target. After he got out of the way, I continued on in to shoot a few rounds. I saw some flashes, but I think that they were from the rear gunner shooting back at me.

When I pulled up from my pass, I looked back on what I can only describe as a Hollywood set. Bombers were going down in flames, bombers were crashing into the sea, with large explosions of smoke and flame, and parachutes were floating everywhere! Our guys claimed eight of the twelve Tu-2s as Destroyed. But a later intel report said that only one made it back to its base. Totals for the day included eight Tu-2s destroyed and two damaged, one MiG destroyed, and three LaGG-9 fighters destroyed. They didn't bother our friendly islands much after that day.

1Lt. Don Jabusch and another 335th Squadron pilot take off from K-14 in 1951 bound for the area of northwest Korea known forevermore as "MiG Alley." The MiGs were based just across the Yalu River and the 4th Wing Sabres had to fly 230 miles to meet them. (USAF)

6 April 1952 MiG killers and wingmen. Lt. Col. Zane Amell, 335th Squadron Commander, congratulates 1Lt. Billy Dobbs on his fourth victory, as (Left to right) 1Lt. Mike DeArmond, 1Lt. Al Smiley, Capt. Phil Colman, and 1Lt. Coy Austin look on. (USAF)

The crew chief of F-86F-10 #51-12962 named "The 6 Mc's", lines up the guns on the harmonization range at K-14 as Col. Harry Thyng taxies past. The mission was eventful as Col. Thyng dropped his tanks, but no MiGs were engaged as the guns show no sign of use. (USAF)

Lt.Col. Willard P. Dunbar, Jr, 336th Fighter Interceptor Squadron
4 July 1952 and 1 August 1952

It was July 4th 1952, and we were going to celebrate the holiday by bombing the North Korean Military Academy graduation exercises at their school about forty miles south of the Suiho Reservoir. I was flying wing with Major Felix Asla. We were John Red 1 and 2. The F-80 and F-84 fighter bombers would do the bombing. We flew top cover. The MiGs were everywhere that day. I vectored us to a single that was going down river towards the MiG base at Antung. Major Asla already had four MiGs and this was his chance to make ace.

There had already been a number of battles in the area and there were a number of chutes in the air. We passed very close to one of them as we started down on the lone MiG. We were close enough to the chute as we went by, to see the brown leather helmet with goggles and leather flying suit that the pilot was wearing. Definitely not one of ours. He had hold of his risers and appeared to be conscious even though he was above 30,000 feet.

As we approached the MiG we had staked out, he suddenly turned left 90°, then quickly turned left another 90° as Major Asla turned in on him. Asla misled the turn and was some 3,000 feet in trail. But he hosed off a few rounds anyway, and I saw fuel come off the MiG in white streaks. Again, the MiG turned left 90°, and headed northwest across the Yalu. Asla again underled the turn, and did not gain on the MiG. I had stayed high and had cut both of them off on every turn, which put me above and forward of both the MiG and Major Asla.

I was sure the MiG had been hit and was slowing down. I asked Major Asla for permission to make a pass on him from my position of advantage. But he said he was low on fuel and that we should break it off and head for home. I had plenty of fuel left, and felt I could have gotten that MiG had I gotten permission to shoot. But orders are orders, and Asla had missed the chance to get his fifth MiG. I still think that one was meant to be 'my MiG'.

The 1 August 1952 mission ended in tragedy. I was flying Capt. Dick Moyle's wing, as John White 1 and 2. We were up on the River and Moyle spotted a MiG far below us. We dropped out tanks and dove down on the MiG at Mach 1. I remember rolling around Moyle during the dive since I couldn't reach the aileron trim on my airplane in this condition and at that speed. I saw the MiG Moyle was after and executed a seven G turn and pull-up as Moyle tried to get on the MiGs tail.

To get this kind of Gs on an F-86A required an unusual technique. I used 1 1/2° of nose-up trim, and held the stick forward against the instrument panel as the airplane executed the high G turn. The MiG rapidly climbed away from us as Moyle fired uselessly at around 3,000 feet. I didn't see it, but the MiG had just shot down one of our guys. It was John Red Lead, the commander of the 336th Squadron, Major Felix Asla, and my leader on the previous mission. Moyle said the MiG hit Asla in the left wing with one of the big 37mm cannon shells, and the whole wing came off. Asla was killed when the Sabre spun in.

Moyle then concentrated on the MiG that had gotten Asla and didn't see any chute. John Red 2, Asla's wingman, had become separated from Red 1 during the battle. We figured that Asla thought that the MiG was Red 2 attempting to rejoin on him since he took absolutely no evasive action as the MiG was closing on him. Major Felix Asla had 4 1/2 MiGs at the time, and had quit logging missions past ninety-eight trying to make ace.

1/Lt. Drury Callahan, 334th Fighter Interceptor Squadron 1 August 1952

The weather finally broke and allowed us to go on a mission. It was a max effort and we sent every airplane we had. We didn't have to do much hunting, however. The MiGs were waiting for us when we got there.

This was my fortieth mission. I was No.2 in Charlie Flight. We started engines at 0841, and were airborne five minutes later. We left Kimpo by flights in one minute intervals. We were the seventh flight. Charlie Flight arrived in MiG Alley about seven minutes after the first flight began their patrol. The radar at Chodo had picked up several MiG flights in our area, and we were searching for them, but no contact yet.

About a minute later Yellow Flight made contact at 40,000 feet over the Suiho Reservoir. They called out "Bandits!", and we headed for that area. My flight was at 25,000 feet, just east of Antung, but headed west. We reversed and started toward the Dam area. Almost immediately, I saw numerous flights above and on both sides of us, but still too distant for identification. But just in case, we dropped our tanks, pushed the throttle full forward, and began to build up some speed and altitude.

I started checking our rear to clear my leader, who was beginning to set up an attack on the bogies to our left, which we'd now positively identified as MiGs. As a matter of fact, everywhere that I looked there were MiGs! Off to one side I caught a glimpse of a MiG spinning violently earthward, spouting smoke and flames. Someone above me had already gotten one, but I didn't have time to watch him go down.

By now, my leader was in a firing position on a MiG and let him have a short burst. I saw his bullets hit on the aft fuselage. The MiG pilot didn't like that at all, and started to take evasive action. We went through a complete turn with him, and my leader got in another burst, hitting the MiG in the right wing and fuselage. But the MiG still wasn't hurt very badly and was still flying. I'm sure we could have finished him off, if it hadn't been for another MiG that made a sudden attack on us.

I saw this other MiG start in on us and called the breaks for Lead as I stayed out of the MiG gun sight. From then on we fought with this fellow for about ten minutes. He just wouldn't let go. This MiG driver was really good. And he seemed determined to give us a hard time. We went through several scissors maneuvers and a couple of Lufberrys with him. Each of us trying to get a firing position on the other. I was real busy trying to see where my leader was going, where the MiG was, and if any other MiGs were closing on us.

After about ten minutes of this, with nobody even getting a shot off, we were getting pretty close to 'Bingo fuel'. We couldn't just break off from the fight, because if we did, the MiG would immediately jump on our tails. But, the MiG must have been getting tired, and being alone, was at a slight disadvantage. We had slowly started to pull lead on him, gradually pulling around behind him. When the MiG pilot saw what was happening, he decided to call it quits. And being in a MiG, he was capable of doing just that at any time. He just straightened out and climbed away from us like we had stalled.

The whole fight had taken place right over the Suiho Reservoir. There were many other fights going on, but this was the only one I was interested in. Due to our fuel situation, we were forced to withdraw. There was still plenty of MiG activity, but we had to break off. Our element, Charlie 3 and 4, became separated from us during the first attack, and they weren't anywhere around to help us. They had their hands full of MiGs anyway. We returned to Kimpo without incident and landed at 10:15 local time.

The results were mixed, with us having a slight edge. We lost one '86 when a MiG blew the squadron commander's wing off. It was Major Felix Asla. Goes to show that even the big wheels can get careless too. Four birds had major damage. One of those that made it back to Kimpo was flown by Earl Brown. He was just lucky to make it back. A MiG got on his tail and put a 37mm cannon shell in his left wing. It blew a huge hole in the wing, and only missed the main spar by inches.

Brown was saved by his flight leader, who pulled in behind the MiG at a range of about 100 feet and opened fire with his six .50s. The MiG exploded and turned into a sheet of flame. This was the MiG I had seen spinning down. We destroyed three, and damaged five more. So we came out on top. We all had to admit though, that we'd have lost more Sabres if the MiG pilots could shoot better. They had their 'first team' in yesterday, because all of them knew how to fly real good!

1 Lt. William F. Loyd, 336th Fighter Interceptor Squadron 13 March 1953

I arrived at Kimpo (K-14) in November 1952, having just finished F-86 training at Nellis AFB – or should I say "survived." There were thirty of us that qualified to fly the F-86 after F-80 training. Ten of the original gang were killed in crashes, and two of us graduated! The rest washed out! After arriving at K-14, I was assigned to Charlie Flight in the 336th Fighter squadron. The pilots in 'C Flight' all lived together in the same tent. It was just like a club. We worked together, played together, flew together, and often died together.

Sometime in mid-November, we got a new flight leader. I can picture his entrance as clearly today as if it had happened just yesterday. It was about 5 pm local time, and we were in our tent waiting for chow, when in he came. But lo and behold, he wasn't wearing a uniform like ours. He was Royal Air Force. And he calmly announced, "I am Squadron Leader Hulse, from Her Majesties Royal Air Force, and I have been assigned as commander of Charlie Flight. Let's dispense with the formalities and have a drink so that we can toast the Queen!" Which we promptly did!

Squadron Leader Graham Hulse had 750 hours of combat time flying Spitfires in North Africa. In comparison, we had about 250 hours total time in all types of aircraft. And very little of it was actual combat time. In our eyes, he was the epitome of the fighter pilot. And lucky me, I was going to be his wingman.

On my seventh mission, Graham was leading and I was

Above: 1Lt. Drury Callahan (334th) next to his F-86E "Erin Go Braugh", F-86E #50-640. Lt. Callahan flew wing for Capt. Bill Lilley on several occasions. Lt. Callahan's regular aircraft was "Erin Go Braugh" (below), an early F-86E-5. (Drury Callahan)

on his wing. We were flying a Yalu River sweep when my main fuel regulator quit and the engine flamed out. I didn't panic and started to go through the procedures of switching over to the emergency system and trying for an air start. Suddenly the radio crackled and it was Hulse calling me. "I know you're a little busy trying to change over to the emergency fuel system, but we better take some evasive action as there're MiGs all round us!"

Hulse broke left and I broke right – still trying to get that damn engine started. There were four MiGs behind me. Me! None of them went after Hulse. One at a time they bore in on me. Just like making a firing pass against the target rag in training. With one hand I was ramming that stick all over the cockpit. The airplane responded well enough that none of the MiG drivers got a good shot at me. All the while that I'm jinking with an unpowered airplane, my other hand is trying to get all the right switches and knobs in the right position to restart the engine. For whatever reason, suddenly the MiGs broke off and went back across the river. My attitude changed considerable after that flight as I knew I could get away from the MiGs if it became necessary.

2nd Lieutenants flew wing most of the time – unless they started scoring right away. In February 1953, I got spot promoted to 1st Balloon. And on the 13th of March 1953, I got to fly my 55th mission – and the first one in a 'lead position'. I was number 3, or element leader. S/L Hulse was again leading Charlie Flight. We saw a pack of MiGs just across the river heading west, back towards Antung.

We were flying a Fluid Four, the standard combat formation commonly called a 'finger four'. The MiGs kept heading west as we passed head-on about five miles apart. Suddenly, eight of them made a sharp turn south, straight across the Yalu toward us. Hulse called to "Drop tanks!", and we turned north into the oncoming MiGs. As we came around on the MiGs, I saw that I was ahead of Charlie Lead. He cleared me to fire and I opened up on the trailing MiGs.

But I was way out of range. The MiG saw me fire and started turning. But inexplicably, he turned into me, which gave me the chance to close on him. We did that about three times, Each time the MiG would break into me. And as he did so, the range between us would close. Finally, although I was still out of range at about 2,000 feet, I fired a good, long burst, which caught the MiG in the tail and up the left side of the fuselage. The MiG pilot ejected at 47,000 feet, and immediately opened his parachute. At that altitude, there was little chance of his survival since the air is so thin. As we went by him, he was already limp.

When we got back to Kimpo, I told Hulse that I didn't mean to cut him out of the pattern. But he simply replied that "it was OK, there were plenty of MiGs for all of us." He said that he was flying the afternoon mission and he'd get one then. But he was shot down that afternoon and didn't come out during the prisoner exchanges at the end of the war. It was a tragic loss to all of us in Charlie Flight.

Capt. Murray 'Buzz' Winslow, 335th Fighter Interceptor Squadron
K-14 Late 1952/Early 1953

On this day I was flying wing on the squadron CO, Lt.Col. Carrol McElroy. Everyone had departed the area, having reached the 'Bingo' fuel state. Col. McElroy and I were alone, but had plenty of fuel left. He decided that we'd make one last sweep northeast up the Yalu. Sometimes the MiGs would wait until the majority of the '86s had departed the area, and then they'd cross the river southbound to try and catch a straggler F-86 that was low on fuel.

Anyway, a flight of MiGs passed underneath us on their climbout, and evidently hadn't seen us, or us them initially. Looking down I was the first to spot the MiGs and Col. McElroy gave me the lead. Diving to gain speed, I made a slow climb up underneath the MiG flight with Col. Mac covering me. At 45,000 feet, the radar gunsight locked on at 2600 feet range, and I managed a perfect radar track on the last MiG. I fired one good burst, which hit the MiG dead center in the fuselage. The MiG rolled over and dove for the ground, smoking and burning. It finally exploded as it hit the lower altitude.

Knowing that it was going in, I had stopped my chasing dive at about 20,000 feet, and leveled off. Col. Mac called me and calmly said "I got a MiG up here." Looking up, I saw two swept wing aircraft in a tight turn to the left about 5,000 feet above me. Looking around quickly to clear Mac's tail of other MiGs, I called to him and told him to take the shot, that he was clear. He quickly retorted "The MiG is shooting at me!" I pulled up into a vertical climb, timing the maneuver to have them fly right over me. As Col. Mac went by, I fired a burst in front of the MiG and then stalled out. But it was enough to scare the MiG off Mac's tail. Neither of us had any problems on the way back, but you can imagine the riding I got back at Kimpo for that radio comment which everyone naturally had heard.

It was 23 October 1952, and I was again flying wing when I got my first kill. And again, it was the result of the MiGs coming across the river as we hit the 'Bingo' state. I can't re-

1Lt. Boothe Holker talks with his hands as he explains to his wingman, 2Lt. Robert W. Smith, how he scored two MiG kills on 25 September 1951. Lt. Smith must have learned well as he made element leader in early 1952 and shot down two MiGs himself. (USAF)

member the name of my leader on that mission. We had headed south and were the last element out of the 'Alley'. About fifty miles south of the Yalu, the radar at Chodo called us and said that we were being trailed. We did a quick 180° turn, heading back north at 40,000 feet.

Several minutes elapsed and suddenly we met a flight of four MiGs head on. I think they were as surprised as we were and we flew right through their formation. The MiGs made a climbing right turn, and we turned left, giving chase from below and behind them. One MiG rolled over into a dive, heading north right in front of us. We started to follow and closed the range. I hesitated a moment and suddenly another MiG dove after my leader. He left me no alternative but to give chase. As I looked back over my shoulder, I could see the remaining pair of MiGs dive after me.

I called my leader and told him that he had a MiG on his tail, but it wasn't close enough to fire. He just said – "Tell me when to break!" There we were, in a line, MiG, F-86, MiG, F-86, two MiGs, all in a dive, with no one close enough to fire. At about 10,000 feet, I told my leader to "Break right now!" At this point, the first MiG pulled up and headed back north. The MiG behind my leader tried to turn with him, but I cut him off in the turn and closed the range rapidly. The two MiGs behind me pulled up and headed north, leaving me the opportunity for a clear shot. Closing still further, I fire a long burst, which hit the MiG heavily in the fuselage. He bailed out almost immediately.

Capt. Murray Winslow and Lt.Col. Norm Green at K-14 in 1952. 'Buzz' Winslow scored 4 victories while flying with the 335th Squadron. He was also assigned to the GUNVAL project in early 1953. (Norm Green)

There were occasions when the MiGs would spend days without coming across the river. We would become frustrated for not being allowed to follow them 'in hot pursuit' back across the river and engage them. But those were the rules. Sometimes a single MiG would just orbit over our area at very high altitude, then return north across the river. There was very little we could do as the F-86 just wouldn't get up as high as a MiG.

Capt. George Love was "Silent George" when he flew this F-86F with the 336th Squadron in late Spring 1953. Capt. Love scored 1 1/2 victories in the war, sharing a MiG kill with his wingman, 2Lt. George Lefevers on 30 June 1953. (Alan Fine)

This, a single high flying MiG, occurred once when I had a lead position in the flight. I spotted him descending back across the river. My radar ranging locked on at maximum range – over 6000 feet. Knowing full well I could never catch him, I caged the gun sight, took a high sight picture for the great distance, and fired a burst. It seemed like ten seconds went by, when to my astonishment and my wingman's, I actually got some strikes on the MiG. The MiG driver was probably as shocked as we were. One more damaged.

Squadron Leader Graham Hulse, RAF, stands with Capt. Stuart Childs under the 336th Squadron torii at K-14 in 1953. S/L Hulse, was a World War II Spitfire pilot, adding a total of two MiGs in Korea. S/L Hulse was shot down on 13 March 1953. (Bob Windoffer)

Captain John Hoye, 335th Fighter Interceptor Squadron Spring 1953

I was assigned to the 81st Fighter Interceptor Group at RAF Bentwaters during the Korean War. But our group voluntarily rotated one pilot from each of our squadrons, to Korea for a three month TDY tour. We wanted to get some experience against the MiG. I got in thirty-three missions with the 335th FIS at Kimpo, and was in an engagement with the MiGs about six times. I only got to fire one time, when I tried to catch a MiG from below. But I couldn't get anywhere near his altitude, even though I was at my max speed and rate of climb.

After completing the course at "Clobber College", I went to Kimpo to fly combat with the veteran 4th Fighter Wing, arriving in the Spring of 1953. As with all new arrivals at Kimpo, I was assigned the wing position on my first combat flights, in spite of my experience flying the Sabre in England. A lot of the wingmen were freshly graduated from The Fighter School at Nellis, and most people had to fly about forty to fifty missions to get to be even an Element Leader. To get a Flight Lead, you might have to go up to seventy-five missions. Since the guys from the 81st FIG were all well experienced in the '86, and many had previous combat in World War II, I got to lead an Element in about ten missions time.

But on one of my first missions as a wingman, the Flight Leader had a 'ratted tailpipe' airplane, which neither I nor the other element pair could keep up with. "Ratting the tailpipe" was the installation of small metal tabs into the tailpipe, which effectively raised the tailpipe temperature and increased thrust, which gave additional speed. Neither the North American or GE reps condoned this, but all the hot pilots did it anyway.

While I was trying to both keep track of my leader, and catch up with him, I was jumped by a pair of MiGs at close range. However, I saw them just in the nick of time, and went around twice with them. I was gaining on both of them on every circle, but they broke off their attack and broke for the River. Had I known at the time what I found out later, that lots of victories were scored on the 'wrong side' of the River, I would have been able to really make hay. But my background with the 81st included a lot of flight integrity. And I obeyed the rules. I had often wished that I had just let my Leader take care of his own tail, since he persisted in running away from the rest of our flight, and that I had followed that pair of MiGs across the River and clobbered them. But that was not how I was taught.

2/Lt. Nelson Allen, 336th Fighter Interceptor Squadron 13 April 1953

It was 13 April 1953. I'd just graduated from flying school and earned my Pilot's Wings. I had a grand total of three hundred hours in the cockpit. I considered myself the World's Hottest Second Lieutenant Fighter Pilot in the famous 4th Fighter Group. And this was my first mission.

Being a FNG (Frigging New Guy), I had flown a half dozen 'low risk' missions just to get the feel of things in Korea, and to get the ultimate nod of approval from the guys who had been in Korea. The training game was over. It was now time to 'sweep' MiG Alley.

On 13 April, I was flying in the #2 position – where an FNG belongs. Our call sign was Anzac Boxer. Anzac Boxer Lead was Captain Dean Pogreba, I was #2, Captain Pete Frederick was #3 and Element Lead, with Lt. Bob Kearse on his wing. We had a max effort that day, forty eight Sabres. We were the last flight in the last squadron off the runway at Kimpo.

Being the last ones off the runway meant we would also be the last flight to retire from the Alley. And that's exactly what happened. After all the flights had withdrawn, Dean called for a fuel check. Then said, "Let's run down the river one more time and see if they'll come across." They did! The next thing I heard was Boxer 3 calling "Heads up Boxer, Bandits at twelve o'clock!"

Being a dutiful wingman, I had been busy watching our tails, the six o'clock position. My job was to protect my leader. And his job was to shoot down the MiGs. So when I turned to check the twelve o'clock position, I damn near had a mid-air with one of the MiGs. Our wingtips actually overlapped! We were at exactly the same altitude and attitude. The only reason we didn't hit was because the F-86 has a low wing, while the MiG had a mid-wing. It was that close."

"The aerodynamic cushion of air under his wing literally 'bumped' my Sabre. We were each pulling about .92 Mach, which meant the closure rate was over 1350 mph! That's about 1700 feet per second. Our cockpits passed within twenty feet of each other. I can still see a clear image of the red helmet that MiG driver was wearing. And that's when it happened."

"We cranked into a hard right turn, and the MiGs cranked into a hard left turn. When this whole thing started, we were heading west and they were heading east. Bear in mind that we were almost above the service ceiling of the F-86. Even though we were pushing Mach One at 46,000 feet, that was right on the ragged edge of stall for the Sabre at that altitude."

"The MiG was a much better airplane at that altitude. So when I say we cranked it around, I meant we coaxed our Sabres into a 180° that probably had a thirty mile diameter. Combat at that altitude is pure finesse, a delicate touch. It's impossible to attain until the man and machine are one, in a sort of rapport. And I was barely on the threshold of that rapport."

"One of the axioms of fighter pilot lore which is <u>almost</u> true <u>almost</u> all of the time is that "If I can see the son of a bitch, he'll never shoot me down!" That's why we were absolutely obsessive about the minimum combat unit in Korea being a flight of two. It was mutual protection, two sets of eyeballs – you check my six, I'll check yours!"

"One of the reasons that I'm here today is that on that day, the contrails were intense and persistent. When I'm looking over my shoulder trying to find a relatively small object like a MiG, he's trailing this enormous plume of white vapor and not too hard to locate."

"Meanwhile, Pogreba was bouncing one of the MiGs. The MiG was in a left turn and Lead was closing on him. Good show! I was dutifully performing like a wingman and trying not to be a spoil sport. There were about thirty MiGs in the fray. The sky was so full of cons that it appeared almost overcast."

"While Pogreba was closing on his MiG, I was becoming a bit anxious about another MiG that was closing on him, or rather us. Being a hardened veteran of six whole missions, I wasn't going to choke up just because the last four Sabres in MiG Alley were playing tag with about thirty MiGs. And one of those MiGs was at our seven o'clock ... but still out of range ... sorta ... it looked like ... kinda ... and he wasn't pulling lead on us ... I thought."

"The problem was that if I called for my leader to disengage and break prematurely in the best interests of our survival, then the MiG he'd staked out would get away. If, on the other hand, I underestimated the threat, there was a high likelihood that neither of us would have the nightly beer call."

"I had all of this in mind as I glanced at Dean and his target. And somewhat nervously focused on 'Ol Beady Eyes' that was closing at our seven o'clock. Being a real cool dude, I advised Dean of the situation in ten words or less, – "We have a bandit closing, but don't sweat the small stuff. But if you don't shoot that MiG now, we're going to have to change our plans forthwith and concentrate our endeavors on ancillary matters such as our own survival ..." Something like that!"

"The hunters were about to become the hunted! Dean obliged my anxiety by firing a few rounds even though he was still out of 'lethal range'. I saw a few strikes on the MiG tail section and left wing root. I thought, 'Man, that's good shooting!' While Pogreba was doing this outstanding bit of long range sniping, I was checking the rear to see what 'Ol Beady Eyes' was up to."

"He seemed intent on ruining what started out to be a rather pleasant morning. Up to this point, we were really in control. I kept checking Beady Eyes. He was still a long way out ... I thought ... and besides ... I couldn't see the belly of his airplane so he couldn't be pulling lead on me ... I thought. Right?"

"Wrong! I don't know how those slobs harmonized their guns (the MiG mechanics), but the first burst from that big 37mm cannon went in front of me! That's when the cool dude flying Anzac Boxer 2, ME! mashed the mike button, adjusted my vocal chords up at least one octave, and yelled "Boxer Lead, break left NOW!"

"I'm sorry to say that I over-controlled, and did sort of a snap-spin thing. I got it flying again, going more or less straight down in a wind-up turn, with as many Gs on that airplane as it could handle up where the air is really thin, thin, thin. But those damn roman candles were still whizzing by, and I was running

A pair of 336th Sabres over North Korea in June 1953. 1st Lt. Cecil Lefevers flew FU-976 named "Speedy Lee", with the 336th Squadron. He shared a MiG kill with Capt. George Love on 30 June 1953. Often a shared kill was between a leader and his wingman if the leader ran out of ammo, i.e. 'fired out', or had some problem that diverted his attention. (via Warren Thompson)

out of ideas. Then Boxer Lead called me and said, "Roll out Two, you're clear!" I rolled right and saw 'Ol Beady Eyes heading for the dirt trailing a beautiful plume of black smoke. The MiG is really a pretty airplane, especially when it's heading down and trailing black smoke."

"Captain Dean Pogreba had saved my butt. I was green, new, a rookie. And on that day, I was dead in the sights of the MiG. Dean had given up a sure victory over the MiG he'd staked out to come to my aid and shoot that beady-eyed sucker off my ass. Dean Pogreba was a good leader. He had balance, judgment, wisdom, skill and guts. When I flew with him, I was ready to go to Mukden or Moscow. I knew if he took me there, he'd bring me out!"

ten

1953: A Year of Slaughter

1953 would be a year of slaughter for the Red Air Force. Slaughter that would be handed out by pilots in the 4th FIG. The Russian instructors were about to turn their North Korean and Red Chinese students loose to face the Sabres in MiG Alley alone. On the south side of the Yalu River, the two fighter interceptor groups would see their numbers double, when the 18th and 8th Fighter Bomber Groups converted to F-86Fs. Many of the newly arriving replacement pilots were combat veterans, from either World War II or previous combat in Korea. And of course, the brand new F-86F-30 arrived in Korea.

The F-86F had been in the theater since early Fall 1952. The biggest change was installation of the J47-GE-27 engine, with 6090 lbs. of thrust available. The additional thrust gave the F-86F the needed boost in rate of climb, top speed, and service ceiling. Although still not the equal of the MiG in any of these vital areas, the F-86F brought the American pilots close enough that the MiGs no longer had a clear cut advantage.

Other changes in the F-86F such as the installation of the A-4 gun sight with the AN/APG-30 ranging radar, gave the pilots a greater chance for a victory through technology. The APG-30 ranging radar could lock on to a MiG at a greater range, and many victories were achieved outside the normal range of previous F-86s. Many a MiG driver was surprised to find their silver steeds being bracketed by an airplane way beyond the range of the MiG guns.

With the F-86F-30, the Sabre had a strengthened wing, and now could carry either the normal pair of drop tanks and a pair of 1,000 lb. bombs, or four drop tanks to increase the range and patrol time over the Yalu. But it was the addition of the so-called '6-3 wing' that sounded the death knell to the MiG advantages. The '6-3 wing' had the wing chord increased six inches at the root, and 3 inches at the wingtip. Along with the increase, the leading edge slats were removed and replaced with a non-movable leading edge, with a 6" tall flow fence at 70% of the wingspan.

The '6-3 wing' gave the pilot an additional usable 1 1/2 Gs maneuvering at altitudes in excess of 35,000 feet. Now the Sabre pilot could turn inside the MiG. And with the new gun sight/ranging radar, pull lead on him in the turn – while closing the range at the same time. The new wing was added to the F-86F production line after the 200th -30 airplane had been built. But North American had the new wing built as a 'kit', which could be retrofitted to virtually any F-86E or F – and was. The first fifty kits were rushed to Korea in late 1952, and were added to many of the leading MiG-killers personal aircraft.

But one of the biggest things to change was the command of the Wing, which took place in November of 1952. On 17 November, Colonel James K. Johnson – "Jimmie K" to everyone that knew him or worked for him – took over command from Colonel King. Colonel Johnson would quickly be named "The Mayor Of Sabre City", and all his deputy commanders and squadron COs were his 'city council'.

Colonel Johnson was another of the many World War II veterans assigned to the 4th. He had over ninety missions in P-47 Thunderbolts with the 404th Fighter Group. Before going to Korea, 'Jimmie K' had commanded the Flying Training Group at The Fighter School at Nellis AFB, Nevada. Col. Johnson actually replaced Col. Thyng, who had rotated home in October 1952. Col. Charles King had been named acting wing commander until Col. Johnson arrived, after which he was appointed Deputy Wing Commander. Col. Johnson brought the aggressiveness of The Fighter School with him when he arrived at Kimpo. And he made sure all his pilots shared with him in that aggressiveness.

The weather in December cooperated, with only six days of limited missions, and only one day when Kimpo was completely shut down. The Group flew 1680 sorties that month, with the following results – seventeen destroyed, eight probables, and twenty-one damaged. The pilots reported that the MiGs seemed to have finally figured out that flight integrity was the key to less losses. The MiGs were now flying an effective element formation, and the wingman usually covered his leader effectively. This led to many of the 4th pilots having to break off their attacks before scoring a deadly hit, or seeing the results of their attack, i.e. either in pilot ejection or possibly seeing the MiG crash or explode.

The biggest day was the 14th, when Group pilots shot down five MiGs and damaged two more. One of the damaged credits went to Colonel Johnson, who got a probable kill the next day. That same day, the forth shot down three more MiGs and damaged another four. But the highlight of the day came when a pair of large, twin-jet aircraft made an appearance near the Suiho Dam. Had the Ilyushin Il-28 medium jet bomber made its entry into the Korean War? If that was true, the Reds had just escalated the entire complexion of the air war.

"BEEN WITH THE FOURTH LONG, SIR?"

Cartoon in 4th newspaper 1953. (Author)

Col. James K. Johnson shakes hands with his Group Commander with the 4th, Col. Royal Baker. Quickly dubbed the "Mayor of Sabre City", Col. Johnson took over command of the 4th Wing at Kimpo on 11 November 1952. (Sylvia Johnson)

Gunval

On 1 January, the first of an experimental F-86F arrived at K-14. These were F-86F-2 Sabres, armed with four 20mm cannon instead of the standard six .50s. It was called Project GUNVAL, and was under the command of Lt.Col. Clayton Peterson from the Eglin Armament Test Center. The GUNVAL project and test team, like the JATO-equipped experiment that preceded it, was assigned to the 335th FIS.

The GUNVAL F-86s were armed with four T-160 20mm cannons, later standardized as the M39 and used in the F-86H and F-100 Super Sabre. Each gun had only 200 rounds as the installation was jammed into a modified standard gun bay. The aircraft had flown extensive tests at Eglin AFB, Florida prior to their deployment for combat tests in Korea.

All the Sabre pilots had long complained of the lack of 'killing power' of the .50 caliber machine gun round against the MiG. These new cannon-armed Sabres should be the answer and all the pilots were anxious to fly them and see what they could do in MiG Alley. But it would soon be discovered that the additional hitting power of the cannon would be offset

The 336th Squadron torii that led to the aircraft told the story in a nut shell. (Ken Haugen)

APO-970, 4th FIW Headquarters at Kimpo in 1953. (Larry Hendle)

somewhat by problems associated with the experimental installation, problems never encountered in the low altitude tests flown in Florida.

North American built ten GUNVAL Sabres, eight of which were sent to Korea for combat testing. In December 1952, the eight GUNVAL Sabres were loaded aboard the USS Windham Bay, arriving at Kisarazu in the last week of the month. Following the usual stripping of waterproofing and decontamination by the 6408th Maintenance Support group at Kisarazu, the aircraft were flown to Kimpo at the beginning of the New Year.

Only highly qualified pilots were assigned to fly the GUNVAL aircraft in combat. The first missions were flown in the second week in January. Almost immediately, problems arose. Major Robert Moorehead was one of the pilots assigned to the GUNVAL tests in Korea. "Around the 10th of January, I led the first mission to combat test the cannon-armed Sabres. It was a standard MiG sweep. I arrived at the mouth of the Yalu, turned right and proceeded up the River, all the while gradually gaining altitude. About 60-70 miles up the River, I spotted four MiGs crossing just ahead of us, and ordered my flight to 'Drop tanks!'"

The "Scoshi Chief" was one of the Group T-33As. The T-33s were used for VIP flights, weather recon, and as director aircraft in which the mission commander could oversee a battle and call for other flights to help out. (Larry Hendle)

Maintenance facilities at Kimpo took a giant stride forward with the construction of the open air flightline shop. At least it didn't rain on you when you were working on the birds. Aircraft FU-836, one of the GUNVAL aircraft, is having an engine change in late March 1953. (Norm Green)

"We were at about 45,000 feet and I slid under and behind one of the MiGs. When we reached 46,000, the MiGs started a left turn and began slowly pulling away from us. They'd probably been alerted by their GCI controllers. Although they were at maximum range, the A-4 sight got a lock and I fired a short burst hoping to slow one of them down. Instead, the MiGs increased their turn rate and continued pulling away. About the same time, my element leader told me that we had MiGs at our seven o'clock – and closing!"

"In desperation, I held down the trigger for a long burst. We had only four seconds worth of ammo! All the time, I watched as cannon tracers passed over my canopy. Almost immediately, I felt a severe vibration, and my 'OVERHEAT' and 'FIRE' lights starting coming on. I had a flameout! I dove the aircraft in a hard left turn, which separated me from my other element. My wingman, Major Rocky Gillis, a Marine pilot on loan to the 4th, thought I'd been hit. And so did I!"

"I headed for the Yellow Sea as briefed, arriving there at about 20,000 feet. There already was a chopper and a Dumbo waiting for me. And ResCAP flights from both the 4th and 51st were on the way. I could see that I'd probably have to leave the aircraft pretty soon if something didn't happen. So I decided to gamble on trying an air start. The engine caught and slowly started to build RPMs until I had enough for at least cruise speed again. I climbed back to 25,000 and nursed the bird back to K-14."

"At the debriefing with Lt.Col. Peterson (the Eglin team leader) and Col. Royal Baker, they suggested that perhaps I'd left my 'alert switch' on. This was an emergency switch used on takeoff in case the engine fuel pump failed. I told them I was sure I'd turned it off. The Eglin team took my bird and test-fired the guns. But they couldn't duplicate the problem that I'd had. So the combat tests continued."

"Six days later, Captain Murray Winslow, a veteran pilot with two MiGs to his credit, engaged a MiG at about 43,000 feet. His aircraft suffered the same problem as mine had. He suffered a flameout, but could not get the aircraft re-started. He was forced to bail out near Chodo and his aircraft, F-86F-2 51-2861, crashed in the Yellow Sea. The GUNVAL project was immediately grounded pending further tests and evaluation."

The problem was finally traced to ingestion of excessive amounts of gun gas from the larger bore cannons, which caused a compressor stall or flameout. Several 'quick fixes' were performed on the combat aircraft, including welding the gun gas bleed doors closed inside the air intake. Holes were then drilled in the aft end of the gun bay doors to alleviate the buildup of gun gas, which could have a disastrous explosion. In addition, a switch was installed in the cockpit, to allow the pilot a choice of firing all four guns, or either the upper or lower pair.

But it was North American engineer Paul Peterson that finally came up with a permanent fix which cured the problem. Close examination of some film taken of firing tests 'at

In January 1953, eight unusual F-86Fs arrived at Kimpo. Project GUNVAL was the combat testing of 20mm cannons in an F-86F-2 airframe. Lt.Col. Clayton Peterson was the project boss, and the GUNVAL tests were flown by 335th Squadron pilots. (Paul Peterson)

GUNVAL crew chiefs make adjustments to the T-160 20mm cannons in Capt. Lonnie Moore's F-86F-2, #51-2836. North American built ten GUNVAL F-86Fs, modifying the gun bay to hold the larger 20mm cannons. Note the painted on 'third gun port' to fool the locals into thinking it was just another F-86. (Paul Peterson)

altitude', showed that the gun gas would actually extend out in front of the nose of the airplane, even at 600+ mph, and then was sucked back into the engine. This became very critical if all four guns were fired at altitudes above 40,000 feet, and could easily cause a compressor stall.

Mr. Peterson studied the films and came up with a small diffuser to break up the gas. It was a simple horseshoe-shaped clip, which was installed in the gun blast trough of the GUNVAL Sabres. The gas would exit the guns and then hit the diffuser clip, which forced it out and away from the aircraft, keeping it out of the air intake. The GUNVAL tests continued with new enthusiasm.

Many high scoring 4th Wing pilots flew the cannon-armed Sabres, including Major Vermont Garrison, Capt. Lonnie Moore, and Lt.Col. George Jones. A second GUNVAL Sabre was lost when Lonnie Moore suffered a compressor stall and didn't get the engine stop-cocked in time. The turbine wheel failed and he bailed out of his Sabre, F-86F-2 51-2803, and was picked out of the Yellow Sea. Two other GUNVALs were hit by MiG gunfire. Major Ray Evans took a 37mm hit just behind his seat, and Lt.Col. Don Rodewald took two 23mm cannon hits – one in the wing and the other in the aft fuselage. But both pilots brought their aircraft back to K-14.

Some of the GUNVAL aircraft remained in Korea into the summer, even though the combat tests were pronounced finished on 30 April 1953. By the end of the test period, the GUNVAL team had flown 365 missions, including 282 combat sorties and 6 air-ground missions against scrap Army trucks and tanks. The remainder were air tests of the guns.

MiGs were sighted on 139 of the combat missions. The GUNVAL pilots got within range and fired the guns forty-one times, with hits observed 22 times. The results were six destroyed, three probables, and thirteen damaged. The guns fired a total of 94,378 rounds. Sounds like a lot of rounds per mission, but orders were that the GUNVAL aircraft were to 'fire out' all remaining ammo on the flight home as part of the tests. The guns had a stoppage rate of 2.13 per 1000 rounds, which was comparable with the M3 .50 caliber machine gun.

Squadron tally board in the 335th Squadron Operations building. The sign shows a pilots total score, including probables and damages. (Bert Beecroft)

The six MiG kills were scored by four pilots – Lt.Col. George Jones got 2 1/2 MiGs (he shared one kill with Col. Johnson in a .50 caliber-armed Sabre), Capt. Lonnie Moore 1 1/2 (he also shared a victory with Maj. Evans), and Majors Vermont Garrison and Ray Evans one apiece. In spite of the problems with the installation, the GUNVAL tests were deemed successful.

The month of January 1953 ended with MiG contacts achieved on only fourteen days. But on several of these days, the MiGs were very aggressive. Group pilots shot down five MiGs on the 14th. And for the next two weeks the weather held. One MiG went down on the 15th, 16th and 17th; and another three were shot down on the 21st. No further MiGs were destroyed that month, although ten were damaged.

On the 30th 1Lt. Russell Kinsey encountered a North Korean twin-engined Tu-2 bomber, dispatching it quickly. The month ended with fourteen destroyed, six probables, and

Lt.Col. George Jones (FU-867) and other GUNVAL pilots climb into the F-86F-2 Sabres in the revetments set aside for the project team. The project began in early January 1953, ending four months later on 30 April. Lt.Col. Jones scored his fifth victory in this GUNVAL Sabre on 29 March. (Paul Peterson)

The 335th Squadron is heading north for another day of MiG hunting along the Yalu River in late March 1953. The nearest aircraft, FU-803, is Capt. Lonnie Moore's GUNVAL Sabre. Capt. Moore suffered a flameout in -803 and had to eject over the Yellow Sea in April 1953. All GUNVAL aircraft had a standard .50 caliber-armed Sabre on the wing. (USAF)

twenty-two damaged. The 4th didn't crown any aces during the month, but the 51st crowned two – Captains Dolph Overton and Harold Fischer, both on the 24th.

In February, the weather over South Korea deteriorated badly, with only ten days of good flying. But again, the MiGs were up and reasonably aggressive. It was during this time that the pilots started noticing a single MiG element that was flying much higher than the rest of the MiG flights. And he just stayed up there. The pilots reasoned that this was a 'honcho', an instructor that was directing his students. The 'honcho' would order certain flights to make an attack, at which time a MiG flight would peel off, dive on the Sabres, then zoom back up 'on their perch' and await their 'grade'.

But the 4th pilots didn't exactly go along with the program. The Sabre pilots didn't simply wait around for the MiGs to make their attacks and leave with impunity. As the MiG 'students' came through the Sabre flights, there were a number of them that didn't make it back to their 'perch'. Or at the very least, they had some pieces missing. Group pilots shot down eighteen MiGs, with three probables and sixteen damaged. for the month.

On the 18th, Pete Fernandez, now a flight commander in the 334th Squadron, got a pair of MiGs, becoming the twenty-seventh jet ace in the war. Col. Johnson exploded a MiG in the same battle, and got another the next day. His score now stood at 4 1/2 MiGs. The 1/2 MiG being one he shared with George Jones in one of the GUNVAL battles.

The first week in March saw very little activity in MiG Alley. When the weather over South Korea cleared, the weather over the Yalu would be lousy. And vice versa. During the second week, the weather and the MiGs got together. But most of the MiGs were in the 51st Group's patrol sector. Col. Royal Baker got his tenth on 8 March, and Pete Fernandez got his seventh the next day.

Maj. Ray Evans returns to K-14 in April 1953 in "Sweet Carol." It's obvious from the lack of drop tanks and smoke stained gun ports that MiGs were engaged on this mission. This aircraft, #51-2836, was damaged by MiG cannon fire in April. Although only six MiGs were shot down, the tests were successful and the cannons were standardized as the M39 and installed in production F-86Hs and the F-100. (Don Miller)

The GUNVAL pilots were busy, getting victories on the 13th and two on the 21st. But again, all were 'shared' victories. The GUNVAL birds had only 200 rounds per gun, which was rapidly depleted in any fight. For this reason, each GUNVAL Sabre flew in an element with a standard F-86F. If the GUNVAL pilot ran out of ammo, the wingman could pull in behind the MiG and finish him off. Major Ray Evans and Capt. Lonnie Moore shared the MiG on the 13th, while Maj. Evans and 1Lt. Joe Ferris shared the first one on the 21st, with Lt.Col. George Jones and Maj. Jack Mass sharing a second MiG on the afternoon mission.

March ended with only nine days of contact with the MiGs. The big days were the 4th and 13th, when four MiGs went down; and the 21st when seven MiGs were downed. The Group destroyed a total of twenty-one MiGs during March. Major Jim Hagerstrom, now flying with the 67th FBS, made ace on the 27th. He had scored two of his victories flying with the 4th. The 67th FBS had just transitioned into the F-86F and were flying MiG Sweeps with the 4th as part of their 'training' when 'Hag' made ace.

On the 28th, only one MiG went down. But it was credited to Col. Johnson, his fifth. "The Mayor Of Sabre City" was the 29th jet ace in Korea. Col. Johnson tells the tale: "I was leading my flight, patrolling the south side of the Yalu River at about 42,000 feet. On my wing was 1/Lt. Robert Carter, who was always on my wing if I had anything to say about it. And, since I was the Wing Commander, I did!"

"Looking down and to the left as we headed up the River, I spotted two MiGs below us heading south. I called Carter and pointed out the MiGs. We dropped our tanks, and went into a dive coming up behind the apparently unwary MiGs. I closed on one of them, and opened fire at about 200 feet. I gave him two real good bursts. The first burst hit the left wing, and walked into the canopy. The second burst went right up his tailpipe.

"The MiG started shedding large pieces, and started to burn furiously. Suddenly the canopy came off and the pilot ejected. The plane headed down, disintegrating as it fell, and crashed just north of the Yalu River." But the day wasn't over for Col. Johnson and Lt. Carter. Lt. Carter – "Col. Johnson had just destroyed a MiG-15, and in the process, had expended all of his ammunition. I took the lead then, and started firing on another MiG, which was climbing to a higher altitude."

"As we were chasing the MiG, between 42,000 and 46,000 feet, Col. Johnson called me to say that he'd lost cabin pressure and was suffering from hypoxia and possibly the bends. I

335th Squadron crew chiefs remove the canopy for maintenance on Maj. Jack Mass' F-86F in May 1953. The scoreboard on the right side of the airplane shows the victories won by all the pilots that flew this Sabre. Maj. Mass shot down four MiGs in Korea. (Norm Green)

1Lt. Peter Frederick sits in the 336th Squadron honor chair, an old ejection seat, following his third MiG kill on 16 May 1953. He wears the 336th white star signifying he has scored a MiG kill. (Bob Windoffer)

Maj. Gene Sommerich was the 4th Group Operations Officer when he flew with the 336th Squadron in 1953. Maj. Sommerich shared a MiG with S/L Graham Hulse on 13 March 1953. (Bob Windoffer)

immediately broke off my attack, and turned back toward Jim's airplane. His Sabre did a split-S, and began to go into all kinds of wild gyrations. I was screaming for him to pull out all the way from about 30,000 feet down to 5,000 feet."

"He finally recovered around 5,000 feet, and I talked him back to K-14 (Kimpo). But he still couldn't read his flight instruments. The lack of oxygen had affected his eyesight. Consequently, I had to talk him down for the landing. He was apparently unconscious from the time he lost pressure until he finally recovered at about 5,000 feet. "Shortly after landing, a TWX arrived at Kimpo and delivered to Col. Johnson. It read:

> fm: CG AF FIVE
> to: CO FTRINCEPWG FOUR
> TO JOHNSON FROM BARCUS. CONGRATULATIONS ON YOUR VICTORY MAKING YOU AN ACE. BEST WISHES AND ALL THE LUCK IN THE WORLD ON YOUR NEXT FIVE. END.

It came from Lt.Gen. Glenn O. Barcus, Commander of 5th Air Force.

The next day, Lt.Col. George Jones got a full credit for a MiG while flying one of the GUNVAL Sabres. It was his fifth, making him the thirtieth jet ace. Lt.Col. Jones had been in and out of Korea for almost two years before making ace. He was initially assigned to 4th Wing Headquarters in the fall of 1951, scoring 1 1/2 MiGs before transferring to the 51st Wing with Col. Gabreski. He shot down two more in the 51st and was rotated home. He came back to Korea in early 1953, and was assigned to the GUNVAL project in the 335th Squadron. He had shared victories on the 13th of January with Col. Johnson, and on the 21st with Maj. Jack Mass. His score stood at 4 1/2 MiGs when he left K-14 on 29 March. When he returned to K-14, the nose of his GUNVAL Sabre was blackened, and his score stood at 5 1/2 MiGs.

In April the action was reasonably light. The MiGs just wouldn't come up to play. Sabres shot down a total of twenty-six MiGs in the month, but only nine by pilots from the 4th. Most of the action was again in the patrol areas of the 51st Group, the luck of the draw so to speak. Lt.Col. George Jones got a second MiG in one of the GUNVAL Sabres, bringing his total to 6 1/2.

Beautiful shot of four 334th Squadron F-86Fs over North Korea enroute to MiG Alley in Summer 1953. All are late model F-86F-30 Sabres with the '6-3 hard wing' that gave the Sabre an increased turning rate against the MiG. (George Amussen)

"7 April 1953. I was scheduled on the mid-morning mission. Although I didn't know it, this was my turn to go at it with a 'Honcho'. A 'Honcho' was a MiG pilot with exceptional skill. A master of air tactics, a daring and aggressive enemy."

"My aircraft was again one of the GUNVAL F-86Fs, a Sabre with four 20mm cannon that fired a high explosive incendiary shell that was many times more effective than the .50 caliber round. However, there were some drawbacks in the test installation. Namely, under certain conditions, firing the guns could cause a compressor stall. And losing all power in the midst of a bunch of MiGs was decidedly inconvenient."

"The briefing for the sweep was the usual – 1000 MiGs north of the Yalu, and we were putting up sixteen Sabrejets. Fighter bomber F-84s were working targets south of us. The plan – make a straight penetration, flights stacked up, twenty seconds apart, and fan out at the mouth of the Yalu hoping to pick off any MiGs that crossed the River."

"My position was Element Lead in King Flight. King was the lead flight for the mission. As the briefing wound down, King Lead had a time hack, then said "Mount up! Let's bust MiGs!" We filed out and headed for the personal equipment shed, where I picked up my Mae West, chute, helmet and oxygen mask. Then we walked down to the waiting jets."

"At my aircraft, F-86F-2 #51-2867, my crew chief, a tall Texan with a ready smile, gave me the word, "She's ready to

Maj. Robinson Risner (left) shakes hands with Capt. Leonard Lilley in early February 1953 as both pilots prepare to leave for home. Robbie Risner, the twentieth jet ace in Korea, scored eight victories; while Bill Lilley scored seven and was the twenty-second jet ace. (USAF)

January 1953, Kimpo AB. Maj. Robinson Risner flew "Little Mike", an F-86E with the 336th Squadron in 1953. The art work on Maj. Risner's Sabre depicts "Bugs Bunny" looking for a discharge – or at least a ticket home from the frigid weather of Korea. (Robinson Risner)

roll sir!", I thanked the sergeant, made a quick pre-flight, climbed in and buttoned up. I glanced at the instruments and the gun sight to make sure the gun camera film was installed. Then it was start engines time."

"King Lead and #2 rolled past, and I followed with King 4, which was Major Ray Evans. We taxied out, skirting a hole in the taxiway, and lined up on the runway. At the green light from the tower, King 1 and 2 rolled. Ray and I ran up full power about 5 seconds later. With my nod, we released the brakes in unison and began a rapid acceleration. The runway rolled by fast. A slight back pressure on the stick brought the nose wheel off and we were airborne. Wheels up, flaps up, and climbing on course."

"In minutes we were over the bomb line and over enemy territory. From now on, your head was on a steady swivel, searching left and right, up and down. We followed the briefing and leveled off at 42,000 feet. There was hardly a sound in the cockpit, just a distant whine like a car running fast over asphalt. Outside, the temperature is 60° below zero! But the cockpit is warm. And although you are moving at over 600 mph, there is absolutely no sense of speed."

"Looking out, an eerie peacefulness prevails. Above, the sky is a bowl of deep blue. Below me is the mountainous terrain of North Korea stretching out hundreds of miles to the north and south. And about forty miles ahead of us lies the Yalu River, snaking its way to the sea. It was high noon in MiG Alley."

Over the radio, we hear our radar site – "Heads up! Thirty-six bandits taking off from Antung!" Then – "Twenty-four bandits crossing out (of Manchuria), altitude unknown!" Excitement mounting, I shift in my seat straining for a glimpse of the MiGs. The sky is empty, but I know they're out there. By this time, the drop tanks are empty and King Lead gives a silent signal to 'Drop tanks!' With the tanks gone, the airplane feels lighter and more responsive. The Mach needle edges up a little."

"Suddenly, a stream of cannon shells pass under Ray's left wing. Six MiGs flash by and now they're gone. Ray and I were flying about 1000 feet higher and 1500 feet out to the side of King Lead. King Lead spotted eight MiGs at eleven o'clock low, starting a turn to get into position for an attack. The MiGs were at 40,000 as King Lead continued his turn. Ray and I followed, holding to the outside."

"Looking straight ahead, I see a string of MiGs coming right at us from twelve o'clock, and the lead MiG was already firing. I yelled over the radio, "King Lead, MiGs at twelve o'clock and firing!" He responded "Roger, take them. You're on your own!" Behind that first group of MiGs was another flight coming in head on and fast. I picked out the number two MiG and started a slight diving turn, getting my sight in front of his nose."

One of the promises that President-elect Dwight D. Eisenhower made was to visit Korea and to end the war. On 3 December 1952, an L-19 Bird Dog landed at K-14 carrying the President-elect. (Sylvia Johnson)

There were signs welcoming President-elect Eisenhower everywhere in South Korea. This is the East Gate to Seoul City. (Dave Eldredge)

"At 300 to 400 feet range, I pulled the trigger and held it down. Hits flashed on the nose of the MiG, and down the middle of his right wing. The rate of closure was terrific. I had to push the stick over in the corner to avoid a collision. "I hit him!", I called, and Ray Evans answered "Roger, I saw it!" Then he yelled "Break right King 3! Break right now!"

"We were being attacked by six MiGs that were pulling in at our six o'clock. I had to turn my attention away from the MiG I'd already hit. (Later I learned that the MiG had exploded behind me.) I turned into the MiGs hard, and they were thrown to the outside. But they stayed. Finally, after a hard diving, turning, spiral, five of the MiGs lost their places and left."

"But not the leader. He was like a shadow, racing through the air and following every move. Then suddenly he pulled up. Maybe he discovered that he was alone. I called Ray, – "Pull out to the side, then continue on course." This put us heading east down the Yalu. Ray and I were flying parallel with the MiG, which was about 2000 feet above and to our right. We had set him up for a squeeze play. No matter which one of us he attacked, the other would come in on his tail. The bait of course, a 'free shot' at one of our Sabres. We waited."

"The MiG pilot sat high on his perch, pausing for a decision. The MiG poised against the sky had a blue underside, which really accented the bold red nose. He had two choices – break right and go home (we couldn't follow him across the River), or break left and attack. I waited and watched, the strain and uncertainty mounting. Ray and I knew he was going to attack, but which way? Suddenly, the impasse was over. He'd made his decision."

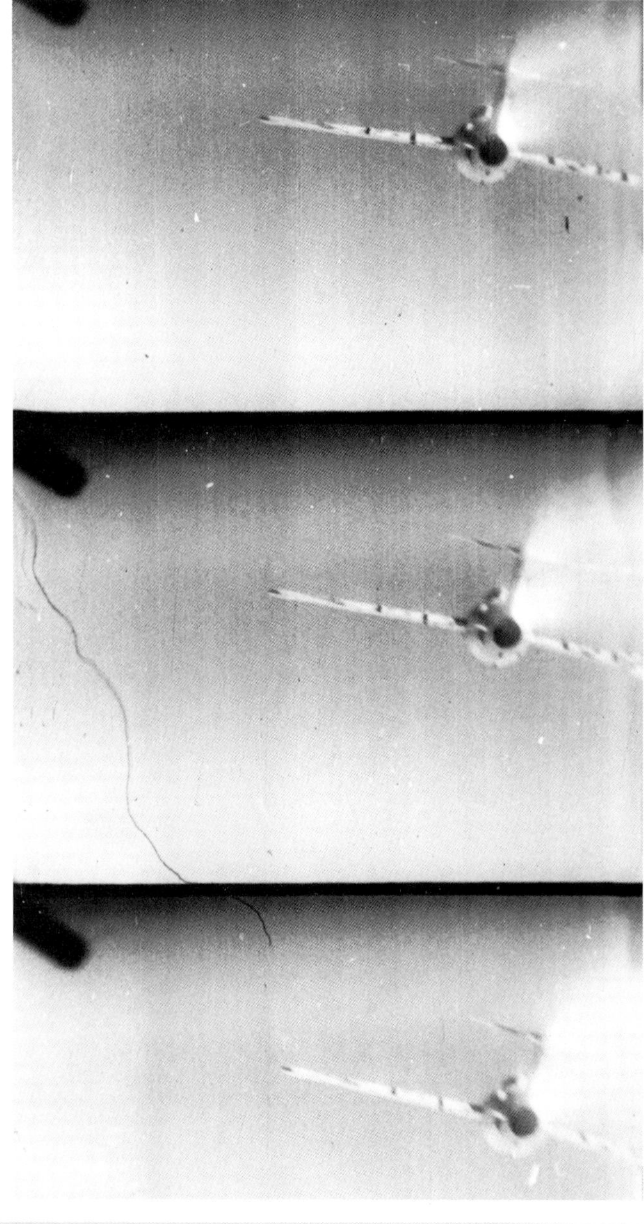

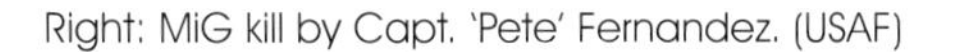

Right: MiG kill by Capt. 'Pete' Fernandez. (USAF)

Below: Capt. Manuel J. 'Pete' Fernandez taxies out for a mission in late October 1952 in Capt. Ryland Dewey's Sabre. The F-86E would become Pete's airplane later in the year and he would make ace in FU-830. The aircraft was heavily damaged by another pilot in late February 1953, while Pete was on R&R in Japan. (Pete Fernandez)

"The MiG plunged down toward us, starting a beautiful, high-side gunnery pass. Roll in, reverse, pick up a target and start a cut-off. We still didn't know which one of us was his intended target. His nose was on a point halfway between Ray and I. He had at least a fifty knot overtake speed from his dive, and was closing fast. Just out of range, the red nose shifted to the right. I was the target!"

"I broke hard into him, and he slid to the outside, trying to pull some lead on me. I pulled harder. Suddenly, orange flashes winked under his nose, and a stream of cannon shells, looking like red golf balls, passed under my right wing and behind my tail. Startled by their closeness, I pulled the stick back for more Gs, and dropped my nose to gain some speed. I was sweating now, and thought – "George, you may have cut this maneuver just a little too thin!"

"Breathing hard, I grunted to Ray – "Get this son of a bitch off my tail!" But Ray was already on his way. Our squeeze play was working. I just hoped he would get there in time. Ray rolled out behind the MiG, and pulled within range, firing a burst which hit the MiG. Ray called me – "I hit him! His canopy just came off!" He then called for me to reverse. But I wasn't sure if the MiG had broken off, so I kept pulling Gs. Then I saw the MiG had pulled off and headed north toward the Yalu, with Ray in hot pursuit."

Capt. 'Pete' Fernandez holds the "MiGs Hava Yes" scoreboard showing his score on 10 May 1953 – 13 1/2 MiGs destroyed. He would add one more victory on 16 May 1953 before being grounded by 5th AF and rotated home with Capt. Joe McConnell of the 51st Wing. (O.C. Wilkinson)

"Moments later Ray called again – "I hit him again and he bailed out!" "Roger", I answered, "Head out of the area and

An element of F-86Fs from the 336th Squadron over North Korea in early summer 1953. The element was the basic combat formation of the UN fighter forces. (John Africa)

rejoin at point Echo." We rejoined at 32,000 feet, and stayed in the Alley another five minutes hoping for another bounce. But nothing showed, and we were both at Bingo fuel. We returned to Kimpo, landed, and my armament chief checked the guns. I had fired a total of ninety-two rounds."

"What of the 'honcho' that Ray had hit? Who can say. For a moment that seemed endless, he scared me plenty! I can still see that red nose MiG all over my tail, with cannons flashing." All in all, April was a slow month. But that would change within days.

May was the beginning of the 'turkey shoot'. What happened was that the Soviet instructor pilots turned their Chinese and North Korea 'students' loose. According to Lt. Kum Suk No, the MiG pilot that defected to Kimpo in September, the Russians stopped flying at the end of April, rotating their squadrons back to Mother Russia. They'd had enough. By their own admission, Russian MiGs that were piloted by Russians, were shot down at a rate of 4:1. Chinese losses were even greater, at least 8:1 according to Soviet sources.

The Chinese and North Korean MiGs came across the Yalu River in large flights, sometimes with a 'honcho' very high above directing the traffic, but usually by themselves. And this time they were in the areas where the 4th was patrolling. In actuality, they were everywhere. There were plenty of MiGs for everyone. The month ended with a total of fifty-six MiGs going down, 32 1/2 being downed by pilots from the 4th Wing.

In April, Jim Jabara returned to Korea, now a Major and assigned to 4th Wing Headquarters. On the 17th he got his seventh victory of the war. He would get Nos. eight and nine on 26 May. Pete Fernandez scored the last of his 14 1/2 kills on the 16th. He was rotated home a couple of days later, with Capt. Joe McConnell of the 51st Group, the top scoring ace in Korea with sixteen. Major Vermont Garrison, the new CO of the 335th Squadron, scored twice, getting his third MiG on the 17th, and his fourth on the 23rd.

Col. Royal Baker talks with the press following his eleventh victory in Korea. Col. Baker was the Group Commander of the 4th. He ended the war with thirteen victories. (Dave Eldredge)

In February 1953, a famous name returned to K-14. Jim Jabara, now a Major, had wrangled another tour in Korea and was assigned as Operations Officer in the 4th Wing. He is congratulating Capt. 'Pete' Fernandez on his 5th and 6th victories, 18 February 1953. (USAF)

Left: 336th Squadron flight commanders in May 1953 – (Left to right) Capt. Stuart Childs, Capt. Houston Tuel, Capt. Thomas Broe, Capt. Peter Frederick, and Capt. Bob Windoffer. (Bob Windoffer)

Capt. 'Pete' Fernandez' second Sabre was F-86F #51-2857, which has his score as of 10 May 1953 under the canopy. The three stars under the crew name block are those victories 'awarded' to the crew chief of 857, A1C L.W. French, and the armorer, A1C R. Holar. (Curt Francom)

Col. Royal 'King' Baker gives thanks to his crew chief, A2C Holland, on the afternoon following his thirteenth and final victory in Korea, 13 March 1953. Col. Baker's aircraft was F-86E #51-2822, named "Angel Face & The Babes/The King."(USAF)

(Left to right) 2Lt. Frank Arbuckle, Maj. James Hagerstom, and 1Lt. Ira Porter lean on Maj. Risner's F-86 following Lt. Arbuckles MiG kill on 21 January 1953. Maj. Hagerstom would score two victories with the 4th Wing, then transfer to the 18th FBG and score 6 1/2 more victories to become the only 'fighter bomber ace' in the Korean War. (USAF)

In June, the slaughter became unbelievable, even to the pilots that were flying the patrols. The MiGs were everywhere, but hopelessly outclassed by the veteran pilots of the 4th and 51st Groups. It was not uncommon for a pilot to get on the tail of a MiG and without firing a shot, have the MiG pilot eject as soon as he saw the Sabre pull within range! Several MiGs also went down when the horizontal tail ripped itself off during violent combat maneuvering. Those that didn't eject or tear themselves apart, were shot down by the dozens.

The total for the month of June was a staggering seventy-seven MiGs shot down, without loss to the F-86s. 4th Wing pilots were responsible for forty-four of the victories. The 4th crowned three aces in June – "The Grey Eagle", Lt.Col. Vermont Garrison, got his fifth on 5 June; while Captains Lonnie Moore and Ralph Parr both made ace on the 18th. Capt. Parr made ace in less than two weeks, getting his first two MiGs on the 7th, and his fifth on the 18th. On the 10th, Major Jim Jabara became a double ace, the Wing's fourth 'double ace' of the war. It wouldn't be his last.

The biggest day was the final day of the month. On 30 June, no less than fourteen MiGs were shot down, all but two by 4th pilots. Jim Jabara and Ralph Parr each got two, although Parr's were on two separate missions. Col. Johnson made 'double' that day, with Lt.Col. Garrison and Capt. Lonnie Moore also scoring that day.

One of the big 'hunters' in the 335th Squadron was Capt. Lonnie Moore. Moore was a double ace with ten confirmed MiG kills. His aircraft, F-86F #51-12972, is one of the Fs that had the '6-3' hard wing' conversion kit added in Korea. Note the unusually large, removable fillet at the juncture of the wing and fuselage. (NAA)

The End Of The Fighting

The final month of the war was both hectic and mundane. It was hectic as the UN Peace Accords stipulated that only those aircraft already in place within the boundaries of Korea, would be considered as part of the active defenses. This was for both North and South Korea. In the North, it was up to the pilots of 5th AF, and those of the 4th and 51st Groups especially, to keep the amount of MiGs allowed to enter North Korea at a minimum. This meant a constant reconnaissance of all the bases within the boundaries of North Korea, literally twenty-four hours a day. All with F-86 escort.

And of course, the other end of the scale was trying to get as many operational aircraft in place at the bases in South Korea as was possible. Aircraft that were AOCP at the Tsuiki REMCO facility, were patched back together for the flight back to Kimpo. It didn't matter if they remained AOCP at Kimpo, just as long as they were on the base. This meant that the Group was brought to above authorized operational strength. Each squadron was supposed to have about twenty-five F-86s in their inventory. But by 27 July, the date the truce went into effect, each squadron had closer to forty airplanes on hand. All four F-86 units in Korea were brought to above authorized strength just prior to the truce.

In the actual air fighting, it was a battle between the MiGs and the Sabres, and the MiGs and the weather, and the Sabres and the weather. The weather during the first week of the month was lousy. It wasn't until the 11th that the weather cleared for both the Sabres and the MiGs – and then they were in the 51st

The main gate and guard shack at Kimpo in 1953, have changed greatly since 1951. (Larry Hendle)

Group area. On the 12th, the weather cooperated, and the MiGs came across the River. 4th Group pilots shot down five of the seven MiGs downed that day – two by Lonnie Moore, and one each by Ralph Parr, Major Stephen Bettinger, and 1Lt. Curtis Carley.

Captain Clyde Curtin and Jim Jabara each got a MiG on the 15th, while Major Stephen Bettinger and 1Lt. Larry Roesler each scored on the 16th. On the 17th only one victory was scored, but it was significant. It was one of the 'Bedcheck Charlies', and it was shot down by Navy Lt. Guy Bordelon,

Col. James K Johnson's Sabre in a revetment at K-14 in early March 1953. Col. Johnson flew F-86F #51-12941 on almost all his ten victories in Korea. Col. Johnson's F-86F-10 has had the '6-3 hard wing kit' installed. (Larry Hendle)

North American Aviation Tech Rep Bill Grover and North American photographer Bill Binder sit on a 335th Squadron Sabre in the Summer of 1953. Binder was at K-14 to shoot publicity photos for North American's Skyline Magazine. (Bill Grover)

CBS-TV reporter H.V. Kaltenborn interviews Maj. Jim Jabara on the flightline at K-14 regarding his return to combat in Korea. Maj. Jabara would score his first victory of the second tour almost two years to the day after he made ace – 16 May 1953. (Don Miller)

You catch a few winks where and whenever you can. The crew chief and armorer of a 335th Squadron Sabre relax on the wing in the summer of 1953. The dark colored underwing tank was one of the Japanese-built drop tanks that had such unfavorable flight characteristics that FEAF ordered them painted olive drab so the pilots knew instantly what type of tanks they were carrying and what evasive maneuver to take when the order came to 'Drop tanks!' (Don Miller)

'The Mayor of Sabre City', Col. James K Johnson, and his crew chief share a moment following Col. Johnson's tenth MiG kill, 30 June 1953. (NAA)

flying an F4U-5N Corsair. Bordelon, and several other Navy and Marine Corsairs, had been given the job of stopping the nightly raids. And they were extremely effective. Lt. Bordelon's victory on the night of the 17th was his fifth since the 29th of June, making him an ace – the only non-F-86 ace in the Korean War.

On the 18th Captain Lonnie Moore, again flying a standard F-86F, and Major Foster Lee Smith, each shot down a MiG. On the 19th, the MiGs came across in large numbers, and suffered the heaviest losses of the month when ten MiGs were shot down. Pilots from the 4th were victorious over seven of the ten MiGs shot down that day. Captain Clyde Curtin got a MiG on the morning mission, and another in the afternoon, to bring his score to five, making him the 38th jet ace. Vermont Garrison and Lonnie Moore each scored, making both men 'double aces'. Other victories on the 19th were by Lt.Col. Jack Best, 1Lt. Frank Frazier, and 1Lt. Robert Strozier.

Three MiGs went down the next day – two by Major Thomas Sellers, a Marine exchange pilot flying with the 336th Squadron; and a single MiG downed by Major Stephen Bettinger. It was his fifth, making him the thirty-ninth and last jet ace of the Korean War. Group pilots didn't score again until the final afternoon of the war.

The last victory of the war came on the last afternoon of the war. It was a straight forward victory, but became an international incident when the Reds claimed that it was, a.) a civilian airliner, and b.) that the aircraft was shot down some sixty miles north of the Yalu River. Capt. Ralph Parr was a pilot in the 335th Squadron that fateful afternoon of 27 July 1953:

MiG kill of Col. Johnson showing the MiG pilot in the parachute. (James K. Johnson)

Opposite: Col. Johnson's fifth MiG victory of the war, 28 March 1953. (USAF)

"The Reds accused me by name, of being sixty miles north of the river, and filed suit against me in the World Court in Holland. I was damn sure where I was at, although many of the other aircraft with my flight, probably didn't realize our exact position. Our mission that day was escort of a reconnaissance

Maj. Jim Jabara in one of the many Sabres he flew in 1953, a 'borrowed' aircraft from the 334th Squadron. Jabby flew whichever aircraft was available, but 319 was one of his favorites. (Gene Sommerich)

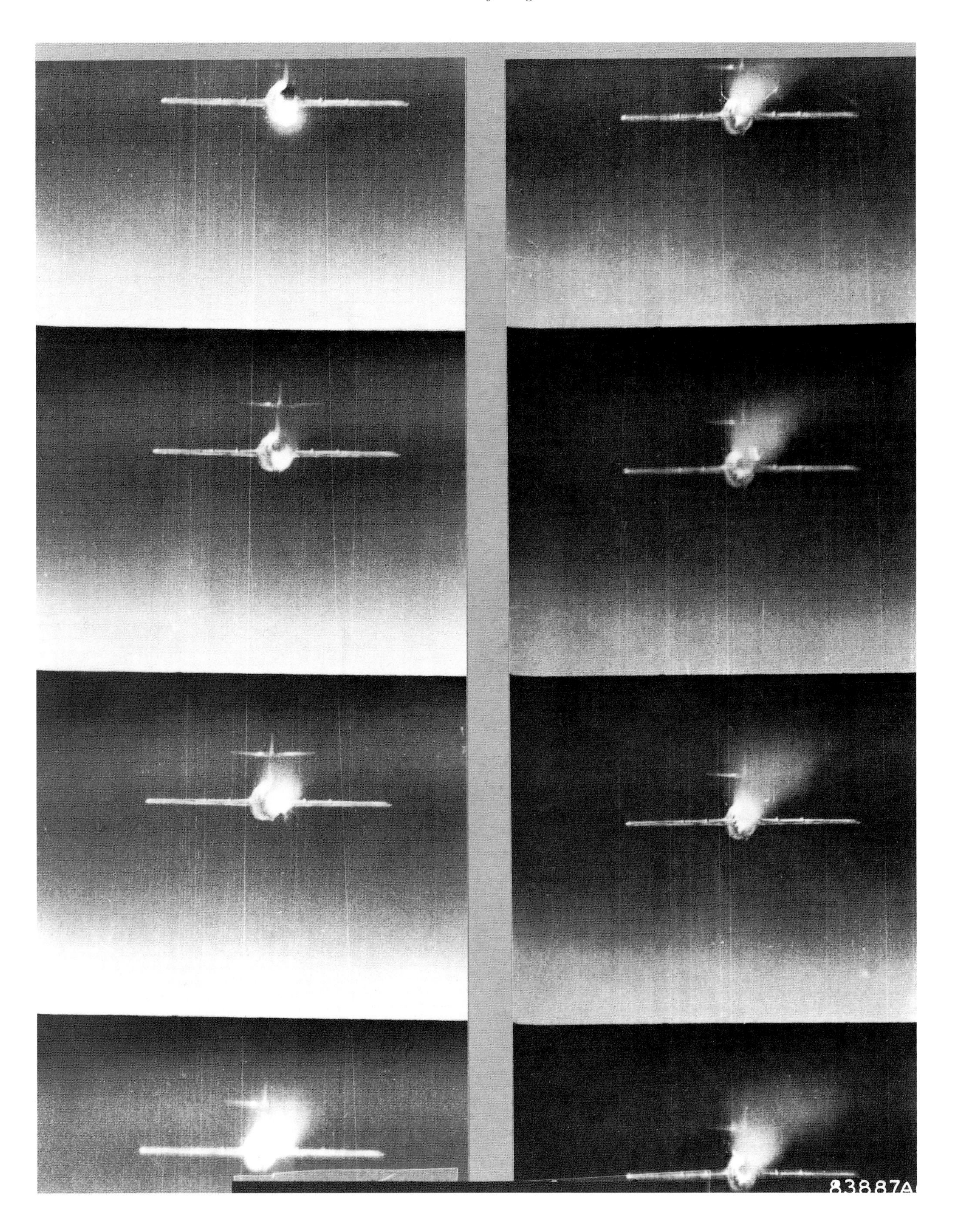
83887A

"The Grey Eagle", Maj. Vermont Garrison, in the cockpit of his F-86F, #51-12959, showing four victories, 23 May 1953. Maj. Garrison was the CO of 335th Squadron in the Summer of 1953, and shot down ten MiGs. He flew with the original 4th FG in World War II. (Norm Green)

aircraft to the Yalu. FEAF wanted some good pictures of the MiG airfields so they could determine how many MiGs had been moved into North Korea, which was a violation of the truce terms."

"A little south of Namsi-Dong on the west coast of Korea, a speck of silver caught my eye. We were at about 30,000 feet and the bogey was real low, down at about 10,000. I took my element and we went down for a quick look at whatever it was. I was hoping for a MiG, but it was an Il-12 transport, similar to a U.S. C-47. It was silver in color, with red stars on the fuselage and wings. Definitely a military bird."

"I double-checked my position to make sure we were inside North Korea. We definitely didn't want to get caught on the north side of the Yalu on this day. Confirming my position as being south of the river, I told my wingman that I was going to take him. He was a sitting duck. I just pulled in behind him and gave him a couple of quick bursts. The Il-12 caught fire, banked over and crashed in the hills below. They'd probably been cutting across that area for months, but today wasn't his lucky day."

"The war ended at midnight and I didn't think any more about it. The claim was confirmed and I was credited with my tenth victory. The next thing I know, I'm being called to FEAF Headquarters. They're asking me about this Russian airliner that I'd shot down 60 miles inside of Manchuria. The Air Force set up a full inquiry into the incident even before we went to World Court. I was called in, as well as everyone else in my flight. The gun camera film was closely examined. I was asked the same questions over and over – "Where were you? What kind of airplane was it? How was it marked? Can you prove it?"

"After examining all the evidence, the Air Force decided that I was right. The airplane was exactly what I said it was, and exactly where I said it was. It was a legal kill and the Air Force would defend me in the World Court. The world press had a hey-day with the investigation. The U.S. press defending me, the Soviet press accusing me of shooting down an unarmed

Left: "The Ceegar Kid." Maj. Jim Jabara and the ever-present stogie. (Don Miller) Right: The scoreboard on Maj. Jabara's Sabre, #52-4519, 18 June 1953, showing twelve victories, three probables, and seven damaged. Jabara would add three more to the confirmed victory column, making him a triple ace. (Larry Hendle)

Capt. Clyde Curtin was the pilot of "Boomer", an F-86F-30 with the 335th Squadron. Capt. Curtin became the thirty-eighth jet ace in Korea on 19 July 1953. (Bert Beecroft)

airliner. In the end, with the evidence piling up in my favor, the Russians dropped the suit. It was a hell of a hassle for one lousy Il-12."

The war ended at midnight on 27 July 1953, three years, one month, and two days after it had began. It began with a North Korea and a South Korea, and it ended the same way. The boundary between the two Koreas was bent a little bit from what it was on 25 June 1950, but it was still essentially the same. The communist forces had lost over a million ground troops in the fighting. U.S. losses were in excess of 54,000 men.

In the air, the Soviet, Chinese, and North Korean Air Forces had lost at least 954 aircraft, including at least 827 MiGs. According to a 5th Air Force communiqué on 29 July 1953, F-86 Sabres accounted for 808 MiGs, with Sabre losses listed at fifty-eight. This was what led to the legendary 14:1 kill ratio commonly referred to whenever talking about the air war in Korea.

However, after the end of the war, some of the victories were down-graded to 'probables'. At the same time, many of the F-86 losses previously listed as to 'unknown cause', were changed to combat losses. The revised figures were 792 MiGs shot down by Sabres, with Sabre losses listed at seventy-eight – a 10:1 victory ratio. Of that total of 893 enemy aircraft 'officially' credited, 4th Fighter Interceptor Wing pilots shot down 502, more than 54% of all the enemy aircraft shot down during the war.

The top scoring ace in the 4th was also the first ace in the 4th – Major James J. Jabara. Captain Jim Jabara shot down his first six MiGs in 1951, then came back in 1953 to shoot down

Another ace that was assigned to 4th Wing Headquarters was Maj. Stephan Bettinger, seen in Capt. Bob Windoffer's F-86E #50-676 in the Spring of 1953. Maj. Bettinger scored five victories between 5 June and 20 July 1953 and was the thirty-ninth and last ace of the war. (Bob Windoffer)

The big hunters at K-14 in the Summer of 1953 included, (Left to right) Capt. Clyde Curtin, five victories; Lt.Col. Vermont Garrison, ten victories, Maj. Foster Lee Smith, 4 1/2 victories, and Capt. Ralph Parr, ten victories. (USAF)

Air Vice Marshall Sanderson, RAF, gets to check over Col. Johnson's F-86F during a visit to Kimpo in June 1953. (Sylvia Johnson)

Capt. Ralph Parr's tenth victory, and the last airplane shot down in the Korean war, a Soviet Air Force Il-10 military transport plane that Capt. Parr caught attempting to slip into North Korea before the peace deadline on 27 June 1953. The Communists tried to sue Capt. Parr and the Air Force in World Court for shooting down a passenger plane. They lost! (USAF)

July 1953. Five doubles and a triple = fifty-five victories. (Left to right) Capt. Lonnie Moore (335th), ten kills; Lt.Col. Vermont Garrison (335th), ten kills; Col. James K Johnson, ten kills; Capt. Ralph Parr (335th), ten kills; and Maj. Jim Jabara (4th Wing), fifteen kills. (USAF)

Capt. Ralph Parr scored his fifth victory on 18 June 1953, becoming the thirty-fourth jet ace of the war. (NAA)

Capt. Parr was assigned to the 335th Squadron and flew "Barbera", F-86F #51-12955. Capt. Parr would shoot down five more aircraft including the last kill of the war, a Soviet Il-10 transport. (via David Menard)

another nine. His total of fifteen was second only to Captain Joseph McConnell, who scored sixteen with the 51st Group. The 4th Wing had twenty-four of the thirty-nine jet aces in the Korean War, including nine of the eleven 'double jet aces'. The top scoring squadron of the war was, by far, the 335th Squadron. The 335th was credited with 218.5 victories, seventy-six more than their nearest competitor, and almost twice as many as any squadron outside the 4th Wing.

Truly, the 4th Fighter Interceptor Wing had lived up to its motto: FOURTH BUT FIRST!

Celebrating the end of the war in Korea are (Left to right) Maj. Foster Lee Smith, Capt. Clyde Curtin (in cockpit), and Capt. Ralph Parr. Curtin is about to depart on one of those 'routine peacetime patrols' up the coast of Korea looking for MiGs even though there was now a truce. (USAF)

eleven

The Post-War Years: The "Truce"

The war was officially 'stopped' at midnight of 27 July 1953. At least the ground fighting was halted at that time. There was no victory, nor any defeat. The Communist armies had been driven out of South Korea and that government was secure in Seoul. Wherever the ground troops were at midnight, was where they stayed. The 'truce' provided for a demilitarized zone, or DMZ, along the lines of the opposing ground troop positions. It was somewhat along the same lines of the 38th Parallel, which was the original boundary between North and South Korea. At Kimpo, Col. Donald Hall relieved Col. Johnson as Wing Commander on 9 August.

But the war in the air continued unabated, at least as far as flying missions. Actual engagements with the MiGs were rare. Beginning on the morning following implementation of the 'truce agreements', FEAF and 5th Air Force began to fly a two-fold mission. First was the air defense of South Korea and Japan. Second was the monitoring of North Korean military facilities, including air bases, as to whether the communists were indeed, following the terms of the 'truce'. The truce terms specifically stated that only that equipment and manpower, including ships, tanks and aircraft, that were in place within the boundaries of North and South Korea, were allowed to remain there. No reinforcements of any kind were allowed.

With that in mind, weather permitting, the mission of the 4th became fighter escort of reconnaissance aircraft that were monitoring the MiG forces in place at the bases nearest the coastline. The recon aircraft had to fly outside the three mile limit. Missions were flown along both coasts, as far north as Antung on the west and Vladivostok, Russia on the east. 4th Wing Sabres escorted RF-80 Shooting Stars and RF-86 Sabres from the 15th Tactical Reconnaissance Squadron, based across the runway at Kimpo; and 91st Strategic Reconnaissance Squadron RB-29s, RB-50s, and RB-45C Tornadoes out of Yokota AB, Japan. The RB-45Cs would usually 'stage through' K-14, refuel, then launch with the Sabre escort flights.

These missions were usually boring and had little results as far as actual MiG engagements. The MiGs would launch and fly parallel to the recon flight. The MiGs and Sabres would be eyeball to eyeball for over an hour without incident. At times the MiGs would feign an attack towards the recon flight, causing the Sabre flights to drop their tanks. Then, just as suddenly, the MiGs would turn away. The 'pucker factor' was high for the entire flight, but usually it was just a long flight up the coast, turn around and return to K-14.

In September 1953, one of the most exciting incidents in the history of the Korean War took place. On the morning of 21 September, Kimpo was alive with activity. Crew chiefs were readying their aircraft for the next mission up the coast of North Korea. Radar Hill was shut down for regular maintenance. And unknown to the crews at Kimpo, so was the radar at Chodo Island. Four F-86Fs were sitting five minute alert at the south end of the runway. And a four ship flight of Sabres was conducting formation flying practice near the base.

Far to the north, shortly after 9 am, a flight of two North Korean MiG-15s left Sunan AB for a training flight that would take them close to the DMZ. As they approached the demarcation line, one of the MiGs dropped slowly behind the other, banked suddenly to the right, and flew straight into South Korea. With both Radar Hill and Chodo shut down, no one had any idea that a MiG had penetrated South Korean air space. The MiGs destination was Kimpo.

The wind had changed and was now coming directly out of the north. The alert airplanes had just finished moving to the south end of the runway. The control tower had just given an inbound F-86 the 'Go' for final approach for a landing from the south. Suddenly there was a jet coming in for a landing from the north! Both aircraft touched down and rolled past each other at well over 100 mph, with barely ten feet between their wingtips. The startled Sabre pilot taxiied to the north end of the taxiway and turned in, complaining bitterly to the Kimpo Tower. The MiG continued down the runway to the south, and taxiied right into the alert ramp full of Sabres!

The surprised alert pilots and crew chiefs had various reactions. Several admit that they thought the little silver jet was some type of Navy aircraft, even though it had several very prominent red stars painted on it. The pilots in the alert birds, immediately bailed out of their cockpits and scrambled to the nearest cover. They thought the MiG driver might have bombs aboard that were wired to explode on landing.

But Lt. No Kum-Suk, a pilot in the North Korean Air Force, meant them no harm. He simply wanted to defect to the United States. And he used his MiG as a vehicle of escape. He had no knowledge of Operation MOOLAH, the $100,000.00 offer that was made by General Mark Clark for the intact delivery of a MIG-15 into the hands of United Nations forces.

Almost as soon as his wheels stopped turning, the 4th Air Police people were alongside him, and whisked him away to the Group Intelligence hut. The MiG was surrounded by 4th APs and U.S. Marines. Several M16 Quad-50 half tracks were set up nearby in case of air attack. Later that day, the MiG was towed up to the concrete main tower building. That evening, an Air Force C-124 Globemaster flew in and taxiied up near the MiG. Several members of the 4th calmly disassembled the MiG-15, and loaded it into the C-124. It was then flown to Kadena AB, Okinawa, where it was reassembled and test flown by pilots from the 4th Wing, as well as Air Force test pilots Tom Collins and Chuck Yeager.

On 9 October 1953, the 4th Wing participated in the FEAF Gunnery Meet that was held at Johnson AB, Japan. Led by Lt.Col. Vermont Garrison and Major Ralph Parr, with Maj. Robert Knapp and Capt. John Roberts completing the team, the 4th lost the high team scoring to the 41st FIS by 1.02 point. "The Grey Eagle" took top individual honors at the meet.

In early 1954, the missions continued much as they had throughout the last half of 1953. Takeoff at 0900 with an RF-86 from the 67th TRW, and proceed up the west coast of North Korea. Or rendezvous with an RB-45C from the 91st SRS for a similar flight. At the mouth of the Yalu River, in the heart of

The Presidential Unit Citation award was presented to the 4th Fighter Interceptor Wing in a ceremony at K-14 on 31 August 1953, for the period from 9 July 1951 to 27 November 1951. (John Africa)

Radar Hill at K-14. The facility was shut down for normal maintenance on 21 September 1953. And unknown to the people at K-14, so was the GCI radar at Chodo Island, leaving the air space over western North Korea completely unguarded. (John Africa)

On 21 September 1953, Lt. No Kum-Sok of the North Korean Air Force, made the decision to defect to South Korea. And he brought a MiG-15 with him! He landed against traffic at K-14, then taxied right into the alert ramp and parked – much to the shock of the alert pilots, the Kimpo tower, and everyone else working nearby. (Royce Raven)

MiG Alley, the recon aircraft would break away from the escorts and make a high speed, low level pass over the target area. Some targets were inside North Korea, some were in Manchuria and Red China, some were even inside the actual Soviet Union. The 4th Wing Sabres orbited nearby, waiting for a call that the recon bird was in trouble. But the call rarely came.

Lt. No Kum-Sok received $100,000.00 for delivering an intact MiG-15 to UN forces in Korea. The offer was made as part of Operation MOOLAH, and had been a standing offer throughout 1953. (USAFM)

Captain Bert Beecroft, 335th Fighter Interceptor Squadron
Kimpo AB, 22 January 1954

I reported to K-14 in mid-April 1953, and started flying combat in June. I had eighteen missions in when the war ended on 27 July. My Form 5 shows a combat mission lasting 1:50 to Sinuiju on the 27th, and a non-combat mission on the 28th. By January 1954, I had been promoted to D Flight Commander. By that date, most of our flights were patrols and escorts up the west coast of North Korea, and training flights in Korea and Japan.

On 22 January, the 335th mission for the day was escort for an RB-45C Tornado, flying a recon mission up the west coast. It was mid-afternoon, and the flight was sixteen F-86F Sabres. My flight was assigned to fly 'high cover'. The squadron was led by Lt.Col. Robert Dixon, who had the 'low flight' or close cover to the RB-45. On my wing was 1Lt. Rod Giffin.

As we crossed the 38th Parallel, the RB-45 was at about 25,000 feet, with my flight at 35,000. Although there were a lot of Sabres around the RB-45, there was nothing but air over

Below: After inspection by 4th Wing pilots and intelligence people from FEAF and 5th AF, the MiG was flown to Kadena AB, Okinawa, where several top U.S. pilots flew it, including Maj. Chuck Yeager, Capt. Tom Collins, Vermont Garrison, and others from both the 4th and 51st Groups. The serial number atop the tail is actually one from the F-86E serial sequence. (USAF)

Capt. Ralph Parr high over the Yellow Sea during an escort mission up the West Coast of Korea in the Summer of 1953. Capt. Parr, now assigned to the 334th Squadron, has ten kills on the nose of his aircraft, "Barb/Vent de la Mort", which was not his aircraft when he was in the 335th Squadron. (E. Sommerich)

Suddenly, the radio silence was broken – "Bandits at three o'clock high!" Then again the radio went silent.

The RB-45 was still flying due north, right up the coastline. I assume he was busy shooting pictures. But not the Sabre pilots. We were all watching the MiGs and trying to remain in our protective screen for the Tornado. Of course, we weren't allowed to pursue the MiGs or initiate any contact with them. But if one of them started to get into firing position, or made a firing pass on either us or the RB-45, then it was 'Katy, bar the door!'. If they started it, we were allowed to finish it.

Suddenly, as we watched with amazement, one of the MiGs left the rest of the bunch, and started down through our formation towards the RB-45. I fell in behind him and had him in my gun sight in case he started shooting. Col. Dixon called for the RB-45 to "Break now!" I called the RB-45 pilot and kept telling him to keep turning as the MiG was firing at him. I could see the puffs from around his 23mm cannon as he fired. The MiG driver fired twice, then three times, then a fourth, all the while I'm still yelling for the RB-45 pilot to "keep breaking, he's shooting at you!" Col. Dixon then called me and said "Get that son-of-a-bitch!"

I responded "Lead is locked on.", and began firing as the MiG broke right and started to climb back over the coastline (We weren't allowed to cross the coast). Since I had been diving to close on him, I was able to stay with him through the first part of his climb to safety. I was firing bursts at him the whole time. Then I saw it, fuel and smoke streaming from the MiG. I called Rod to see if he also saw him smoking.

About that time the MiG started some turns which were easy to stay with, and I was still firing when my guns suddenly quit. I thought that maybe I had 'fired out' (fired all the ammo), but the guns had jammed. I called Rod and said that I had fired out, then flew on past the MiG which was still smoking and had slowed considerably. Rod then said that he'd seen the MiG pilot bail out. Col. Dixon then called us and ordered us to return to K-14. My gun camera confirmed the kill.

In September 1954, the 4th FIW was removed from combat in Korea. The 334th and 335th Squadrons took their aircraft and crews to Chitose AB on the island of Hokkaido, Japan, while the 336th Squadron went to Misawa AB on North-

Following the Korean Ceasefire on 27 July 1953, many of the 4th Wing aircraft were sent through the REMCO facility at Tsuiki for much needed IRAN procedures. Any F-86F that did not have the '6-3 hard wing', was brought up to the latest F-86F standard, including addition of the new wing leading edge. FU-857 is Capt. 'Pete' Fernandez' old Sabre. (USAF)

On 6 October 1953, FEAF held a gunnery meet at Johnson AB, Japan. The 4th FIG team, comprised of Lt.Col. Vermont Garrison, Capt. Ralph Parr, Maj. Robert Knapp, and Capt. John Roberts, lost the meet to the 41st FIS team by a scant 1.02 points. However, 'The Grey Eagle' – Lt.Col. Garrison, was the top individual scorer. (USAF)

ern Honshu. The 335th Squadron was the last unit to leave K-14. It was Thanksgiving 1954. The missions from the Japanese bases were similar to those from Kimpo – air defense of northern Japan, with an occasional recon escort as far north as Vladivostok.

Captain George Amussen was assigned to the 334th Squadron at the time. He was Revamp Rifle Flight Leader. He recalls an incident that took place in December 1954. "We moved to Chitose in September, and began flying air defense missions over the northern part of the island. In December, a 91st SRS RB-50 was shot down by Soviet MiGs off the coast of the Kurile Islands. The RB-50 crew got out of the airplane before it crashed into the Sea of Japan, and a major rescue effort took place."

"I had one of the lead flights of Sabres that were covering the rescue effort. Just as the Dumbo (Grumman SA-16 Albatross') was ready to pick up the survivors, a couple of MiGs out of Vladivostok came down to see how things were going along. And to interrupt the rescue attempt if they could. But our radar alerted us to their presence and we chased them back to the Kuriles, with one of them streaming smoke after we got in some decent hits. From that time on, all the RB-29/RB-50 missions had a MiGCAP flight all the way to Russia."

On 30 June 1954, Col. Neil Newman took command of the wing. He was in command for six weeks before being replaced by Col. Alvin Hebert on 10 August. The Group Commanders were Col. Henry Tyler on 28 December 1953, Lt.Col. Dean Dutrack on 19 July 1954, and Col. William Gilchrist on 9 August.

During the winter of 54-55, the Red Chinese began flexing their muscles over the islands of Matsu and Quemoy. FEAF was forced to commit several units to the crisis, including some that had been withdrawn from Korea. In late January 1955, the 4th Wing again deployed to "The Land Of The Morning Calm", when the 335th Squadron moved to Osan AB (K-55), just south of the Korean DMZ.

The 4th FIG team at the 1953 FEAF Gunnery Meet. (kneeling) unknown and Capt. John Roberts; (standing left to right) Capt. Ralph Parr, Maj. Robert Knapp, and Lt. Col. Vermont Garrison. (USAF)

In November 1953, newly-elected U.S. Vice President Richard M. Nixon visited the troops in Korea. Capt. Ralph Parr 'checks out' Vice President Nixon in the F-86F on the ramp at Kimpo. Nixon holds Col. Don Hall's helmet. (John Africa)

1Lt. Bruno Giordano makes a last minute remark to the crew chief of "Patricia", before leaving for a 'training' mission up the west coast of Korea in December 1953. At least one of these 'training missions' went all the way up the east coast to Vladivostok, as a show of force to the Soviet MiG forces there. (USAF)

1Lt. Robert Stonestreet, 335th Fighter Interceptor Squadron

Osan AB, 5 February 1955

I was assigned to the 335th in May 1954. At the time we were based at Kimpo. But in the Fall of 1954, the 4th Wing moved back to Japan. During the winter of 1954-1955, Red China

Left: The old 336th Squadron torii that said "MiG Alley – 200 Miles", had a new sign installed signifying where the O-Club at K-14, commonly referred to as "Swig Alley", was located. (Left to right) Pilots H.P. Johnson, Ken Haugen, and Gobel James ham it up for the camera in early 1954. (Kenneth Haugen) Right: The 'theater of temperate climate' didn't get any warmer even though the war was over. "Tootsie", a 336th Squadron Sabre, is covered in snow in a Kimpo revetment in January 1954. (Tom Clark)

started making noises about invading the islands of Matsu and Quemoy, which were under the control of the Nationalist Chinese. FEAF immediately deployed several squadrons back to Korea, and my squadron, the 335th, went to Osan (K-55). The whole time we were at K-55, we maintained a five minute alert status with four airplanes.

On 5 February, twelve of our F-86s were scheduled to fly escort for an RB-45C Tornado. The RB-45 was going to fly up and down the west coast to shoot the North Korean airfields. The mission called for the RB-45C to fly at about 30,000 feet, parallel to the international boundary, which was about three miles off the coast. The Sabre escort was about 2000 feet above and behind the RB-45C, with 2000 feet separating the Sabre flights. Since the RB-45C flew at a considerably slower speed than the F-86s, we were required to fly a continuous S-turn or weave, to maintain our position and still keep our speed up above .82 mach.

We took off at 1300 hours. Our flight was Shark Flight, with Captain Jack Kimball leading. Lt. Giles 'Pockets' Charliebois was Shark 2, Lt. Chuck 'Fish' Salmon was Shark 3, and I was Shark 4. The RB-45C was Osage 111. Almost as soon as we left the runway at K-55, we were handed off to

Col. Donald Hall flew "Dottie", when he commanded the 4th Wing in August 1953. Note the red, yellow, and blue 'command stripes', signifying the Wing Commander's aircraft, around the fuselage and drop tanks. (Tom Clark)

BADGER Control. During climbout, and after crossing the coastline south of Inchon, we test-fired our guns, then started north.

As was always the case when our birds would start up the west coast, the MiGs would take off and climb to altitude, which was always above us. On several missions up the west coast, and at least one up the east coast that we flew, we always had a MiG escort. But usually they stayed inland. Most of the time all we could see of them were contrails.

The ground radar like SATAN Control, would monitor their flights, and advise us of the 'bandit' count. At a certain point up the coast, BADGER would turn us over to SATAN Control, a radar site on Cho-Do Island in the Yellow Sea. Cho-Do was a UN facility, located some seventy miles behind enemy lines. SATAN's radar coverage reached all the way to the Yalu and beyond, and they could track the MiGs almost as soon as they took off from Antung.

During Thanksgiving 1954, the 4th Wing moved from Kimpo to Chitose AB, Japan. (Left to right) Lts. Don Thiel, Chuck 'Fish' Salmon, Giles Charliebois, and Ike Coleman are seen at K-14 just prior to the move to Chitose. Lt. Salmon, promoted to Captain, shot down a North Korean MiG on 5 February 1955. (Bob Stonestreet)

Flying north this day, everything seemed routine. SATAN was giving us continuous info on the MiGs. The whole flight continued north to the mouth of the Yalu River, then turned west, before making a 180 and heading back towards the Yalu. Over the mouth of the river, we again turned south, maintaining a position in international air space, but as close to the three mile limit as we dared. As we passed Pyongyang, SATAN suddenly called 'Heads up! MiGs very close!' And suddenly all hell broke loose.

Shark Flight was in a shallow turn to the right, and were about to cross directly behind the RB-45 when someone started yelling "Hey, there're MiGs up here!" Then "Hey, those f—ers are shooting at us!" Instantly I looked back and saw four MiGs swooping down behind us at about 2000 feet, closing fast. The MiG leader was firing at the RB-45C and his No.3 was firing at me!

The first MiG element continued down under us heading straight for the RB-45. The second MiG element broke off to their right. At this time, our radio chatter turned from 'highly professional' to using nicknames. Except for one call which I remember distinctly. Fish Salmon was as calm as he could be when he suddenly asked, "Shark lead, this is 3. May I take the

"Sullie's Whip" and "Pappy's Pet", a pair of 334th Squadron F-86Fs, on the alert ramp at Chitose in 1956. The mission of the 4th FDW was air defense of northern Japan. Note the 334th Squadron 'Pissed-Off Pigeon' insignia has now been moved to the vertical tail. (via Mike Fox)

The 335th Squadron returned to Korea in January 1955 to bolster FEAF air defenses in South Korea. This time the squadron called K-55, Osan AB, home. The 335th made the deployment during the Formosa Crisis of January 1955. (Author)

bounce?" At which time, Jack Kimball just replied, equally calm, "Roger Shark 3."

Fish called me then, "Stoney, are my tanks clear?", and he punched off his drop tanks. I punched mine off as I answered him in the affirmative. He was already rolling over and pulling down into an inverted dive. I was on his right, in trail and trying to hold my position. Fish rolled out behind the two MiGs as they broke hard left over land. But Fish was in good shape and gave the trailing MiG a burst. As far as I could tell, he hit him with that first burst.

Both MiGs then reversed and made a hard climbing turn to the right. Not a smart move because now Fish could pull lead on him easily. He let go with another burst, which caught the MiG all around his tailpipe. I could see the little 'blinks' all around the fuselage as Fish's six .50s started scoring. The MiG started to smoke. At this point, both MiGs broke left again and rolled level in a shallow dive. Fish kept asking me "Stoney, are we still clear?" I was constantly looking around for the other two MiGs and assured him that indeed, we were still clear.

During this two or three minute melee, there was a lot of other radio traffic. We knew that at least eight MiGs had bounced us, with at least one scoring a hit on Lt. Don Phillips' Sabre. The MiGs had started their pass on the top Sabre flight, then made a climbing turn back to safety. Phillips' Sabre made it back safely, with minimal damage. Captain George Williams, leader of one of the other flights, shot down another MiG.

On 5 February 1955, the 335th Squadron was escorting an RB-45C photo recon bomber up the west coast of North Korea, when eight MiGs attempted to disrupt the mission. Capt. Charles 'Fish' Salmon (right) demonstrates how he shot down a MiG to Lt.Col. Chester Wine, Commander of the 335th Squadron, as Capt. George Williams listens. Williams also shot down a MiG on this mission. (USAF)

Right: Lt. Robert Stonestreet was Capt. 'Fish' Salmon's wingman on the 5 February MiG-killing mission. (Bob Stonetreet)

After our two MiGs rolled out over land, they headed east in a shallow dive. Fish and I continued the chase "in hot pursuit." Only that week the 'rules of engagement' had been changed to allow us to chase them back over land. Fish kept firing. The MiG was really starting to smoke now. I was now right up beside Fish's right wing as he kept asking for me to clear his tail. I was also now directly behind the other MiG and in good firing range.

Looking up to our left, I suddenly saw a fighter rolling in from nine o'clock high. I was about to call it as a bandit, when I realized it was a lone F-86. It was Lt. Leroy Crane and he pulled in directly in front of me and started firing at the other MiG. My MiG! I moved to the left and positioned myself between Fish and Leroy, trying to keep us all clear. Leroy was firing but he wasn't hitting anything. Then I heard Fish call that he had 'fired out' (was out of ammo), and for me to move over and take the MiG that he'd already hit several times.

The MiG was burning pretty good by this time, but the pilot hadn't ejected yet. As Fish moved out, I pulled in behind the burning MIG. Then Leroy called that he too, had 'fired out'. I now had my choice of either MiG. I remember thinking about which one to take, when the radio came alive. It was Harpoon One, "Break it off and return to base." Fish and Leroy immediately pulled up and to the right. As a wingman, I had no choice. I had to break it off too, without ever firing a shot!

1Lt. Leftwich and his family stand next to his 335th FBS F-86F named "Texas Traveler", on the snowy ramp at Chitose in March 1956. With the war over, FEAF allowed many of the men to bring their families with them to Chitose. (Ken Buchanen)

We had fought those MiGs from above 30,000 feet to below 5,000, and had flown about fifty miles inland over North Korea. Fish, Leroy and I joined up and the rest of the flight home was uneventful. As we approached the end of the runway, Fish asked to do a victory roll over the base but was denied. That night at the O-Club, we had quite a celebration. It

Lt. James Jenson was the pilot of "Irva-Jean", a 335th Squadron Sabre that is sitting on jacks in the gun harmonizing pits at Osan in early 1955. The 335th re-deployed to Korea during the Red Chinese attempted capture of the islands of Matsu and Quemoy in the Formosa Straits. (Author)

At Chitose, the 4th Wing had an additional squadron assigned, the 339th FIS equipped with F-86D all-weather interceptors. The 339th Squadron was attached to the 4th Wing between 18 September 1954 and 7 December 1957. (via Mike Fox)

was somewhat akin to what they have after winning a Super Bowl. Even the RB-45 crew, enlisted guys and all, partied with us.

Fish Salmon and Willie Williams flew out the next morning for Tokyo and a big news conference. We never did hear anything from the Reds as to whether they had lost a couple of MiGs. Nor did we find out whether or not the MiGs were North Korean or Chinese. All they said was that we had violated their airspace, and were over North Korea at the time of the 'incident'. But the camera film doesn't lie. Scratch two MiGs!

From this time on, the wing supplied pilots and airplanes for a variety of missions throughout the Far East Theater – wherever a crisis required a U.S. presence. Most of the missions were air defense or escort of a reconnaissance or rescue flight. There were routine return deployments to Korea, usually a detachment or (rarely) an entire squadron. And occasional deployments to places like Okinawa or the Philippines to support units that were engaged in the on-going crisis over Formosa.

Officially, the mission of the 4th Wing changed from air superiority to strike on 8 March 1955 when the designation was changed to 4th Fighter Bomber Wing. That mission was changed again a year later. On 26 April 1956, the 4th FBW was re-designated the 4th Fighter Day Wing. A 'fighter day wing' mission was air superiority, the same mission the wing had been flying since 1940.

1Lt. Wally Carson interviews Col. George Ruddell, Commander of the 4th Group, during the 1955 FEAF Gunnery Meet held at Suwon AB in mid-April. Col. Ruddell was a jet ace in the war with eight MiG kills that he scored with the 51st Group. (USAF)

Col. Grover Brown took command of the 4th Wing at Chitose on 1 May 1955. His aircraft, "Trouble IV" has a three-color nose and winged 4th emblem, with each color representing the three squadrons in the 4th Fighter Bomber Wing. The 4th took on a fighter bomber mission on 8 March 1955. (via Mike Fox)

In May 1957, the 4th Wing undertook one of their most important missions during the deployment to the Far East – training Japanese Air Self Defense Force pilots to fly the F-86F Sabre. The initial batch of Sabres for use by the JASDF, were transferred directly from the 4th FBW to the JASDF 1st Fighter Wing. (via Mike Fox)

Col. Grover Brown took over command of the 4th Wing on 1 May 1955. At the same time, a Korean combat veteran took over command of the 4th Group. He was an ace with eight MiGs – but not from the 4th Wing. Col. George Ruddell had scored all his victories when he commanded the 39th FIS in the 51st Fighter Wing at Suwon. He knew how to make tigers of the new pilots coming into the 4th, and soon had them training on flying the F-86 right on the edge. Col. Robert Montgomery took command of the Wing on 17 August 1956, with Col. Earle Myers relieving him on 6 June 1957.

In May 1957, the men of the 4th Wing helped organize and train the first classes of jet pilots and mechanics for the soon-to-be-created Japanese Air Self Defense Force at Chitose. The JASDF would be equipped with F-86F Sabres, which were being license-built in Japan by Mitsubishi Heavy Industries. But their first aircraft were transfers from the 4th Wing.

On 2 July 1957, Col. James Shelly took over the reigns of the 4th FDW. He would be the last commander the wing would have in the Far East. In the late fall of 1957, the wing was alerted that they would be going home. Well not quite. The 4th FDW designation was going back to the United States. The pilots and airplanes remained in the Far East, assigned to other units in Japan and Korea. On 8 December 1957, the 4th Fighter Day Wing was permanently and instantaneously, moved from Chitose AB, Japan, to Seymour Johnson AFB, North Carolina. The 4th Group was inactivated that same day.

The three stripes around the nose of "Hallie's Comet", indicate that Maj. W.H. Rice was the Commander of the 334th FDS during the training of JASDF pilots at Chitose. The 4th became a Fighter Day Wing, again maintaining an air superiority mission, on 25 April 1956. (via Mike Fox)

The 'short TDY to a country of temperate climate' was finally over. The 4th Wing had been in the Far East for slightly over seven years. It wouldn't last. Slightly less than seven years hence, the squadrons of the 4th would again be involved in a shooting war in a far off land. This time in Southeast Asia in a place called Vietnam. Following a truly short TDY in 1964-65, the squadrons went back to Southeast Asia in 1972 for the LINEBACKER operations.

twelve

Vietnam and Beyond

When the 4th Wing returned to the United States on 8 December 1957, they took over the aircraft and mission of the 83rd Fighter Day Wing at Seymour Johnson AFB, North Carolina. Once again, the 4th was flying their beloved F-86 Sabres, this time in the F-86H. But it wouldn't last long as the 83rd was already beginning the transition to the North American F-100C Super Sabre. When the 4th arrived, there were five F-86Hs and twelve F-100Cs on the base. The 4th also acquired a fourth squadron – the 333rd Squadron 'Lancers'. On 1 July 1958, the 4th Fighter Day Wing was redesignated as the 4th Tactical Fighter Wing, and all four assigned squadrons were redesignated as tactical fighter squadrons.

The 4th TFW flew the F-100C (and F-100F trainer) for less than a year before transitioning began into the second Century Series fighter aircraft, the Republic F-105B Thunderchief. On 19 June 1959, the first four F-105Bs arrived and were assigned to the 334th TFS. Not only was the 334th Squadron the first to transition to the new Thunderchief, they would also be conducting the Category II Operational Flight Tests at Eglin AFB, Florida. On 11 December 1959, Brigadier General Joseph Moore, Commander of the 4th TFW, set a new World Speed Record for the 100 kilometer closed course, with a speed of 1167.35 mph in a production F-105B, then improved on that with a 1216.4 mph run the next day.

The 4th TFW, the only F-105B unit in the Air Force, was just beginning both testing and transition into the new F-105D when CIA U-2 spy aircraft uncovered the fact that Soviet ICBMs were being installed on the island of Cuba, just ninety miles from Florida. The entire U.S. Armed Forces were put on maximum alert for a possible invasion of Cuba; or worse, a nuclear war with the Soviet Union. On October 18th, 1962, the 4th TFW deployed to McCoy AFB, FL. Their mission during the Cuban Missile Crisis would be air superiority, even though the aircraft that they flew was a tactical nuclear strike fighter. When the crisis ended, the 4th Wing went back to the business of training for the war that hadn't come.

Disaster struck on 22 November 1963, when President John F. Kennedy was assassinated. The 4th TFW provided a thirty-five aircraft flyover for the President's funeral. One month later, on 25 December 1963, the first F-105F trainer was delivered to Seymour Johnson. In January 1964, the first production F-105Ds arrived from Republic, and the F-105Bs were transferred into the New Jersey Air National Guard. On 23 June 1964, the Wing was completely equipped with new F-105D and F-105F aircraft. And just in time to meet the next crisis. Another Asian war was brewing half way around the world from the United States. This time the country was South Vietnam.

On 2 August 1964, North Vietnamese Navy patrol boats attacked U.S. Navy destroyers that were patrolling in the Gulf of Tonkin off the coast of North Vietnam. Thus began eleven years of conflict in Southeast Asia. The personnel of the 4th TFW continued their training until late Spring 1965, becoming very proficient in the new F-105D, when the 335th TFS was alerted for another short TDY to "a country of temperate climate." This time the alert order was correct. The TDY would actually be short, and Southeast Asia was a 'temperate climate', although tropical was closer to the truth.

On 3 July 1965, the 335th deployed to Yokota AB, Japan, under Operation TWO BUCK 13. They would take the place of the squadrons at Yokota that were already operating against North Vietnam. On 28 August 1965, the 4th Wing again went

When the 4th FDW unit number was transferred to Seymour Johnson AFB, NC, on 8 December 1957, they inherited the remaining F-86H assets of the 83rd FDW. It was the final F-86 variant that the 4th Wing flew. The next step was the supersonic F-100C Super Sabre. (Col. Hess Bomberger)

to war, when the 334th TFS deployed to Takhli RTAFB, Thailand. The 334th began flying missions against North Vietnamese targets right away, and suffered their first loss on 20 September when Captain Willis Forby was shot down and taken prisoner. And on 30 September, disaster struck the 334th when a North Vietnamese SAM missile exploded the F-105D flown by the Commander of the 334th, LtCol. Melvin Killian. LtCol. Killian died in the explosion of the Thunderchief.

The 335th TFS deployed from Yokota to Takhli on 3 November 1965. Both squadrons eventually came under the operational control of the newly activated 355th TFW at Takhli. The first of the TDY squadrons, the 335th TFS, returned to Seymour Johnson on 15 December 1965, leaving their aircraft and ground crews behind. The 333rd TFS took over the aircraft and ground crews of the 335th at Takhli, and was permanently re-assigned from the 4th TFW to the 355th TFW on 8 December 1965.

Although the 333rd would remain assigned to the 355th Wing until de-activation in December 1970, the 334th Squadron would return to Seymour Johnson on 10 October 1966. By the end of the TWO BUCK deployments to the war in Southeast Asia, the 4th Wing had lost eight aircraft – one from the 335th and seven from the 334th. Four pilots did not return from Southeast Asia – LtCol. Killian (334th) and Capt. Thomas Reitman (335th) were killed in action; while Capt. Forby (334th) and Capt. Jon Reynolds became prisoners of war. LtCol. Killian's remains were not returned until 8 June 1985.

An F-100C of the 334th TFS at Andrews AFB in May 1958. The 4th Wing transitioned into the F-100C in early 1958, again taking over the assets of the 83rd Wing that preceded them at Seymour Johnson. Note the early positioning of the national insignia on the nose of the F-100. (Ron Picciani)

An F-100F from the 333rd TFS in 1960. The 333rd was activated on 8 December 1957 when the 4th Wing moved into Seymour Johnson. The 9th AF Firepower Team markings were applied for a gunnery meet at Nellis AFB. (Col. D. Elmer)

When the 334th TFS returned to Seymour Johnson in October 1966, they also did not bring their aircraft with them. The remaining F-105Ds and F-105Fs were assigned to the 355th TFW at Takhli, and would soldier on until that unit was deactivated on 10 December 1970. A total of 334 Thunderchiefs would be shot down over the next few years by the vastly improved North Vietnamese defenses.

It was just as well, however, as the 4th Wing was about to transition to a new aircraft – the McDonnell Douglas F-4D Phantom II. On 27 January 1967, Col. Robert Spencer, Commander of the 4th Wing, delivered the first F-4D to Seymour Johnson. It was the beginning of a twenty-two year love affair between the 4th and the F-4 Phantom. By June 1967, the 4th was completely equipped with the F-4D.

Six months later, the Wing was once again alerted for possible combat duty. And it was a very familiar name this time – Korea. On 23 January 1968, the North Korean Navy seized the U.S. Navy intelligence ship USS Pueblo, and its entire crew of eighty-three men. On 27 January 1968, the 4th TFW returned to Korea as part of Operation COMBAT FOX. The Wing was in place at Kunsan AB, South Korea in a matter of days. The 4th remained in Korea until June 1968 before returning to Seymour Johnson. The 335th TFS returned on 28 June, the 336th on 11 July, and the 334th on 30 July 1968. Col. Chuck

A 336th TFS F-100C on the Langley AFB ramp in January 1959. The aircraft was flown by the Commander of the 4th TFW, Col. Timothy O'Keefe. Col. O'Keefe took command of the 4th Wing on 5 January 1959, and his aircraft had three color stripes bordering the white nose and tail bands. (MSGT Merle Olmsted)

F-105Bs from the 334th TFS over Seymour Johnson in 1959. The 334th TFS was the first unit to be equipped with the F-105B Thunderchief, flying the Category II Operational Test Program at Eglin beginning in June 1959. (USAF)

Yeager, new Commander of the 4th TFW, remarked that, "we engaged no enemy, shot down no aircraft, and underwent no bombardment. But we moved an entire wing (seventy-two aircraft, 2000 personnel, and more than 1000 tons of equipment) 9000 miles in a matter of a few days."

On 16 April 1970, the first four F-4E Phantom IIs were delivered to Seymour Johnson. The F-4E differed from the D model in having an internal 20mm Gatling Cannon to augment the air to air missile capabilities. Nine months later, on 16 February 1971, the Wing was completely equipped with the latest model of the F-4 Phantom. Transition training continued into early 1972. The training was interrupted on 30 March 1972, when the North Vietnamese launched their Easter Invasion of South Vietnam. President Nixon immediately ordered Operation CONSTANT GUARD, which sent a number of Air Force squadrons to Southeast Asia to bolster the strength of the squadrons in Thailand that were trying to stem the tide of the North Vietnamese invasion.

One of the first units alerted was the 4th Wing. On 12 April 1972, the 334th TFS deployed to Ubon RTAFB, Thailand, returning to Seymour Johnson on 21 July 1972. The 336th TFS went to Ubon on 13 April, staying until 30 September. The 335th TFS relieved the 334th at Ubon on 20 July, returning on 21 December. It was a rotational deployment as the 334th returned to Ubon to relieve the 336th on 21 September; who were in turn, relieved by the 336th on 9 March 1973. The end of the 4th TFW CONSTANT GUARD deployments came on 11 September 1973, when the final 336th F-4E returned to Seymour Johnson.

During the CONSTANT GUARD deployments, 4th Wing air crews flew more than 8700 combat sorties in the LINEBACKER I and II operations, of which 1300 sorties were over North Vietnam. The wing lost eleven aircraft in combat. Five air crew were rescued, while eight became POWs. Capt. Samuel Cornelius was declared killed in action, when his F-4E was shot down over Cambodia on 16 June 1973 (the war in Cambodia did not end until 15 August 1973). Captains Frederick Sheffler and Mark Massen (336th) shot down a North Vietnamese Air Force MiG-21 on 15 August 1972, recording the first MiG kill since the Korean War. On 14 April 1973, the last 4th Wing POWs returned to Seymour Johnson and were greeted by more than 1000 people.

But it was from the frying pan into the fire for the crews of the 4th, as they began delivering 4th Wing F-4Es to Israel during the October 1973 Yom Kippur War under Operation PEACE ECHO. Many of the aircraft were armed enroute to Israeli air bases, with live bombs and cannon shells, and delivered that ordnance on Egyptian and Syrian targets along the way.

Over the next fifteen years, the Wing deployed squadrons to bases all over the world on a regular basis. In October 1977, the 4th TFW became one of a few Air Force units to have a 'dual base capability', with the 4th calling both Seymour Johnson and Ramsten AB, Germany 'home'. Exercise CORONET VIKING sent the 336th TFS to Bodo AS, Norway to sup-

The 335th TFS was the second squadron to have the F-105B. Brigadier General Joseph Moore flew a 335th TFS F-105B to a new World Speed Record on 12 December 1959, covering the 100 km course at 1167.35 mph, then going 1216.4 mph the next day. (MSGT Merle Olmsted)

A 335th TFS F-105D at Wright Patterson AFB in 1962. The 4th 'officially' began conversion to the D model Thunderchief in January 1964. However, the 335th had several test aircraft assigned when they deployed to McCoy AFB during the Cuban Missile Crisis in October 1962. (Maj. Gene Sommerich)

A 334th TFS F-105D carries a full load of M117 750 lb. General Purpose bombs as the pilot prepares to take on fuel from a waiting SAC KC-135A tanker in October 1965. SAC tankers were essential for all F-105 operations from Thai bases into North Vietnam. (Dave Graben)

port NATO. The 335th deployed to Spangdahlem AB, Germany under CORONET SPA. Competing in the Aerospace Defense Command exercise known as WILLIAM TELL '76, the 4th TFW took home 1st Place in the F-4 category. On 12 September 1981, the Wing placed 1st in the GUNSMOKE '81 competition held at Nellis AFB. On 1 April 1982, the Wing activated a fourth squadron, the 337th TFS, which was inactivated again on 1 July 1985.

On 6 January 1987, Air Force announced that the 4th TFW would be the first unit to equip with the brand new F-15E Strike Eagle. The first aircraft, "Spirit Of Goldsboro", F-15E #87-0178, arrived at Seymour Johnson on 29 December 1988. The first squadron to be fully equipped with the F-15E was the 336th TFS, which completed the transition from F-4E to F-15E on 20 April 1989. The 335th TFS followed on 1 March 1990, with the 334th completing the transition on 1 January 1991. Just in time to participate in still another Asian war. The last F-4Es departed Seymour Johnson on 7 January 1991.

Armorers remove the 20mm ammunition drum from a 335th TFS F-105D on the ramp at Takhli RTAFB in late 1965. The 335th deployed initially to Yokota AB, Japan in August 1964, then moved to Takhli in November 1965. (USAF)

Below: A pair of 334th TFS F-105Ds prepare to taxi for takeoff at Takhli in 1965, armed with bombs and rocket pods. The first camouflaged aircraft reached Southeast Asia in late 1965. Both aircraft remained in Southeast Asia after the 334th went back to the United States, being assigned to the 333rd TFS. Both aircraft were shot down in mid-1967. (USAF)

An F-4D assigned to the 335th TFS over North Carolina in mid-1967. The first F-4Ds were delivered to Seymour Johnson in January 1967. Initially, no tail codes were applied to the aircraft. The F-4D carries AIM-7 Sparrow missiles and a SUU-23 Gatling Gun Pod on the centerline station. (USAF)

The war this time was in Southwest Asia against a tyrant named Saddam Hussein. The country to be defended, or rather retaken, was Kuwait. Hussein had ordered the Iraqi army into neighboring Kuwait on 2 August 1990. President George Bush initiated Operation DESERT SHIELD to protect Saudi Arabia from attack by Iraq and interrupting the flow of vital oil supplies from Saudi Arabia. On 9 August 1990, the 336th TFS deployed the first of twenty-four F-15Es to Thumrait AB, Oman, before moving to Al Kharj AB, Saudi Arabia in December 1991.

Col. Chuck Yeager, 4th TFW Commander, talks with his air crews on the flightline at Kunsan AB, South Korea in May 1968. The 4th TFW deployed over 9000 miles to Korea during the Pueblo Incident, which almost resulted in a full resumption of hostilities in Korea. (USAF)

On 20 December 1990, the 4th TFW(Provisional) Headquarters was established at Al Kharj, which was located about fifty miles southeast of Dhahran. The 335th TFS joined the

A 334th TFS F-4E on the ramp at Ubon in August 1972 during Operation LINEBACKER. President Nixon ordered Operation CONSTANT GUARD to bolster the forces in Southeast Asia trying to stop the North Vietnamese takeover of South Vietnam. (John Poole)

336th at Al Kharj on 27 December, bringing the total number of F-15Es deployed to DESERT SHIELD to forty-eight aircraft. Something big was in the works – the Allied Coalition military action that would drive the Iraqi troops out of Kuwait. At 0300 local time on 17 January 1991, after months of fruitless negotiations with Hussein, President Bush ordered Operation DESERT STORM.

The F-15Es from the 4th TFW(Provisional) would be among the first waves of attacking aircraft hitting targets throughout Iraq and Kuwait. The F-15E air crews hit suspected Scud missile launching sites, aircraft bunkers, bridges, and command and control structures, guiding the latest smart bombs right in through an open door or window, and some that were closed. The Gulf War ended on 28 February 1991 with the liberation of Kuwait and the complete humiliation of Saddam Hussein and his vaunted Republican Guard armored force.

During DESERT STORM, the 336th TFS flew 1088 combat sorties, dropping some 6.5 million pounds of ordnance, including standard 'dumb bombs', cluster bombs, and laser-guided munitions. The 335th TFS flew 1097 combat sorties, dropping 4.8 million pounds of ordnance. The 335th TFS recorded one air to air victory during the Gulf War when Capt. Richard Bennett (Pilot) and Capt. Daniel Bakke (WSO) downed a hovering Iraqi Hughes 500 helicopter near Al Quaim, Iraq, using a Mk 82 500 lb. laser-guided bomb. The date was 14 February 1991.

The 4th TFW(Provisional) lost three F-15Es during the eight month DESERT SHIELD/DESERT STORM deployment.

A 336th TFS F-4E laser bomber on the Ubon ramp armed with Mk 84 2000 lb. laser guided bombs. Using LGBs, the 4th TFW air crews struck hard targets like bridges and bunker complexes during the LINEBACKER raids in the Summer of 1972. 4th TFW air crews left Ubon in late 1973, turning their aircraft over to crews from the 31st TFW. (John Poole)

A 335th Squadron F-15E Strike Eagle on the Seymour Johnson ramp with the LANTIRN pod under the fuselage and carrying AIM-9L Sidewinder air-to-air missiles under the wing. The first 'operational' F-15E arrived at Seymour Johnson on 20 April 1989. (Robert F Dorr)

Right: 4th TFW ground crew personnel pull the wheel chocks from a 336th TFS F-15E on the ramp at Thrumrait AB, Oman, in September 1990 during Operation DESERT SHIELD, the buildup of aircraft that would eventually combat Iraqi forces in DESERT STORM. (Robert F Dorr)

Right: F-15E combat operations against Iraq were flown from Al Kharj AB in Saudi Arabia. The first targets were hit beginning at 0300 hours on 17 January 1991. The LANTIRN pod is under the right fuselage. This aircraft was assigned to the Commander of the 4th TFW(Provisional), Col. Hal Hornberg. (Robert F Dorr)

Below: Five 4th TFW(P) aircraft fly over destroyed Iraqi aircraft bunkers. 4th TFW(P) F-15Es, using precision guided munitions, knocked out many of this type of target during the Gulf War. The F-16s are from the New York and South Carolina Air Guards, while the 'BT' coded F-15C is from the 36th TFW at Bitburg AB, Germany. (4th Wing/PAO)

Maj. Peter Hook and Capt. James Poulet were killed when their F-15E crashed in Oman on 30 September 1990. Maj. Thomas Kuritz and Maj. Donnie Holland (335th) were killed in action shot down on the first night of the air war – 17 January 1991. Col. David Eberly and Maj. Thomas Griffith (4th TFW Staff) were shot down by an Iraqi SAM on 19 January 1991 and captured. Both pilots were released from captivity by 5 March 1991.

On 13 March 1991, the 4th TFW(Provisional) was inactivated at Al Kharj and returned to Seymour Johnson. Although the combat squadrons returned to Seymour Johnson, rotational deployments continued throughout the 1990s as part of Operation SOUTHERN WATCH, and were based at Dhahran International Airport.

On 22 April 1991, the first of two major Air Force reorganizations took place. The 4th Tactical Fighter Wing became the first of the new 'composite wings, equipped with several different types of aircraft. The new unit was called simply, the 4th Wing, and they were equipped with seventy-two F-15E Strike Eagles and twenty McDonnell Douglas KC-10A Extender tankers.

The 4th Wing was re-organized with five squadrons attached – the 334th, 335th and 336th Fighter Squadrons with F-15Es; and the 344th and 911th Air Refueling Squadrons with KC-10As. Finally, on 1 June 1992, after thirty-five years in Tactical Air Command, the 4th Wing was assigned to the new Air Force Air Combat Command, which had control over all the offensive and defensive forces within the Air Force, including the old Strategic Air Command bomber force.

But no matter what official unit designation was carried, or what command the unit was assigned to, they would always be:

"FOURTH BUT FIRST!"

The only air to air 'victory' that 4th pilots got in the Gulf War was by 335th TFS air crew Capt. Richard Bennett (Pilot) and Capt. Daniel Bakke (WSO) used a 500 lb laser guided bomb to down an Iraqi helicopter on 14 February 1991. (Tim Zick)

4th TFW(P) aircraft flying over the burning oil wells that Iraqi troops set afire in Kuwait during DESERT STORM. The 4th Wing is the only Air Force wing to fly combat in every major conflict since World War II. (4th Wing/PAO)

A 916th ARW KC-135 refuels a pair of 4th FW F-15Es. The 916th Air Refueling Wing is based at Seymour Johnson AFB, and is an Air Force Reserve unit. (4th WING/PAO)

The Commander of the 4th Wing, and all four squadron commanders, flying formation with a 911th Air Refueling Squadron KC-10A in 1994. The 911th Squadron was assigned to the 4th Wing when it was still a composite wing. (4th Wing/PAO)

Appendices

IN MEMORIAM
4th Fighter Interceptor Wing Pilots Killed In Action

1Lt Eugene G. Aldridge, 335th Squadron, 11 July 1953
1Lt Conrad M. Allard, 335th Squadron, 11 July 1951
Major Felix Asla, Jr, 336th Squadron, 1 August 1952
1Lt Carl G. Barnett, Jr, 336th Squadron, 26 September 1951
2Lt Albert W. Beerwinkle, 335th Squadron, 11 February 1953
1Lt Austin W. Beetle Jr, 335th Squadron, 4 July 1952
1Lt James D. Carey, 334th Squadron, 24 March 1952
2Lt Max H. Collins, 335th Squadron, 4 May 1953
Captain Troy G. Cope, 335th Squadron, 16 September 1952
1Lt Albert Cox, 335th Squadron, 11 July 1953
LtCol George A. Davis Jr, 334th Squadron 10 February 1952
1Lt Thomas Hanson, 336th Squadron, 5 June 1951
1Lt Charles B. Hogue, 334th Squadron, 13 December 1951
1Lt John W. Honaker, 335th Squadron, 14 March 1952
Squadron Leader Graham S. Hulse, RAF, 336th Squadron, 13 March 1953
1Lt Paul J. Jacobson, 335th Squadron, 12 February 1953
1Lt Robert H. Laier, 336th Squadron, 19 June 1951
Captain John F. Lane, 336th Squadron, 20 May 1952
1Lt Laurence C. Layton, 335th Squadron, 2 September 1951
2Lt Joe A. Logan, 336th Squadron, 15 September 1952
1Lt Joseph E. McElvain, 336th Squadron, 7 November 1952
1Lt Howard P. Miller Jr, 336th Squadron, 28 November 1951
1Lt Robert F. Niemann, 334th Squadron, 12 April 1953
1Lt Lester F. Page, 334th Squadron, 6 January 1952
Captain Charles W. Pratt, 334th Squadron, 8 November 1951
1LtWilliam F. Prindle, 334th Squadron, 15 December 1951
1Lt Donald R. Reitsma, 335th Squadron, 22 December 1952
Major Thomas M. Sellers, 336th Squadron, 20 July 1953
1Lt Charles R. Spath, 335th Squadron, 3 February 1952
1Lt Ward L. Starkweather, 335th Squadron, 28 December 1951
2Lt Bill J. Stauffer, 336th Squadron, 26 January 1953
2Lt James E. Swenson, 336th Squadron, 7 November 1952

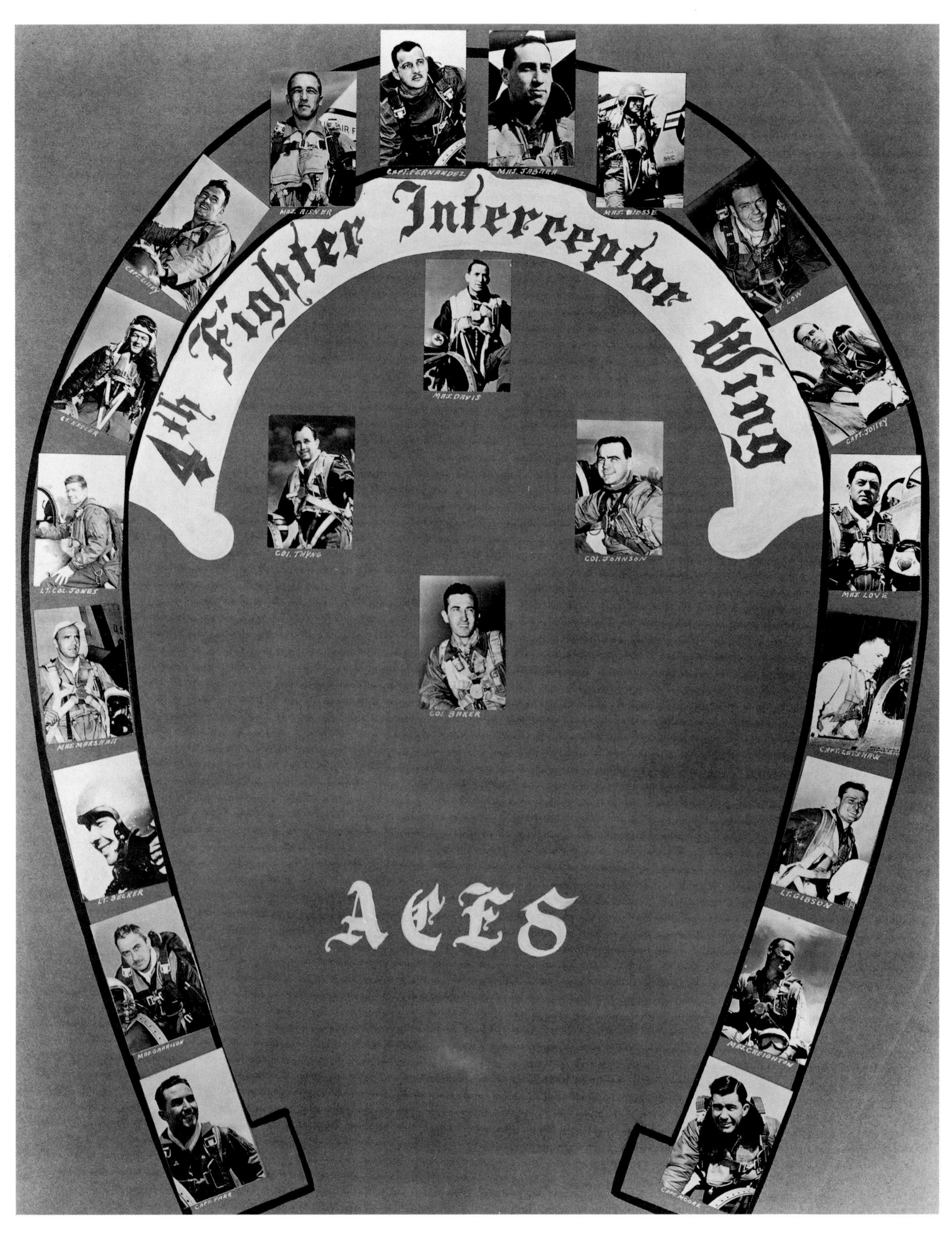

4th FIW aces in a horseshoe photo. (USAF)

4th Fighter Interceptor Wing Aces In The Korean War

Ace #	Name, Rank & Squadron	1st Victory	5th Victory	Final Score
1)	James J. Jabara, Captain, 334th	3 April 1951	20 May 1951	
	Major, 4th FIW (10th victory-10 June 1953)			
	(15th victory-15 July 1953)			15.0
2)	Richard S. Becker, Captain,334th	22 April 1951	9 September 1951	5.0
3)	Ralph D Gibson, Captain, 335th	18 June 1951	9 September 1951	5.0
4)	Richard D. Creighton, Major, 336th	18 June 1951	27 November 1951	5.0
5)	George A. Davis, Major, 334th	27 November 1951	30 November 1951	
	(10th victory-13 Dec. 1951)			14.0
6)	Winton W. Marshall, Major, 335th	1 September 1951	30 November 1951	6 1/2
11)	Robert J. Love, Captain, 335th	20 March 1952	21 April 1952	6.0
13)	Robert T. Latshaw, Jr., Captain, 335th	25 January 1952	3 May 1952	5.0
15)	James H. Kasler, 1Lt., 335th	1 April 1952	15 May 1952	6.0
16)	Harrison R. Thyng, Colonel, 4th FIW	24 October 1951	20 May 1952	5.0
17)	James F. Low, 2Lt, 335th	8 May 1952	15 June 1952	9.0
18)	Clifford D. Jolley, Captain, 335th	4 May 1952	8 August 1952	7.0
19)	Frederick C. Blesse, Major, 334FIS	25 May 1952	4 September 1952	
	(10th victory-3 October 1952)			10.0
20)	Robinson Risner, Captain, 336th	5 August 1952	21 September 1952	8.0
21)	Royal N. Baker, Colonel, 4th FIG	20 June 1952	17 November 1952	
	(10th victory-14 Feb. 1953)			13.0
22)	Leonard W. Lilley, Captain, 334th	30 August 1952	18 November 1952	7.0
27)	Manuel J. Fernandez, Jr., Captain, 334th	4 October 1952	18 February 1953	
	(10th victory-21 March 1953)			14 1/2
29)	James K. Johnson, Colonel, 4th FIW	13 January 1953	28 March 1953	
	(10th victory- 30 June 1953)			10.0
30)	George L. Jones, Lt.Colonel, 4th FIW	2 November 1951	29 March 1953	6 1/2
32)	Vermont Garrison, Major, 335th	21 February 1953	5 June 1953	
	(10th victory-19 July 1953)			10.0
33)	Lonnie R. Moore, Captain, 335th	13 March 1953	18 June 1953	
	(10th victory- 19 July 1953)			10.0
34)	Ralph S. Parr, Captain, 334th	7 June 1953	18 June 1953	
	(10th victory- 27 July 1953)			10.0
38)	Clyde A. Curtin, Captain, 335th	11 October 1952	19 July 1953	5.0
39)	Stephen L. Bettinger, Major, 336th	5 June 1953	20 July 1953	5.0

Total number of aces in 4th Fighter Wing	**24**
Total number of enemy aircraft downed by aces	**197 1/2**

Victories by 4th Fighter Interceptor Wing pilots

Major Foster Smith, 334th & 335th FIS 4 1/2
Major Felix Asla, 334 & 336 FIS 4
Captain Ralph Banks, 336 FIS 4
1/Lt Charles Cleveland, 334th FIS 4
Captain Philip Colman, 335th FIS 4
1/Lt Billy Dobbs, 335th FIS 4
1/Lt Walter Fellman, 336th FIS 4
Lt.Col. Louis Green, 336th FIS 4
Captain Brooks Liles, 336th FIS 4
Major Jack Mass, 335th FIS 4
Captain Conrad Mattson, 335th FIS 4
Captain Milton Nelson, 335th FIS 4
Colonel Benjamin Preston, 4th Group 4
Captain Murray Winslow, 335th FIS 4
Major Zane Amell, 335th FIS 3
Lt.Col. William Cosby, 336th & 334th FIS 3
Captain Karl Dittmer, 335th FIS 3
Major Franklin Fisher, 4th Group 3
Captain Peter Frederick, 336th FIS 3
Major Alex Gillis, USMC, 335th FIS 3
Flt/Lt Ernest Glover, RCAF, 334th FIS 3
1/Lt Ira Porter, 335th FIS 3
1/Lt Merton Ricker, 335th FIS 3
1/Lt Albert Smiley, 335th FIS 3
Captain Houston Tuel, 336th FIS 3
Captain George Dunn, 334th FIS & 4th Grp 2.5
Captain John Taylor, 335th FIS 2.5
1/Lt Coy Austin, 335th FIS 2
Major Richard Ayersman, 334th FIS 2
1/Lt Raymond Barton, 334th FIS 2
1/Lt John Burke, 334th FIS 2
1/Lt Charles Carl, 336th FIS 2
1/Lt Charles Christison, 336th FIS 2
Captain Theodore Coberly, 334th FIS 2
Major David Davidson, 334th FIS 2
Captain Ryland Dewey, 334th FIS 2
1/Lt Alfred Dymock, 334th FIS 2
Lt.Col. Glenn Eagleston, 4th Group 2
1/Lt Ivan Ely, 334th FIS 2
1/Lt Douglas Evans, 336th FIS 2
Colonel Francis Gabreski, 4th Group .... 2 (+4 1/2 w/51st Group)
Major James Hagerstrom, 334th & 335th FIS .... 2 (+6 1/2 w/18th Group)
Lt.Col. Bruce Hinton, 336th FIS 2
1/Lt Booth Holker, 334th FIS 2
1/Lt John Hanaker, 335th FIS 2
Sq/Ldr Graham Hulse, RAF, 336th FIS 2
Captain Jere Lewis, 334th FIS 2
1/Lt Justin Livingston, 335th FIS 2
Captain Freeland Mathews, 336th FIS 2
Lt.Col. Carroll McElroy, 335th FIS 2
1/Lt Thomas McQuade, 336th FIS 2
Colonel John Meyer, 4th Group 2
1/Lt Claude Mitson, 336th FIS 2
1/Lt John Hoore, 335th FIS 2
Captain James Nichols, 335th FIS 2
1/Lt Arthur O'Conner, 336th FIS 2
Major Charles Owens, 336th FIS 2
Major Lewis Powers, 335th FIS 2
1/Lt Lawrence Roesler, 335th FIS 2
Captain William Ryan, 334th FIS 2
Major Thomas Sellers, USMC, 336th FIS 2
1/Lt Robert Smith, 335th FIS 2
1/Lt George Spataro, 334th FIS 2
1/Lt Robert Straub, 335th FIS 2
Major William Whisner, 334th FIS .... 2 (+3.5 w/51st Group)
Captain Nelton Wilson, 334th FIS 2
1/Lt Ronald Berdoy, 334th FIS 1.5
1/Lt Joseph Fields, 336th FIS 1.5
1/Lt Frank Frazier, 336th FIS 1.5
1/Lt Harry Jones, 335th FIS 1.5
Captain George Love, 336th FIS 1.5
2/Lt John McKee, 335th FIS 1.5
1/Lt Richard Pincoski, 334th FIS 1.5
Captain Vincent Stacy, 335th FIS 1.5
1/Lt Robert Strozier, 335th FIS 1.5
1/Lt William Yancy Jr., 336th FIS 1.5
1/Lt Robert Akin, 336th FIS 1
2/Lt Frank Arbuckle, 336th FIS 1
Major Edward Ballinger, 334th FIS 1
1/Lt Martin Bambrick, 335th FIS 1
1/Lt Robert Barnes, 334th FIS 1
Lt.Col. Jack Best, 336th FIS 1
1/Lt Duane Bryant, 335th FIS 1
Captain Paul Bryce, 4th Group 1
1/Lt Curtis Carley, 335th FIS 1

1/Lt Robert Carter, 335th FIS 1
Captain Kenneth Chandler, 336th FIS .... 1 (+4 ground victories)
1/Lt David Copeland, 335th FIS 1
2/Lt Al Cox, 335th FIS 1
Captain William Craig, 334th FIS 1
1/Lt Henry Crescibene, 335th FIS 1
1/Lt William Dawson, 336th FIS 1
Captain Daniel Dennehey, 336th FIS 1
1/Lt Forest Dupree, 336th FIS 1
Captain Van Eisenhut, 335th FIS 1
1/Lt Joseph Ellis, 334th FIS 1
Lt.Col. Benjamin Ellis, 335th FIS 1
Major Raymond Evans, 335th FIS 1
Lt. Simpson Evans, (USN) 336th FIS 1
Major Edward Fletcher, 334th FIS 1
Major Westwood Fletcher, 334th FIS 1
1/Lt Richard Frailey, 334th FIS 1
Captain Henry Frazier, 334th FIS 1
1/Lt David Freeland, 336th FIS 1
Captain Tom Garvin, 334th FIS 1
1/Lt Bruno Giordano, 334th FIS 1
1/Lt Robert Goodridge, 335th FIS 1
1/Lt Otis Gordon, 335th FIS 1
1/Lt John Green, 336th FIS 1
1/Lt Donald Griffith, 335th FIS 1
2/Lt Richard Guidroz, 335th FIS 1
Captain William Guss (USMC), 336th FIS 1
1/Lt James Heckman, 335th FIS 1
Captain Erwon Hesse, 4th Group 1
Major William Hoelscher, 335th FIS 1
1/Lt Donald Hooten, 334th FIS 1
Captain James Horowitz, 335th FIS 1
Lt.Col. William Hovde, 4th Wing 1
2/Lt James Howerton, 336th FIS 1
Captain Richard Johns, 335th FIS 1
Lt.Col. Ralph Keyes, 336th FIS 1
1/Lt Raymond Kinsey, 335th FIS 1
1/Lt Arthur Kulengosky, 336th FIS .... 1 (+ 2 w/51st Group)
Captain Howard Lane, 336th FIS 1
Flt/Lt J.A.O. Levesque (RCAF), 334th FIS 1
1/Lt Charles Loyd, 334th FIS 1
1/Lt William Loyd, 336th FIS 1
1/Lt Gerald Lyvere, 336th FIS 1
1/Lt William Mailloux, 334th FIS 1
Captain Cleve Malone, 335th FIS 1
Major James Martin, 334th FIS 1
1/Lt John Martin, 334th FIS 1
1/Lt Robert McIntosh, 334th FIS 1
Captain Robert McKittrick, 336th FIS 1
1/Lt Alfred Miller, 335th FIS 1
1/Lt Russell Miller, 335th FIS 1
Captain Richard Moyle, 336th FIS 1
Flt/Lt J.M. Nichols (RAF), 335th FIS 1
Captain Michael Novak, 335th FIS 1
1/Lt Waymond Nutt, 334th FIS 1
1/Lt Conrad Nystrum, 335th FIS 1
1/Lt George Ober, 335th FIS 1
Captain John Odiorne, 334th FIS 1
1/Lt Orren Ohlinger, 334th FIS 1
Lt.Col. George Ola, 4th Group 1
Lt.Col. John Payne (USMC), 336th FIS 1
Captain Alphonso Pena, 335th FIS 1
Captain Samuel Pasecreta, 4th Group 1
1/Lt Jimmie Pierce, 334th FIS 1
Captain Dean Pogreba, 336th FIS 1
Lt.Cmdr. Paul Pugh (USN), 4th Group 1
Lt.Col. James Raebel, 334th FIS .... 1 (+ 2 w/51st Group)
1/Lt Dayton Ragland, 336th FIS 1
Captain Richard Ransbottom, 336th FIS 1
1/Lt Kenneth Rapp, 336th FIS 1
2/Lt Philip Redpath, 335th FIS 1
2/Lt Samuel Reeder, 335th FIS 1
1/Lt Charles Riester, 336th FIS 1
Captain James Robert, 335th FIS 1
Captain Jack Robinson, 334th FIS 1
1/Lt Gene Rogge, 334th FIS 1
1/Lt Robert Ronca, 335th FIS 1
2/Lt Len Russell, 334th FIS 1
Captain Jack Schwab, 335th FIS 1
Captain Alfred Simmons, 336th FIS 1
1/Lt Bobbie Smith, 335th FIS 1
1/Lt Herschel Spitzer, 336th FIS 1
Captain Maynard Stogdill, 334th FIS 1
Lt.Col. Stephen Stone, 334th FIS 1
Major William Thomas, 335th FIS 1
1/Lt Loyd Thompson, 336th FIS 1
Lt.Col. Chester Van Etten, 335th FIS 1
Major Philip Van Sickle, 335th FIS 1
Lt.Col. Francis Vetort, 335th FIS 1

Captain Herbert Weber, 334th FIS 1
1/Lt Elbert Whitehurst, 334th FIS 1
Captain Robert Windoffer, 336th FIS 1
1/Lt George Wood, 336th FIS 1
1/Lt Vernon Wright, 336th FIS 1
1/Lt William Angle, 336th FIS 5
2/Lt Marshall Babb, 334th FIS 5
1/lt Garold Beck, 336th FIS 5
Captain Lewis Blakeney, 334th FIS 5
1/Lt Clifford Brossart, 334th FIS .... .5 (+ 1 w/51st Group)
Captain Bewey Durnford (USMC), 335th FIS 5
2/Lt Joe Farris, 335th FIS 5
2/Lt Samuel Groening, 335th FIS 5
Lt.Col. Julian Harvey, 336th FIS 5
2/Lt Merlyn Hroch, 334th FIS 5
2/Lt Cecil Lefevers, 336th FIS 5
1/Lt John Ludwig, 335th FIS 5
1/Lt Roy McLain, 334th FIS 5
1/Lt Donald McLean, 336th FIS 5
1/Lt Ernest Neubert, 336th FIS 5
1/Lt Robert Perdue, 336th FIS 5
1/Lt Edgar Powell, 335th FIS 5
1/Lt Paul Roach, 334th FIS .... .5 (+ 2 w/51st Group)
1/Lt Harold Schmidt, 336th FIS 5
2/Lt William Schrimsher, 335th FIS 5
Major Eugene Sommerich, 336th FIS 5
2/Lt Charles Spath, 334th FIS 5

Summery Of Credits

Unit	CREDITS		
	Air-Air	Air-Ground	Total
Squadrons			
334th Fighter Interceptor Squadron	142 1/2	-	142 1/2
335th Fighter Interceptor Squadron	218 1/2	-	218 1/2
336th Fighter Interceptor Squadron	116 1/2	4.0	120 1/2
Group Headquarters			
4th Fighter Interceptor Group	20 1/2	-	20 1/2
Wing Headquarters			
4th Fighter Interceptor Wing	4.0	-	4.0
Total enemy aircraft downed	502.0	4.0	506.0

4th Fighter Interceptor Wing Awards - Korean War Era

Campaigns

Chinese Communist Forces Intervention	3 November 1950/24 January 1951 FEAF GO 78, 14 February 1952
First United Nations Counteroffensive	25 January 1951/21 April 1951 FEAF GO 78, 14 February 1952
Chinese Communist Forces Intervention	22 April 1951/8 July 1951 FEAF GO 78, 14 February 1952
United Nations Summer/Fall Offensive	9 July 1951/27 November 1951 FEAF GO 500, 3 October 1952
Second Korean Winter	28 November 1951/31 April 1952 FEAF GO 500, 3 October 1952
Korean Summer/Fall 1952	1 May 1952/30 November 1952 FEAF GO 114, 5 March 1953
Third Korean Winter	1 December 1952/30 April 1953 FEAF GO 114, 5 March 1953
Korean Summer/Fall 1953	1 May 1953/27 July 1953 FEAF GO 383, 7 October 1953

Decorations

Disntinguished Unit Citation (First Oak Leaf Cluster), Korea	22 April 1951/8 July 1951 DAF GO 34, 31 August 1953
Distinguished Unit Citation (Second Oak Leaf Cluster), Korea	9 July 1951/27 November 1951 DAF GO 34, 31 August 1953

Special Honors

Republic Of Korea Unit Citation	1 November 1951/30 September 1952 FEAF GO 83, 17 February 1953
Republic Of Korea Unit Citation	1 October 1952/31 March 1953 FEAF GO 121, 9 August 1954

Commanders of the "Fourth But First"

4th Fighter Wing (organized on 15 August 1947)

15 August 1947/17 February 1949 .... Brig. Gen. Yantis H. Taylor
17 February 1949/26 April 1949 .... Col. Arthur C. Agan, Jr.
26 April 1949/14 June 1949 .... Col. Robert W.C. Wimsatt
14 June 1949/13 August 1949 .... Col. Henry B. Fisher
13 August 1949/22 August 1949 .... Col. Albert L. Evans
22 August 1949/3 October 1949 .... Col. Bela A. Harcos
3 October 1949/31 May 1951 .... Brig. Gen. George F. Smith

(Redesignated 4th Fighter Interceptor Wing on 20 January 1950)

31 May 1951/1 November 1951 .... Col. Herman A. Schmid
1 November 1951/2 October 1952 .... Col. Harrison B. Thyng
2 October 1952/11 November 1952 .... Col. Charles W. King
11 November 1952/9 August 1953 .... Col. James K. Johnson
9 August 1953/30 June 1954 .... Col. Donald P. Hall
30 June 1954/10 August 1954 .... Col. Neil A Newman
10 August 1954/1 May 1955 .... Col. Alvin E. Hebert
1 May 1955/17 August 1956 .... Col. Grover C. Brown

(Redesignated 4th Fighter-Bomber Wing on 8 March 1955)

(Redesignated 4th Fighter-Day Wing on 26 April 1956)

17 August 1956/5 June 1957 .... Col. Robert P. Montgomery
6 June 1957/2 July 1957 .... Col. Earle R. Myers
2 July 1957/8 December 1957 .... Col. James M. Shelly

(Returned To Seymour Johnson AFB on 8 December 1957)

4th Fighter Group Commanders Korean War Era

September 1946 .... Col. Ernest H. Beverly
August 1948 .... Lt.Col. Benjamin S. Preston, Jr.
June 1949 .... Col. Albert L. Evans, Jr.
1 September 1950 .... Col. John C. Meyer
May 1951 .... Lt.Col. Glenn T. Eagleston
July 1951 .... Col. Benjamin S. Preston, Jr.
18 March 1952 .... Col. Walker M. Mahurin
14 May 1952 .... Lt.Col. Ralph G. Kuhn

1 June 1952 .... Col. Royal N. Baker
18 March 1953 .... Col. Thomas D. DeJarnette
28 December 1953 .... Col. Henry S. Tyler, Jr.
19 July 1954 .... Lt.Col. Dean W. Dutrack
9 August 1954 .... Col. William D. Gilchrist
4 May 1955 .... Col. George I. Ruddell

(The 4th Fighter-Day Group was inactivated at Seymour Johnson AFB on 8 December 1957)

Squadron Commanders
Korean War Era

334th Fighter Squadron - "The Fighting Eagles"

(reactivated at Selfridge Field on 9 September 1946)

9 September 1946 .... Major Jacob W. Dixon
25 April 1949 .... Major Benjamin H. Emmert
20 June 1949 .... Lt.Col. Jacob W. Dixon
5 July 1949 .... Lt.Col. Benjamin H. Emmert
28 July 1949 .... Major Charles J. Hoey
26 August 1949 .... Lt.Col. John A. Carey
31 May 1951 .... Major Edward C. Fletcher
June 1951 .... Lt.Col. Goerge L. Jones
3 October 1951 .... Major William T. Whisner
November 1951 .... Major George A. Davis, Jr.
17 February 1952 .... Major James F. Martin
May 1952 .... Major Theodore S. Coberly
June 1952 .... Lt.Col. Richard L. Ayersman
February 1953 .... Lt.Col. William J. Cosby
July 1953 .... Lt.Col. Henry J. Pascho
10 January 1954 .... Major J.E. Wisby
February 1954 .... Major Magnus P. Johnson
3 May 1954 .... Lt.Col. Val W. Bollwerk
6 September 1954 .... Lt.Col. Dean W. Dutrack
3 January 1955 .... Major Magnus P. Johnson
January 1956 .... Major Warren H. Rice
mid-1956 .... Major Bruce W. Carr
1 September 1957 .... Major Lucien B. Shuler

335th Fighter Squadron, "The Chiefs"

(reactivated at Selfridge Field on 9 September 1946)

1 March 1947 .... Lt.Col Nathan M. Abbot
27 July 1948 .... Major Clay Albright

5 August 1948 .... Major Bruce H. Hinton
23 June 1949 .... Lt.Col. Harvey L. Case, Jr.
June 1950 .... Lt.Col. Donald W. Nance
31 May 1951 .... Lt.Col. Benjamin H. Emmert
19 August 1951 .... Major Winton W. Marshall
10 January 1952 .... Major Zane S. Amel
25 April 1952 .... Major Philip H. Van Sickle
6 September 1952 .... Lt.Col. Carrol B. McElroy
early 1953 .... Lt.Col. Vermont Garrison
Summer 1953 .... Lt.Col. Robert J. Dixon
12 March 1954 .... Major Robert H. Knapp
12 June 1954 .... Lt.Col Chester B. Wine
4 March 1955 .... Lt.Col. John S. Stewart
January 1956 .... Major Howard F. Hendricks
early 1957 .... Captain Kenneth A Runeberge

336th Fighter Interceptor Squadron, "The Rocketeers"

(reactivated at Selfridge Field on 9 September 1946)

1 February 1949 .... Major Benjamin H. King
1 June 1949 .... Lt.Col. Benjamin S. Preston, Jr.
1 January 1950 .... Lt.Col. Bruce H. Hinton
July 1951 .... Major Richard D. Creighton
10 March 1952 .... Major Felix Asla, Jr.
1 August 1952 .... Major Louis Green
July 1953 .... LtCol Edward Weed
1 July 1954 .... Lt.Col. Donald H. Ross
23 October 1954 .... Major Leo D. Sill
23 December 1954 .... Captain Harry E. Krig
1 January 1955 .... Major Bruce W. Carr
August 1956 .... Major Richard J. Condrick

4th Fighter Wing Stations

9 September 1946-15 August 1947 .... Selfridge Field, Michigan (4th Fighter Group)
15 August 1947- 26 April 1949 .... Andrews Field (later Andrews AFB), Virginia
26 April 1949-8 September 1950 .... Langley AFB, Virginia
8 September 1950-19 November 1950 .... New Castle County Airport, Maryland
28 November 1950-7 May 1951 .... Johnson AB, Japan
7 May 1951-23 August 1951 .... Suwon AB, South Korea
23 August 1951-1 October 1954 .... Kimpo AB, South Korea
1 October 1954-8 December 1957 .... Chitose AB, Japan
8 December 1957-Present Day .... Seymour Johnson AFB, North Carolina

Index